Welcome To

Excellent Cycling Adventures in Southern Alberta

Part of the Cycling Adventure Series

By

Marg Archibald

The Monday Communications Group Ltd.

When you are ready to feed your spirit of adventure as you travel, you are ready to see the world on a bicycle. Bicycle travel lets you experience the local scale of the countryside, meet the people and animals on their turf and see what others do not. All while you increase your fitness, re-discover skills you forgot you had and develop pride in yourself.

Southern Alberta is one of the best places to start. Roads are paved. Travel is safe, even alone. And details of getting around like food, accommodation, currency exchange, bike repairs and directions are easy to come by. You have a choice of terrain and even weather conditions.

Welcome to Southern Alberta cycling.

Published by:
The Monday Communications Group Ltd.
Office: 424 11A Street NW
Calgary Alberta Canada T2N 1Y1
Fax: 403 - 283-5983
Email: monday@nucleus.com

Canadian Cataloguing in Publication Data

Archibald, Marg, 1946 -
Welcome to excellent cycling adventures in Southern Alberta

(Cycling adventure series)
Includes bibliographical references and index.
ISBN 0-9682100-0-7

1. Cycling--Alberta--Guidebooks. 2. Alberta--Guidebooks.
I. Monday Communications Group. II. Title.
III. Title: Excellent cycling adventures in Southern Alberta.
IV. Series: Archibald, Marg, 1946 - Cycling adventure series

GV1046.C32A42 1997 917.123'4043 C97-900510-8

Designed by Robin Albright, Two Birds, One Stone Design, Calgary.
Custom Digital Mapping by Nadar Salloum, Map Town Publishing, Calgary.

All the information in this book is completely independent. There have been no discounts or payments accepted in exchange for positive coverage.

We would like to be infallibly reliable and ever current so regret that we cannot guarantee that. Please let us know of updates, errors and new ideas that you have.

Author and publisher is not responsible for any problems, mishaps or accidents that may occur while using this guide or cycling in Southern Alberta.

THIS BOOK IS DEDICATED,

WITH LOVE AND ADMIRATION

TO MY MOTHER,

EV ARCHIBALD

WHO MADE THIS POSSIBLE IN

EVERY WAY.

Contents

Contents Continued

Routes back into Calgary

City exploring:

Multi day trips

Marg Archibald's Excellent Cycling Adventures in Southern Alberta

The pleasures of cycling in Southern Alberta

Welcome to the wonderful world of paved road cycling in rural Southern Alberta. When you want exercise that is more interesting than aerobics and you think that jogging may be hard on the bones, you are ready to try the fun and adventure of cycling to small towns. It satisfies the explorer in you. It feeds new parts of yourself.

There are plenty of paved roads in Southern Alberta that are in excellent condition. Most of them have wide shoulders and many of them have very little traffic. This is the legacy of a province that enjoyed the affluence of the oil boom and the attitudes of Texas developers: everyone deserves a paved road to the end of their driveway. So rural voters got roads and roads and roads. And these roads make for cycling that is amongst the best in the world.

You can choose the drama and challenge of cycling in among the Rockies or the wide-open vistas and rolling terrain of prairie. You can cycle for hours in close-to-isolation and you can book Bed & Breakfasts that offer surprising professionalism, comfort and pleasure.

Solitary travel by bicycle offers escape and a new dimension of self-exploration. It is a pleasure to learn to trust the little voice that comes from who-knows-where inside. As one enthusiast describes, it is just you and your freedom machine. Cycling alone is as safe in Southern Alberta as anywhere on the planet.

Cycling with a partner, friend or group offers camaraderie and shared decision-making. You learn new things about each other, build a history of shared adventure and have someone to take your picture. It only matters that you do what you like and use the opportunity to explore what gives you pleasure.

These wonderful cycle excursions in Southern Alberta offer fun, adventure and enormous pleasure. They will make you proud of yourself. They will make you feel athletic even if you aren't. They will make you a courageous adventurer, which we don't get enough chance to be while we are scratching out a living in our urban lives.

Growing to the Challenge

We are quick to say we couldn't possibly go that far and couldn't manage on our own. We feel concerned about safety when isolated on a rural highway. We worry about dogs and carloads of drunken teenagers. We worry about weather.

I had all those worries so it was years of slow evolution to get from cycling on city cycle paths to venturing out of town. First an afternoon on the edge of the city. Then day trips. Eventually, as I went further afield looking for new places to explore, I tried a route that was too ambitious for a day trip. The destination was Mossleigh - a dot on the map. I had never seen it so it offered a chance to explore.

I had been merrily cycling, eating my snacks, singing along to my tunes, enjoying nature since 5:00 AM. I had enjoyed the ever-warming sun for eight hours. Then I came to a highway junction at which the sign said, "Calgary 86 K." Hmmm. It was going to be a long, hard ride back.

I then decided I had cycled everywhere I could from Calgary and still get back in one day. Now I wanted to go further. See more. Draw more red lines on maps. I wanted to know more routes, to make them mine. The next weekend I booked Bed & Breakfasts for Friday and Saturday night. Life has never been the same since.

The rush mentality

The subtle pressure exerted by the question "How far do you go each day?" is working against your best interests in bicycle travel. This is particularly hard for competitive men to deflect. And if seeing how far you can go appeals to you, fine. But a bicycle holiday provides the opportunity for you to learn about more than speed and self-discipline.

Most touring cyclists average 15 to 20 K an hour and rack up 150 to 170 K each day. I heard a New Zealand cyclist boast of cycling 380 K in one day. I average 10 to 12 K per hour and anything over 120 K in a day is a long ride for me.

You can ride slowly and steadily or fast and furiously. You can ride for long days or brief ones. Sometimes you will cycle so slowly you are truly meandering on your bicycle. Maybe it'll be because you are tired, maybe your are feeling philosophical or just want to drink in every moment of a special spot. Sometimes you will clip along and feel powerful and fast. The important thing is that you do what feels right for you at the moment and that's why solo cycling works so well. You get to know what you like and that's how you ride. This is a chance to learn the elusive skill of being in the moment.

You will rush until you get used to the fact that you do get there, wherever "there" is. And you will eventually get used to picking destinations each day so that you can cycle to them without feeling rushed. It is the leisure to stop and snack and change clothing layers and buy treats and drink water, relish a view and follow your whims - this is what makes the journey worth doing.

Stopping lots is also easier on the crotch, however kind your bicycle seat. You'll be able to ride a lot longer if you just ease yourself off your seat from time to time for a view, a drink, a whatever.

Cycling from your doorstep

You can load your bike into a vehicle, drive it out to the edge of Calgary and start your cycling in the country, but that means you have to return the same route to re-connect with your vehicle. Or you can get a designated driver to drop you off and pick you up. This is cumbersome. Your final rendezvous time and place will circumscribe your whole trip.

For complete independence and flexibility you can start each trip by cycling your way from your doorstep, hotel, Bed & Breakfast or airport to the edge of the city. There is a certain satisfaction when the whole trip is door to door on your bike. You can pick and choose your city exit and entry routes depending on where you live. The routes shown here give you ideas. Adapt them.

Most routes, in light traffic, take about 1 1/2 hours from the centre of the city to the edge. The exception is when you exit straight south, which takes closer to 2 hours just because of the shape of the city.

To help you out, whatever your preferences, this guide offers cycle routes, drop-off/pickup spots and places to park at the edge of town if you drive yourself out and leave your vehicle. If you are planning to park and start riding early in the morning, you may have to negotiate the latter ahead of time with a business or resident in the area. We advise against leaving a vehicle beside the road for several days. It could be considered abandoned and towed away.

From the airport you are in such an ideal location to exit the city north immediately that, even if you have chosen a journey south of the city, it makes sense to exit north and then turn and travel south once you are outside Calgary. This is covered under exit routes.

During July and August you can take bicycles on the C-Train if it isn't rush hour. This provides another option for getting in and out that is described at the beginning of exit and entry routes.

Navigation is easier than it sounds

All these route descriptions sound more complex than they really are. The maps provide the easiest way to find your way around. These written descriptions provide answers to questions you may have when you compare the real world and real world signs to the maps.

It's all made a bit confusing the first time because we have roads and highways that stop abruptly and then continue on somewhere else - not necessarily in the same direction. We also have routes with more than one name and routes that change name. In that case we have tried here to use all the names: Highway 22/22X/Marquis of Lorne Way. Be assured that when you have traveled any of these routes once, they will be yours. In the meantime, the maps plus the directions may be helpful.

Traffic volumes change

Comfort with vehicular traffic varies enormously from one cyclist to another. In general, the more you ride, the less it bothers you. Even in the course of one dayís riding, by the end of it you may be less bothered by traffic then you were at the beginning.

The fact is, however, that traffic isn't pretty, doesn't sound soothing, doesn't smell good and doesn't relax you. So the rides here aim for minimal traffic all the time. Occasionally, to get you from one minimal traffic situation to another, descriptions guide you through traffic. The guide will tell you what to expect and get you out of it as fast as possible.

Your experience with traffic volumes may not be the same as others', particularly on the routes in and out of Calgary. One new subdivision changes traffic patterns and often the roads too. These can be in process for two or even three years. Then the final result may be better for cycling, or worse. Road planners have different priorities than cyclists.

The guide incorporates all these changes in regular updates. Notify me of any you notice.

Road surface

The routes here, both inside the city and in the country, are chosen because they are paved. There will, however, be the odd brief stretch of gravel. And some rural road pavement will be updated with oil and aggregate that can be quite rough to ride on. Some of the road surfaces are old and chewed up but if there is little traffic you can weave through that easily. For the most part, the route surfaces suggested here are a pleasure to be on.

Leave early

In spite of suggesting that you fight the urge to rush, your pleasure in riding will increase if you minimize dealing with traffic and that means leaving the city early. Even from the middle of Calgary, you can avoid heavy traffic by leaving early, particularly on weekends. If you start out by 6:30 AM on a weekend you will be out of the city with very little traffic because the shopping frenzy has not yet begun. If you leave by 5:00 AM, when the sun is up in mid-summer, you will have a very peaceful exit.

On a weekday, if you leave at 6:30 AM traffic will already be starting to build at the edge of the city. If you are not a morning person, use the cycle paths, consider a lift to the outskirts drop-off described for each route, take the C-Train or accept that traffic may get heavy, depending on the route. You could also try leaving in the evening and just going to a close town and then starting out a full day of riding the next day.

In and out of Calgary

The best routes out of Calgary aren't necessarily the best routes back in. A route that is deserted at 6:30 AM may be hectic by 3:00 PM or even 9:30 AM. Some of this is unavoidable but certain routes (like Highway #2 entering the city from the south) are completely unacceptable when busy.

Only you know your tolerance for traffic. Some cyclists pride themselves in coping with the thick of it without flinching. As always in cycling, know yourself and your preferences and cater to those. The guide gives you as vivid a description as possible on conditions at the time of writing.

Weather

There is no such thing as a reliable weather forecast. Meteorologists do their best. When you call the 1-900 number in Calgary you get better detail and therefore more accuracy than from the phone number with the recorded message. But wind shifts of a few degrees can have enormous effects on cycling. And suddenly spawned rainstorms may be isolated but if you are in them, they are huge. I have experienced heading out to a forecast of mixed sun and cloud and plus 12 degrees C and cycled home mid-afternoon the same day, in snow, gale force winds and temperatures of minus 12 degrees C.

In spite of this, a weather forecast could help you decide which route to take. When you are choosing between heading southwest or northeast from Calgary there can be quite a difference, even within the distance you can travel on a bicycle in two days. A forecast can improve your odds of weather within your comfort range.

Calgary is at a high elevation: 1084 metres/3400 feet. The proximity of Southern Alberta to the mountains results in dramatic weather changes in a short time and weather differences from one local area to another. You can experience several weather patterns in an afternoon. One of the local climatologists reports he has experienced a 7 or 8 degree temperature drop in the space of one footstep while hiking. So be prepared for variety.

But there's nothing worse than discovering you could have been riding in great conditions, within reach on your bicycle, but instead you are fighting gusty winds and heavy overcast. So talk to the weather experts. Apart from their current forecast, there are some overall patterns worth knowing about.

Chinooks:

Calgary's weather is dominated by a fohn wind called chinooks. They blow over the Rocky Mountains, which drain out all the moisture they carried from the West Coast. They then descend the inland slope of the Rockies warm and dry, racing down onto the prairies. Not only can these winds bring rapid weather change they can also blow very strongly. Heading west into a chinook is hard work. The forecaster will tell you if chinook conditions are expected.

Snowstorms year round:

At the risk of frightening you, Southern Alberta has recorded snowstorms in every month of the year. It is unusual but it can happen. Summer snow is wet and doesn't last, but it happens. The main point is to be prepared for anything, enjoy what you get and be ready to stage an unplanned stopover when conditions call for it. The further you get from the mountains, the less likely that is.

Thunderstorms:

Thunderstorms can be wonderful to watch build and unfold. Apart from keeping dry during a thunderstorm, you need to be careful about lightening in Southern Alberta. If you are out on your bike and a storm hits, stay away from isolated stands of trees. Look for bushes that are lower than the surrounding vegetation. If necessary get down in a ditch and lie your bike down. Keep low. One of the most common causes of lightening fatality is rural fencing. You may feel like you aren't even in a storm that is a kilometer away when its lightening travels along a fence you are leaning on and kills you. Stay away from fences when there is storm activity around.

You can do a bit of your own forecasting if you see cumulous clouds building along the mountains. Watch for sunny spots. That's where the air will heat up and feed a storm. Likewise, when you see clouds building in the mountains, wind coming hard from the west and it meets an east wind of heated prairie air you can get storm activity where the two meet.

Alberta thunderstorms tend to bring the heaviest downpour during June and early July. But don't blame me when you get drenched in August.

Warm southeast corner of the province:

The southeast corner of Alberta is warmer and dryer than the rest of the province. It also tends to be breezier and may get more mid summer hailstorms. As early as April, when the rest of the province is still shedding winter, you can start good weather cycling south and east of Drumheller. You may still be surprised by a freak coldsnap but it consistently warms sooner. And you can usually continue cycling there into the stable fall conditions of late October.

Summer:

The area within roughly 200 K east, south and north of Calgary is wettest in June. Short of a sudden cold front, however, you can ride there comfortably from May until mid October with September and October being the most stable. The closer you get to the Rocky Mountains in the west and southwest of the province the more changeable, cooler and unpredictable the weather. Sudden snowstorms even in mid-summer, forceful winds and rainsqualls all come with mountain riding.

The southwest wind funnel:

The strip from Crowsnest Pass to Fort MacLeod and Lethbridge can generate fierce wind tunnel conditions. If you have a topographic map and can identify an east-west low spot in that area through which wind could pick up speed, you may want to avoid it. This is certainly a strip where westerlies out of the mountains and hot easterlies from the drier corner of the province can build storms.

In general, in Alberta the east wind is not as strong as the west but often brings long cold spells. You'll get an east wind about 20% of the time. A north wind brings storms.

Ideal fall conditions:

Weather all over southern Alberta is sunnier, drier and more stable in the fall. Many locals consider it the best season. But evenings will cool off quickly and mornings may have frost.

Ask the experts

In Calgary you can call the weather office (1-900-565-5555) and pay by the minute to talk to real live weather people. You can explain your route options and tell them what matters to you. You can ask which of your options is least likely to have major winds and changeable weather. Then, if all routes qualify, which will be warmest. They can tell you this and give you specific suggestions. Once they know you are cycling, they throw themselves into finding a route that meets your preferences.

If you arrive at the airport with your bicycle ready to head out, you can call them from an airport payphone and bill it to a credit card.

Without any charges, you can call 299-7878 in Calgary to hear a recording of expected conditions. The forecast will mainly dwell on Calgary and will include any weather warnings of extreme conditions.

The fact is, however, that you cannot count on great weather all the time. So you become philosophical about dealing with what happens around you. And given adequate clothing, (see Keeping warm: page 235 or Keeping cool: page 240) you can be comfortable and find new kinds of beauty in unexpected conditions. There is enormous pride in weathering a storm - whether you are smart enough to find a friendly farm kitchen or tough enough to just keep pedaling.

This is your adventure so pick conditions you prefer.

Maps

International cycling magazines recognize Calgary as offering one of the best and most extensive, in-city, cycle path systems in the world. There are wonderful spots in the city that you can only get to on this path system. The City's annually updated cycle path map (*Calgary Pathway and Bikeway Map*), is usually available in sponsor outlets by May. This means you can get them in most cycle shops and some newsstands, Canadian Tire Stores and The Flying Bear Coffee Den. It can't be beat for in-city cycling - whether you use the roads or cycle paths. It also highlights many cycle repair shops and points of interest such as the Zoo. To fit the whole city on one sheet, the type is quite fine so the Glasses Generation will need glasses.

When you are cycling inside Calgary, if you want to keep off roads and away from traffic as much as possible, you will want to get one of these maps. Some of the routes in this guide incorporate sections of the cycle path routes but don't give the same amount of map detail.

When you venture out of town, it helps to have maps that inspire you. Routes in this guide have maps. When you want additional maps, Map Town on 6th Avenue and 6th Street SW (downtown) can open new doors. They carry the city cycle path map and *The Country Key*: a great map-set to start exploring outside Calgary. This delightful booklet covers the country roads around Calgary and includes street maps of the adjacent small towns. It can get out of date, but can't we all.

Map Town also sells big, government sectional maps that are necessary when you go further afield. These maps indicate all the roads and whether they are gravel or paved. They are only updated periodically so you will find discrepancies but the amount of detail can be handy to determine whether two roads really do link up.

For some reason some of us get a great deal of pleasure from drawing a red line along routes as we travel them. Claiming them as our own. Then, as we explore new ones and get new routes pronounced ours, we colour them too. And what a thing of pride and beauty - a coloured map - which in the process has become battered, wet and dry several times, ripped and frayed. The urge to fill all the maps and all the routes is almost as strong as the urge to be out there exploring.

Places to stay

Camping is an economical option but involves carrying at least sleeping bag, mat and tent. That increases weight and necessitates building in time to set up camp and break camp in the morning. Some camping sites are included here but do not consider this guide a knowledgeable source on Southern Alberta camping.

We recommend Bed & Breakfasts in rural Alberta. In some towns they are the only places to stay. Between towns they are often farms or ranches and even those that do not live up to the romantic image of little house on the prairie are excellent accommodation and value.

You'll see some named with the service lists right after the route description for each ride. You can find others through several avenues, none of which list them all. So draw on several.

-*Alberta Campground Guide*: annual listing by location, quite comprehensive. Call Travel Alberta: **1-800-661-8888** to get a copy or consult their new website:
http://www.AlbertaHotels.ab.ca/campgrounds

- *Alberta Accommodation & Visitors Guide*: annual listing with description that includes motels and hotels and, at the back B&Bs. This is the most comprehensive listing of these free-spirit businesses and easy to use because the location name is prominent and listing format is consistent. Order yours through Travel Alberta: **1-800-661-8888**.

- *Travel Alberta*: (**1-800-661-8888**) is in operation from 9:00 AM to 4:30 PM, Monday to Friday during the summer, but they say, "subject to change", so you'll find variations. You probably won't find them available weekends or evenings. Their telephone service can give you information on accommodation but they do not book it. They are knowledgeable and help both plan routes and find accommodation when the pickings are scarce.

- *Alberta Bed & Breakfast Association Directory of Member Bed & Breakfasts*: available from Travel Alberta: **1-800-661-8888**. This guide lists Bed & Breakfasts in six regions of Alberta, shows their location on a map and briefly describes costs, highlights and how to contact them. Unfortunately the booklet is amateur looking but the B&Bs aren't.

- B&B leaflets: a local store in small towns often stocks B&B leaflets for quite a wide geographic area.

- Other B&B owners: they know about each other but motel and hotel owners rarely know about B&Bs.

Book ahead. A local wedding or reunion fills accommodation in small towns. It is often too far to cycle to an alternative before dark or before you are tired.

Throughout this guide, regardless of the correct full name of a Bed and Breakfast, it is always abbreviated to B & B. It is too cumbersome to keep writing it out in full. My apologies to B&B owners who dislike this.

Your bike and equipment

Twenty-one gears and cantilevered brakes are wonderful but I managed fine for 20 years on my Sears five-speed lady's bicycle and had a great deal of pleasure from it. I only bought up when one of my knees complained. You don't need to wait that long but don't feel you have to go high-end or the latest technology to enjoy cycling. Start with what you have now. If you already have a bike your are happy with, stick with it. Familiarity breeds comfort in bicycles.

Putting a bike together

Your cycling equipment needs to fit your cycling preferences. As with all else - suit yourself. If you don't like wearing cycling shoes or using toe clips, don't. If you don't want to wear skin-tight lycra and you don't want to cycle leaning on a cowcatcher in front of your handlebars - don't.

If your bike has downturned handlebars, or is a mountain bike and you like that, that's fine. On long rides, you can rest your back and shoulders by riding with your hands on top of down-turned handle bars. You can install less knobby, light tires on a mountain bike to get a smoother ride. Your seat can be adjusted fore and aft as well as up and down to experiment with the optimum position. Likewise brake levers and handlebars can be adjusted. It is important not only for comfort but also for safety that your bike fit.

If you need to buy a bike, don't let the cycle shop staff bully you into a bicycle you don't want. If you learned to ride on a lady's bike and feel uncomfortable on a man's, insist on a lady's frame. There will be fewer choices but the increased riding confidence will be worth it.

If you are shopping, consider a few of the following:

- The bicycle frame size needs to fit your body. In general, mountain bikes have too long a reach for most women. A formula isn't going to help much. Just try several. Your body will know when it feels comfortable.

- You will want indexed gears by a reputable name. Most bikes, except the cheapest, come with Shimano but even Shimano gears vary in price and quality. Gear shifters can be built into the handgrip like a motorcycle, which is popular with some people. For touring the gears should have three rings in front, not just two. The smaller the smallest gear in front and the bigger the biggest gear at the back, the better for climbing hills. You want to know that whatever terrain you ride you have all the hill-climbing help you can get.

- All new bikes have cantilevered brakes. They make a huge difference to arm and shoulder fatigue on long downhills and are the only kind of brakes that stop you cold on really steep grades.

- A light weight bicycle costs money but is increasingly worthwhile the more you ride and the more you drag your bike up and down steps. (Packing light helps with this one too.)

- Well-padded handgrips reduce vibration and therefore fatigue.

Try three or four bikes to get the feel of the fit. Try different sizes. Ignore the colour and go for fit and comfort. If you are having trouble getting what you want, enlist a sympathetic cycle expert to help you put together a bicycle that is right for you.

Tires and flat tires

The larger and knobbier the tire, the tougher terrain it can handle. Skinny, smooth racing tires are the fastest but will cut into soft terrain like a knife. You want to get a balance between them for pleasurable touring. Consult with your cycle shop and be clear whether you will stick to pavement or will be cycling dry creek beds. Even if you intend to ride on pavement, you'll get forced onto gravel from time to time with a detour or incorrect directions. A hybrid tire works in all these cases.

Apart from thorns, which really play havoc with tires, you shouldn't get flats often. If you do, the most common cause is not having enough air in your tires. You want them inflated to the point of being hard.

Anne Sustoe, a retired English headmistress started out around the world on her bicycle without knowing how to change a tire. I rode for 15 years without the vaguest idea and no tools. So don't let it stop you if you aren't a grease monkey. However once you know how to change a tire yourself you have one less thing to worry about. It isn't hard and you don't have to be particularly strong, although it seems like you do until you get the knack. See page 245 for a description of the tire-changing process or, better yet, get a kid to show you. They all know how and they're usually patient teachers.

Bicycle seats

The bicycle seat is so important to cycling pleasure that it is worth insisting on your preferences. Be particular about the seat and its suspension. In spite of what cycle shop employees say, you can get a wide, soft, springy seat. This minimizes crotch discomfort as you re-acclimatize to your bicycle each spring and gives you increased comfort on long rides. Be stubborn and don't take their word for it. It's your crotch, not theirs.

Women definitely find a wide, cushioned seat suits them best. Many men agree that the knife-edge seat doesn't work for them either. "Dreamt up by some sadistic Italian", one male cyclist smirked.

Lady's bikes, old-fashioned handlebars and a basket on the front are not hot items with thieves. People who steal bicycles wouldn't be caught dead riding them and you are content knowing that your "street sleeper" is just what you want.

Panniers

You will want panniers that are light, durable and have handy accessible compartments. There are some strong German ones that may be a bit heavy and English-made Caradice have a good reputation. Cannondale makes panniers that are hard to improve on. Unfortunately, they are not waterproof. Even lining them with strong plastic bags doesn't keep things dry. The plastic bags get pinholes through which your clothes soak up water like sponges.

The only brand of pannier that claims waterproofness does not look very practical for quickly getting things in and out of while riding. They also do not offer handy exterior pockets nor have the Cannondale volume capacity.

In New Zealand, where cyclists know how to deal with rain, they line pannier pockets and the main storage space with white or light coloured plastic bags that are big enough to fold over at the top. The light colour makes it easier to see what's inside while they keep things dry. Then they put all the other contents inside separate, smaller plastic bags and zip-loc baggies. You get used to packing and locating things this way quite quickly.

The same applies to your front handlebar bag. Line it and have individual items wrapped separately. If you pack this way all the time, in a sudden rainstorm all you need to do is slip your camera and current map into their individual plastic protection and put on whatever raingear you want.

Cannondales lock on pretty securely, although retracing my route 9 K in Russia taught me that it is worth checking their security after you have lain the bicycle down on the ground with the panniers on. If the top hook gets misaligned and you are on rough road it's just a matter of time before they jiggle off.

They are durable enough to stand up to years of use.

If you are going to be carrying your panniers any distance by hand, which can happen if you ditch your bike for a while and keep travelling around, consider replacing the standard handles with reinforced ones. Otherwise they feel as if they will cut your fingers off when you carry them for long. A luggage repair shop can install padded handgrips.

Water bottles

Have at least two water bottles and holders. There will be times you need more water even than that. Never hold back on getting plenty of water. Be serious about your water carrying equipment.

Fenders

Add fenders to your bike if you don't like cycling with a strip of mud up your back. Again, sneered at by many aficionados.

Handlebars

If you want old-fashioned handlebars you can still get them and they do provide a nice sight seeing position. Mountain bike configuration is popular and many people think that it is their only option. Bicycle stores may support this assumption. Try them out. Go for comfort.

Kilometer counter

Even though they are a fiddly nuisance, it is helpful to have a kilometer counter. The instructions here and verbal directions you get on the road often depend on you knowing how far you have traveled.

Having said all this, don't be intimidated by any of it. Use common sense, buy comfort, try things out and gradually develop equipment that works for you. You are your own expert.

Things to take

You will find a list of things to take along on page 223 to help first-timers but you'll quickly settle on your own choices. Use the list for ideas particularly when you are trying to reduce baggage weight by only taking versatile, absolute musts. That's the hard part. Your preferences should prevail.

Food

You will eat tons and drink copious amounts of water while cycling. You will get stronger and feel healthy. The healthier your snacks and picnics, the more you will build lean, strong muscles.

Food is most accessible in the handlebar bag. When your picnic doesn't fit there, leave some behind. In Alberta you will rarely ride more than two hours in daylight without finding a place to buy some food. Maybe not healthy food, but food.

As everywhere, the easiest food to buy on the road is sweet or fat. I personally love sweets and when I find myself gobbling them it is a sign that I need to slow down. Then I build in other comforts: a lazy day, a non-cycling day, a conversation with someone local, and an afternoon of reading - things that balance the adventure with safety, comfort and stability.

Powerhouse nutrients

Magnesium and potassium are good for endurance. You find them in almonds, cashews, figs, apples, raisins, oranges, bananas and sunflower seeds. Apricots have vitamin A, which is an antioxidant, and dates are bursting with iron, which helps carry oxygen to muscles.

Power Bars are useful in emergencies and they are low in fat but don't plan to live on them. They are constipating.

Sandwiches

Sandwiches are portable and deliver several food groups. Salmon and tuna sandwiches work well. If you don't eat breakfast before leaving, take four. If you take along olives pickles, hard-boiled eggs, chunks of cheese, crackers, etc it feels like a picnic. Buns usually hold together better than bread. Muffins and scones travel well if you don't try and put anything in them.

If you have them made to order on the road, sandwiches can be as low fat, vegetarian, whole grain, flavourful, full-meal-deal, as you want. Ask your B & B host to make them to order for an additional fee. Ask when you arrive or even when you book. They may be willing to buy ingredients. Most restaurants will make to order too.

Fruit

Fresh fruit availability ranges with the season and location. For most of the summer the wonderful fresh fruit from the BC Okanogan is trucked directly to most of Southern Alberta: apricots, nectarines, peaches, plums and the ultimate - cherries. Look for roadside trucks selling fruit. Their prices are usually as good as you'll find anywhere.

Bananas and apricots can get beat up very quickly on the road, however carefully you pack them. Apples are resilient and plums that aren't too ripe survive riding well. Peaches are particularly good when heated by half a day in a sun-warmed handlebar bag. But you'll want plenty of Kleenex, cotton handkerchiefs, napkins or even the pre-moistened handy-wipes to deal with succulent peach aftermath.

Economy meals on wheels

Without packing along cooking utensils, you can keep costs down by creating simple meals on the road. Pick up fruit and yogurt for breakfast, even if you have to get them the night before for an early start. At noon you can try out the local bakery or buy sandwiches from a convenience store. At dinner you can buy the makings of a salad, cut them up and toss them around in a plastic bag and even eat from that. Add some cheese, bread and juice and you have a healthy dinner. These are all ingredients you can find almost anywhere in Alberta.

Snacks

You can go strictly healthy if you take it all with you or plan carefully to get to towns with real grocery stores, not just convenience stores, before they close. Apart from fruit, it is tricky to buy healthy as you go. Snacks are everywhere. Easy and not particularly healthy but lots of fun. Chips, cookies, candy, gum, ice cream, chocolate. I buy candy, ice cream and cookies. I love these things. Particularly when cycling. You'll never have any trouble satisfying those needs.

Trail mixes are loaded with fat but they are useful in small quantities as a treat and as emergency rations and as an intense dose of some of those nutrients mentioned above. They travel well under most conditions, just don't keep the same stash of nuts going day after day in hot weather. The oil in them goes rancid. Dried figs, dates and apricots are also handy, pack-able mainstays.

The boxed breakfast cereal, *Mini-wheats*, is surprisingly low in fat and very portable. If sugar isn't an issue, try them. Easy to pop into your mouth and satisfying.

Bakeries

Many towns have bakeries that offer fresh, wonderful treats. You may not find however, much in the way of whole grain, low fat goods in rural Southern Alberta bakeries. And the truth is now out about muffins, the old cyclists' standby. They contain as much fat as a full steak dinner with sour cream on the potato, so we are not as quick to pop a muffin.

Hot food

It is nice to have one real meal each day. Cyclists usually choose breakfast or, more commonly, dinner. Sitting down in a restaurant, getting hot food on a real plate feels like a nice reward and gives you a chance to relax and reflect.

If it turns cold or you need comfort, you'll want a restaurant to get soup, chili, and macaroni - those comfort foods. But you can get hot coffee everywhere and tea almost everywhere.

Water

Shortage of water quickly moves from uncomfortable to dangerous and potentially fatal. Drink all you can get inside yourself. If you don't like the taste of water from a water bottle, particularly once it gets warm, try inserting a small lemon wedge. Does wonders.

You will usually find places to refill your water bottles whenever you need to. Always refill when you are half way through your water. Refill every chance you get when you are going into a long stretch without a town or when it is hot and windy. And buy extra bottled water to carry with you.

If you get low between towns, stop at a farmhouse, go to the door with your water bottles and ask if you can refill. If no one is around and you try refilling from their hose they may approach you with caution when they see you doing this. A quick explanation has them immediately helpful.

Tap water is safe all over Alberta. Although well water tastes odd in some places, it is usually safe to drink. Do not refill your water from streams, rivers or ponds. Some of this water causes beaver fever from the industrious Canadian national critter.

Taking the children

Children seem to be natural born cyclists. Shortly after you stop running behind to steady a kid on a two-wheeler, they appreciate the power of this freedom machine. But it's a while after that before they have the strength and stamina to ride for several hours. Short stretches on the cycle path can start early but most kids will be teenagers before they can handle travel by bike.

And what perfect timing. Imagine the effect on all of you to hit the road and be adventurers together. Children can be involved in the planning and the on-the-road decisions. Once you have a bit of experience together, an enthusiastic teen can do the planning while you bring home the bacon. Then, at lift-off, you walk in the door, put on your cycle clothes and helmet, step up to a fully packed bike and head out. Think what a thrill it would be for a kid to plan the trip and take you on an unfolding bike holiday that they planned themselves. They learn responsibility and your learn to hand over control.

> ***Brett and his girls***
>
> *There they go. You'll see them on the highways in the interior of BC: Brett in front on the tandem, 13 year old Michelle behind him and, on the trail-a-bike behind that, 8 year old Melissa. They have a little bell and rear view mirror for communicating. They have an orange whipper flag. They all wear helmets and they have fun. "I have to make sure they have food and water all the time. The little one burns it up really fast. They need to start with a good breakfast. We take breaks once an hour for them to do stretches. They get more out of it that way. They love it. It's awesome."*

Be careful about asking too much of your kids. If they get overtired when you first cycle together they may be put off permanently.

If your child is old enough to have the stamina for bike travelling they probably already have some sense of road safety but they may not yet be car drivers so their perspective is limited. Get a copy of *From A to Z by Bike* by Barbara Lepsoe. It teaches bicycle safety to children. It covers things we do automatically and they need to think about such as riding in a straight line and shoulder checking and how to turn left in front of traffic. Talk with them about what they will face sharing the road with cars and trucks. Talk about situations as they come up on the road. When you first include your children, focus on rides with minimum traffic exposure, listed below.

For the parent looking for a fun, healthy, economical way to share adventure with their children, travelling by bicycle may just be it.

Rides to try

For minimum traffic contact:

-Start with cycle paths on the *Calgary Pathway and Bikeway Map*. You can get a copy at most cycle stores in Calgary, starting sometime in May

- Then try day trips: around the northwest and northeast parts of the city in two separate jaunts (pages 101 & 107). Do these either really early in the morning or in the evening. And remember daylight hours are long in Calgary during June and early July.

- The Chestermere ride (page 112) going out on the cycle path along the canal and returning on Highway #1A in the evening when 17th Avenue SE is quiet.

- The Balzac day trip (page 116) if you leave early and return on Highway #782/Centre Street or Simons Valley Road.

- Acme-Carstairs (page 180) is an excellent multi-day trip with minimal traffic that increases slightly on a long-weekend Friday afternoon.

For great scenery

- For a brief ride within Calgary, go north on 10th Street NW to 13th Avenue NW. It leads immediately onto Crescent Road, on the right, that curves around to the bluff overlooking the river and downtown core.

- Then try the cycle path south along the Elbow River to Stanley Park and then further down to Sandy Beach - a secluded, natural spot in the middle of the city. Take the Bow River cycle path south to Fish Creek Park. This is a huge park with large meadows and completely natural vegetation. Get a *Calgary Pathway and Bikeway Map* for details of these.

- Try the westbound cycle path on the south side of the Bow River out to Edworthy Park. But be advised that even as late as May when the weather has been hot, the heavily shaded path may still have ice on it due to the build-up of seepage from the steep bank run-off. Hard to believe but trust me. And watch this on a Saturday or Sunday afternoon when it will be heavily populated with other cyclists and rollerbladers. This pathway is beautiful in the fall, particularly if you can ride it on a quiet weekday.

- For your first multi-day trip try Bragg Creek and around the south end of the city, (page 142). It gives you a taste of getting into Rocky Mountain forest and takes you past world famous Spruce Meadows where horse jumping championships draw people from all over the world.

- When you want more of the Rockies, spend three or four days on the High River & Millarville ride (page 169). Parts of this feel like alpine pastures and parts feel like forest.

- If you like the badlands environment spend three days on the Drumheller ride and exploring Drumheller on the second day (page 162).

For minimum hill climbing

- If you start near the Bow River in Calgary, you start your trip with a climb because Calgary is in the bottom of the river valley. If you live or are staying toward the edge of the city, pick a route that goes directly out from there, don't cross the valley.

-Try cycle paths that run parallel to the valley such as along the edge of the Bow River and then turning north at the Zoo up Nose Creek. Or south along the Bow River and then through Fish Creek Park - although be warned there is one major hill on that ride. Get the *Calgary Pathway and Bikeway Map*.

-Day trips with minimal climbing are Balzac (page 116) and Chestermere (page 112)

- Multi-day trips north, east and south have less climbing then those to the west and closer to the Rockies, but there will be prairie valleys - called coulees to cross on all of these. Try Mossleigh (page 135), Acme & Carstairs (page 180) and Vulcan (page 149)

For maximum hill climbing

-We've got mountains and if you want a workout in Alberta you can find it.

-Highwood Pass, page 74.

-World famous mountain rides, page 110.

For delightful adventures

- On bike paths (you'll need the cycle path map) cycle all the way west along the Bow River (some jogging on streets required in Montgomery which is why you'll have trouble doing it without the city map) to Bowness Park. Wonderful path, often far away from roads. In Bowness Park you can rent a canoe or paddle boat and drift around the lagoon, feed ducks, buy snacks that are bad for you, lie on the grass under the many trees, stare into space, stroll and barbecue a picnic in the firepits. Bowness Park is particularly wonderful in the fall to get a satisfying, crackly leaf walk. You can get there eventually following the alternate NW Crowchild exit description (page 59), on Northwest ride, page 101.

- For an ambitiously long day ride or leisurely multi-day ride, you can cycle out to Cochrane (page123) for the dozens of flavours of MacKay's Cochrane Ice Cream that draws crowds from Calgary on summer weekend afternoons. You can stroll the traveler-friendly streets for crafts and antiques. You can go 1 K further west for a look at the Cochrane Historical Ranch and have a picnic there. From there you can go 1 K north on Highway #22 to the Western Heritage Centre. And if you don't feel like climbing the big Cochrane hill on your return to Calgary you can go south on Highway #22 and return to the city on Highway #8 (page 89). You could stay in Cochrane over night and return the next day.

- Another ambitious day ride or multi day holiday is to ride out Highway #8 to Bragg Creek (page 142) where you can also get serious ice cream, candy, cappuccino, lunch and real groceries as well as antiques and crafts. It's a beautiful town to ride around in with houses tucked away among large evergreen trees. Then you can return via Highway 22/22X (page147). Again, it would be worth staying in a Bragg Creek B & B overnight and cycling to Elbow Falls, and up the Elbow Falls Road, farther west before starting home.

-When you are serious about multi-day, you can invest three days going to Vulcan and back (page 149) - and enjoy many delights. Cycle to High River, get a B & B and explore this dignified little town. Have prime rib at the RoadHouse Tavern on a Saturday or Sunday evening. Try country dancing in the bar. These are real working cowboys and ranchers you are sharing the floor with. The next day explore odd little Cayley and it's geodesic domes, then Nanton's Aviation Museum and antique stores. After that cycle on to Vulcan and explore the town and its shops before heading 8 K north of town to the best kept B & B secret in Alberta: Prairie Past Bed &Breakfast. It should really be called Noah's Ark. Kittens, lamas, cashmere goats - you've got the idea. And the incongruity of a beautifully restored interior within a dilapidated farm house. Ask about the history of the owner's grandfather who homesteaded there. Day three you can try to catch the incomparable fun of a small town prairie baseball game in Carsland and enjoy a rest and snacks on the huge deck of the Wyndham-Carsland Park Store while making the long dash back to Calgary. Or you can plan to stop overnight in Strathmore to keep it relaxing. This is truly bicycle holidaying at its finest.

Let the adventure begin!

USING THIS GUIDE

This guide is designed to get you started, to introduce the joys of seeing part of the world from a bicycle. If you are leaving from Calgary, your first order of business is to get out of the city. So the next section outlines several exit routes. They are chosen to keep you away from traffic as much as possible. Routes back into the city are listed right after them.

The route descriptions include the symbols of various services available there. Then, right after the route description, a detailed list of service outlets shows the services available at each outlet. These are listed in the order that you will encounter them on the ride. The legend below clarifies any symbols that aren't obvious. For quick reference, the legend appears again on the inside back cover. This is designed to make it easy for you to find the things you need, with the minimum page flipping, while on the road.

Bicycle repair options are few and far between in rural areas. You may find a hardware store that sells bicycles and someone working there who assembles them may be able to give you some help. Many farmers and ranchers are used to improvising fixes and might give you a hand. A few cycle shops are listed here, but be warned that they change hands, close down and change their hours. Within Calgary the yellow pages and the city cycle path map, on which cycle shop sponsors are listed, will yield several.

When you see the symbol for groceries (🍎) it indicates more than a convenience store. A convenience store is primarily a source of snacks. The line between them is often blurred in the case of some of the large convenience stores and some of the tiny, independent grocery stores. If you can buy sweets, salty things and fast foods you'll see (▪). If you can buy a full range of groceries you'll see (🍎). And sometimes our judgement won't be the same as yours.

The symbol for accommodation (🛏) does not specify if it is B&Bs, motels or hotels. Camping is just - (⛺). The service list at the end of each ride provides at least one phone number you can call about accommodation in that location. This is either a place with which I have first hand experience or completely random.

Ideas on things worth watching for as you travel are just inserted into each ride. You can ignore these if you want to do your own discovering.

Reference material at the back lists things to consider taking and provides some additional information for people from out of town. That's also where you will find reading ideas for those who like that sort of thing.

Service symbols:

- Bathrooms
- Water
- Snacks
- Ice cream
- Fancy coffee
- Restaurant
- Groceries
- Liquor outlet
- Picnic
- Service station
- Accommodation
- Camping
- Bike repairs
- $ Cirrus/Interac bank machines
- Fun shopping
- Emergency medical services
- Telephones
- Tools

It won't be long before you start planning your own rides and routes. To help you get started, here are a few things to look for in routes and rides you plan.

- Paved road
- Uncrowded roads, the lower the vehicular traffic the better.

- A distance that you can comfortably ride in a day, which means 60 to 120K per day until you know what works for you and 30 to 60 K when you are breaking in.
- New routes, new places - to feed the explorer.
- Old familiar routes to cycle without paying attention.
- Not continuous steep hill, as in crossing the Rockies.
- A B & B or alternative accommodation that can be booked ahead.

And you'll catch on quickly that routes can be combined and interwoven to get variety or for alternatives that help you manage wind shifts and length of time you have to ride.

Alert: Accuracy of kilometers will vary. Many of these rides were repeated several times without an odometer so information was taken from maps and road signage. On rides measured with an odometer, the odometer stopped counting for part of the trip (Don't ask). Maps are hard to measure accurately, even with a string, and road signage varies depending whether it is measuring from city centre or city limits.

Care has been taken to give you accurate measurements here but the exact start location, route and stop location that you use as well as the above discrepancies will mean variations.

Oh... and By the Way...

There are some briefly described rides included here that are physically demanding due to hills, or require camping, or for some other reason I have not done yet. But they are popular and you may enjoy them. So they are added to give you the idea. In all cases, you will want to gather more information before attempting these rides.

Routes out of Calgary

When you start out-of-town trips, whether one-day or multi-day, you want to get in and out of the city as efficiently as possible with minimal vehicular traffic. City-managed bicycle paths minimize vehicular traffic and can be beautiful. They also can be convoluted and on sunny weekends the most popular stretches are so busy they become time consuming. They will be jammed with pedestrians, joggers, preschoolers with training wheels, baby strollers, dogs with leashes extended across the path, roller-bladers who take long, gliding strides into your side of the path and traffic jams that rival rush-hour on the street. This doesn't happen until late morning so you have four hours grace that you do not get on the road.

If you decide to always use the bicycle paths, which is just fine, buy the *Calgary Pathway and Bikeway Map*. You can get it from one of Calgary's cycle shops or from Map Town on 6th Avenue and 6th Street SW downtown or phone the City Parks and Recreation Department that produces the maps and ask them where to find a copy: 268-2300. We have excerpts here but the full map gives you all your path options in more detail.

A word about headwinds and tailwinds when you are going out and back in one day. Some people would rather struggle against a headwind in the morning and get all the wind advantage that they can coming back. On the other hand, you may feel you are stronger and ready to face more later in the day. If these things matter to you, check the forecast the morning you leave. They might be right.

All the exit and entry routes here leave from the 10th Street NW area of the city and return you there. You'll find enough of them in every direction that wherever you are located you will have at least one exit and one entry option convenient to you.

They are listed here starting with due north and then around the compass clockwise. It seemed a logical order. It means nothing about which routes are better than others. The all-around most reliable route, any time of the day, any day of the week, for both leaving Calgary and getting back in is the Simons Valley Route.

Because 10th Street is the centre of the universe in this book, it doesn't make sense to repeat the list of services available there in each route. They are listed below.

Services - 10th Street NW -

Named the Kensington area (after one of the two main streets), the Hillhurst/Sunnyside area (after the two communities there) and the 10th Street area, this is Calgary's lotus land. There are many cappuccino and bagel shops, fancy restaurants, happening bars, a frozen yogurt bar, shops with books and clothing, both new and used, bakeries and chocolate shops.

Beautiful, treed Riley Park is on the corner of 10th Street and 5th Avenue. Apart from stunning flowerbeds, gigantic old trees, Sunday afternoon band concerts and cricket, Riley Park also has a gigantic wading pool. This pool is so big there is an island in it with trees growing on it. Consider a foot-cooling wade and the most entertaining and joy-filled people watching anywhere in the city.

Of the enormous number of fancy coffee shops, some are open early but none *really* early. Check ahead. *Second Cup* on the corner of 10th Street and 4th Avenue NW is open 7 AM to 11 PM seven days a week.

The Shell Service Station at 5th Avenue and 10th Street NW opens at 7 AM weekdays and 8 AM weekends.

For groceries, the Safeway across the street is open 9 AM to 10 PM, Monday to Friday, 8 AM to 10 PM Saturday and 10 AM to 9 PM Sunday. You can get a full range of fresh fruit, ready-to-go deli, cold drinks, buns, cheeses etc.

This is the hub of bicycle shops in Calgary but you may have trouble talking them into doing repairs on the spot. None of them open early so you'll have better luck getting your needs looked after on your way back into town. They will probably have copies of the *Calgary Pathway and Bikeway Map.*

Kensington Wine Store, at 1257 Kensington Road NW is west of 10th Street. Kensington Road Ts into 10th Street just north of Memorial Drive, north of the River. Fun shopping extends along several blocks of Kensington Road.

A repertory movie theatre, The Plaza, on Kensington Road in the first block west of 10th Street draws a loyal crowd.

Out on the C-Train

One option for getting to the edge of the city is to take the C-Train. You can take your bike on the C-Train during July and August as long as it isn't rush hour. However the end of the north line is the only really helpful one that takes you beyond busy traffic. The south end-of-line station still leaves you with heavy exit traffic to brave.

It you are an out-of-towner, **phone 262-1000** to find out where to get a C-Train map and where to catch the train relative to where you are staying.

The northbound C-Train is called Whitehorn. It takes you to the end of the line at 36th Street and Whitefield Drive NE, which is beyond busy traffic. To get out from there, cycle north on 36th Street NE to McKnight Blvd, which has a stoplight. Go right (east) at McKnight to 68th Street NE. From 68th Street you can go south to connect with south and east rides (Northeast - page 107, Chestermere - page 112, Strathmore & Langdon - page 119, Okotoks - page 129, Mossleigh - page 135, Vulcan - page 149, Drumheller - page 162, Acme & Carstairs - page 180 and the Grand Tour) or north to get to 112th Ave/Country Hills Blvd/Highway #564. This takes you to any east, north or west rides, Cochrane Triangle - page 123, Bragg Creek & Elbow Falls Road - page 142, High River & Millarville - page 169.

The southbound C-Train is called Anderson. The end-of-the-line last stop is at Anderson Road and MacLeod Trail. If it is early in the morning you can then cycle south on MacLeod Trail, which becomes Highway #2 out past Midnapore and you are away, see page 47. If MacLeod Trail traffic has built to its chaotic roar you may prefer to take the 37th Street SW route, outlined as an entry point. Turn to page 87 and read the ride up to the left turn from Anderson Road onto Elbow Drive. You are going to do that ride backwards and get to it by just cycling west on Anderson Road and keep going to the westernmost end of the street before turning left (south).

This puts you on 37th Street SW, heading down across Fish Creek and out of the city to Highway 22/22x on the southern boundary. From there any of the ride maps will show you routes close to Highway #22/22X that you can easily connect with, in some cases, doing the ride backwards..

N Centre Street Exit

Total route to the city limits: 20 K
Total time: 1 1/4 hours
Challenges

On this route you have the brief 10th Street NW climb and another climb on Centre Street North at the edge of the city. The latter stretch has no shoulder, is narrow and can be hectic with traffic. But even at is worst it doesn't last long and as soon as you turn onto Country Hills Blvd or pass that intersection you are away from traffic, and you are soon going downhill and either have shoulder or the road to yourself. The rest of the route is in residential areas and is not affected by whether or not other people are leaving town.

Route: N Centre Street Exit

You start on 10th Street NW ($). Go north on 10th Street up to the crosswalk at 13th Avenue NW. The Southern Alberta Institute of Technology is on your left. Turn right and then immediately right again (east then south) which puts you onto Crescent Road NW.

Alert: Don't turn the corner off 10th Street during rush hour (7:00 to 9:00 AM and 3:30 to 6:00 PM) on weekdays and Saturdays unless you are riding on the sidewalk. And the sidewalk disappears after you turn the corner so it doesn't do you much good. The point is that cars are not allowed to turn here during rush hour and if you are riding on the road, you are subject to the same rules as they are. And this happens to be a spot that is policed vigilantly. Your best option is to ride up the hill on the sidewalk, stop at the 13th Street corner and walk your bike up the 10 meters of grass to Crescent Road. Then start riding again when you get back on the road, facing south on Crescent Road.

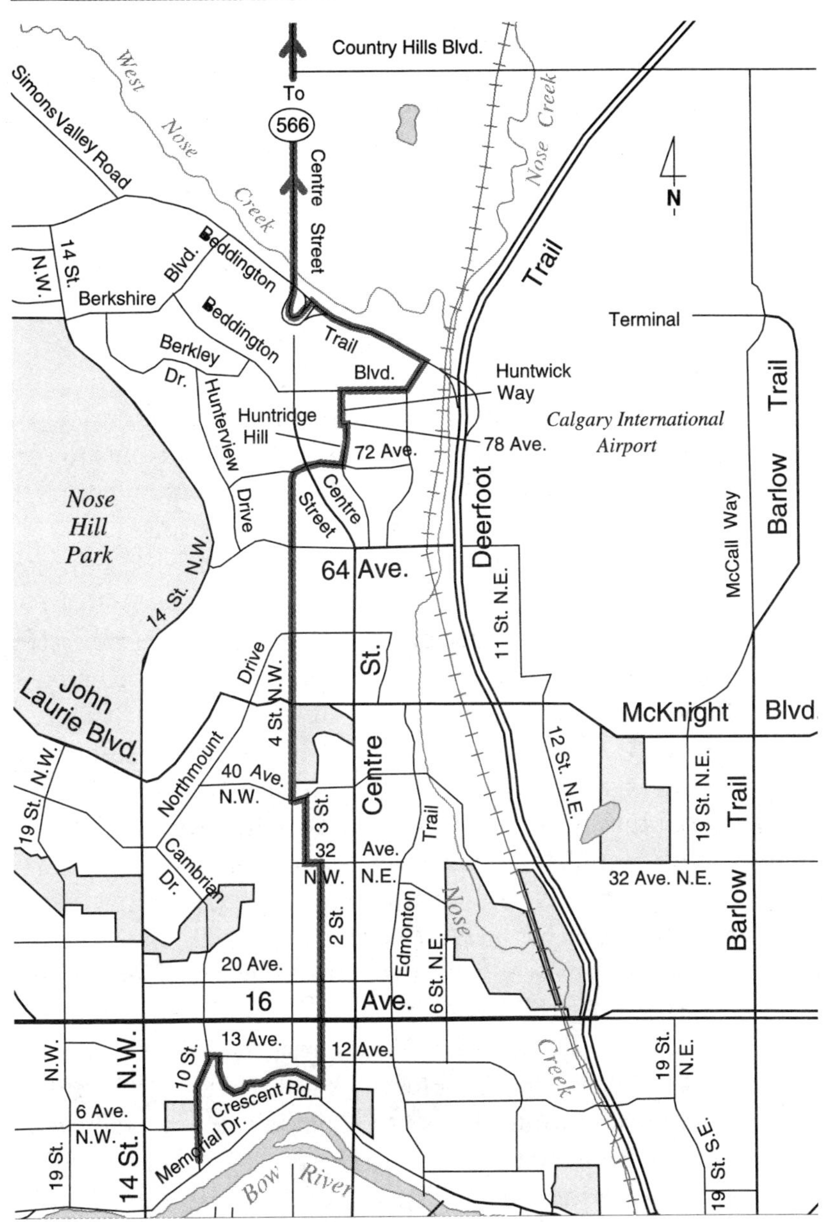

Crescent Road will curve you around above the city. There's a grand view regardless of the weather. You are perched over the downtown core, the Bow River and McHugh Bluff. This is where the buses bring tourists to look at Calgary. They stand in rows beside their buses with their friends lined up on the path and take pictures and videos of each other with the cityscape behind them.

When you pull yourself away from that scene, continue east on Crescent Road until you get to 2nd Street NW. Turn left (north) onto 2nd Street, which is never busy. In fact, on the city cycle path map you'll see that starting at 2nd Street, some of this route is part of the on-road cycle path route. It has been well chosen. It is a residential street that carries you painlessly north. Don't get confused in four blocks when the road turns east and you face a parking lot with a paved path on the left of it. Take the path. Second Street re-appears on the other side of the parking lot.

The path jogs again, west at 32nd Avenue, which puts you on 3rd Street continuing north. Then, again, a one-block jog west takes you around James Fowler High School on 40th Avenue. This takes you down a hill to 4th Street. Turn right (north again) onto 4th Street, and continue north.

Fourth is busier but not fast and never feels hectic except maybe 4:00 to 6:00 PM weekdays. Clustered around Northmount Drive you get your last chance at extensive services ($). Further up 4th Street at 68th Avenue and just before 72nd you get more. Once past here, you won't hit any more stores, without turning off this route, until the next town.

You continue going north on 4th Street until it curves from north to east and crosses Centre Street. Cross Centre, stay on the same street, which is now, called 72nd Avenue NE. In a couple of blocks there is a school on the corner. Turn left (north) there onto Huntridge Hill.

Now you meander a bit through residences to 78th Avenue, then left for half a block to Huntwick Way. This is all well marked with blue and white cycle path signs so you have additional guidance. Turn right (north) onto Huntwick Way. Huntwick Way continues north a long block and then turns east and runs like a service road, beside Beddington Blvd. Stay with it until it turns south again. There is a colourful children's' playground in front of you at that point. Now you leave Huntwick and ride up the sidewalk ramp (on your left) which is on the south side of

Beddington Blvd. Continue east on the cycle path/sidewalk beside Beddington Blvd.

The cycle path/sidewalk is ramped at each street for continuous riding. This is still part of the on-road, bicycle path route. You stay parallel to Beddington Blvd and wind around to a T-intersection at Beddington *Trail*. Turn left (west) onto Beddington Trail. In a short time you'll see a sign marking Centre Street North and indicating that you go left. This circles you under Beddington onto Centre Street leaving town. Do not be confused by other signage about Centre Street North that leads *into* town. Also, be careful about the city cycle map. It looks like you can just ride straight up Centre Street from the middle of town, cross Beddington Trail and head out. You can't. Once you circle around under Beddington Trail and are going north on Centre you continue north to Country Hills Blvd.

Along this stretch, Centre Street is really just a bumpy country road. No shoulder and there can be steady traffic as people dash in and out to their country-living-experiences. It can feel hectic for a couple of K. At the same time the surroundings make this part of Centre feel rural even though there is a subdivision further beyond.

At Country Hills Blvd you can turn right (east) which takes you on the overpass across Deerfoot and east out of the city. You can also continue straight north, which is renamed Highway #782. Both are excellent routes for going north, northeast, or northwest.

This is a fine return route if the country/city commuters have settled in at home instead of tearing in and out on that short, busy stretch. In the next few years this stretch will change as the city upgrades these roads to handle the increased residential development out there. Don't be surprised if you find it a bit different.

Services

10th Street NW – see page 32

4th Street & Northmount

- Shell Service Station: (🚻 ⛽ 🚗) on the west side of 4th Street, (5623 4th Street NW) open 7 AM to 11 PM seven days a week

- Safeway grocery store ( )
- CIBC (bank) with two bank machines ($)

4th Street & 68th Avenue

- 7/11 Convenience Store ( ) open 24 hours, payphone on corner of lot

4th Street & 72nd Avenue

- Zellars ( ) open 8 AM to 10 PM, Monday to Friday, 8 AM to 9 PM Saturday and 9 AM to 6 PM Sunday.

Drop-off

Your best drop-off options are either east or north of the intersection of Country Hills Blvd and Centre Street. It can be a busy intersection and there is no room to pull off. There are some rough, gravel pull-off bays that you could use but you would be better to continue along Centre Street North past Country Hills Blvd. You see traffic drop right off after that. Likewise on Country Hills Boulevard, get past the intersection to get away from traffic and find some shoulder.

Parking

Houses are sparse north on Centre outside the city limits. You are better off to negotiate with residents along Country Hills Blvd, which has a suburb on it. You could contact the Country Hills Golf Course, on Centre Street, or the Harvest Hills Golf Course, on Country Hills Blvd, to see if you could use their parking lots. You also could use the Park & Jet near the airport, (9707 Barlow Trail NE) at the corner of Barlow Trail. They charge $4.95 per day. There is a second lot, Park 'N Fly, at 9100 Barlow Trail NE and they charge $5.75 per day. If you park in either of these, then just cycle north on Barlow Trail and west on Country Hills Blvd.

NE Airport Exit

Total route: 21 K

Total time: 1 1/2 hours

Challenges

Traffic can be heavy on this route if you are later than 9 AM on a weekend, or 7:30 AM on a weekday, particularly along McKnight

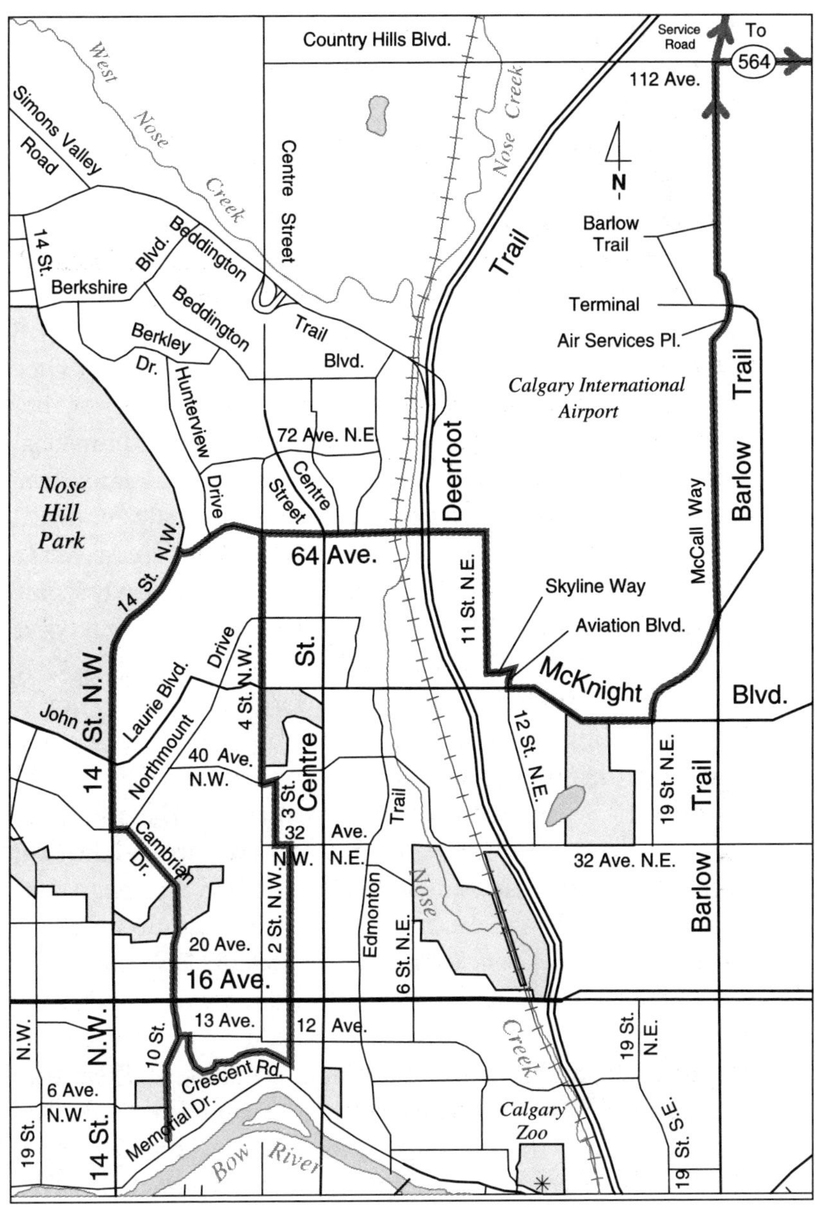

Blvd. There is, however, plenty of shoulder there. The 10th Street and 14th Street hills are steeply graded but still manageable. The shoulder is stingy in places but the traffic lanes are wide enough that you will not feel crowded.

Route: NE Airport Exit

You go north on 10th Street NW ($) and cross 16th and 20th Avenues at the stoplights. Tenth Street then cuts through Confederation Park and when it curves west is renamed Cambrian Drive. It takes you to 14th Street NW where there is a stoplight, ( ).

Turn right (north) onto 14th Street and travel up the hill. Near the top of the 14th Street hill you cross a major east-west throughway: John Laurie Blvd. Immediately north of John Laurie, there are some services in a strip shopping centre on your right ( ).

After that you'll see the road narrow and the commercial activity disappear as the road turns northeast and goes around the spur of Nose Hill Park. Stay with 14th Street as it curves around the park to 64th Avenue NW. Then you turn right (east) at the stoplights at 64th and travel downhill across 4th Street NW.

Continuing east on 64th avenue you cross Centre Street ( ) and pass Hunterview Plaza Shopping Centre (plus a wonderful International bakery) on the north side of 64th. You continue on 64th over the Deerfoot Trail overpass all the way out to where 64th ends at a T-intersection. Turn right (south) there on 11 Street NE. You are now in the northeast, having crossed Centre Street. Eleventh Street takes you around the back of the postal depot, a low building with a red roof. This street ends in a cul-de-sac. To get over to McKnight, that you can see across the grass ahead of you, turn left onto Skyline Way then right onto Aviation Blvd., which ends at the stoplight at McKnight Boulevard.

You then need to go left (east) and travel along McKnight for less than 2 K. Due to the heavy traffic, McKnight isn't fun unless it is really early in the morning but you are not on it long and it is the only way to get to McCall Way. This is well marked with a big green sign on your right, a double left turn lane and a traffic light.

And once you turn left (north) onto McCall, you'll see that it was worth it. You pass some aviation hangers that give you an inside glimpse on small aviation operators and then McCall Way becomes a lovely, quiet road between the east side of the airport runways and Barlow Trail. Leisurely cycling, grassy fields, birds, airplanes. Suddenly you are in the country.

McCall Way ends at a T-intersection with a stop sign. You go right (east) onto Air Services Place that curves 1/4 circle around to where it intersects with Barlow Trail, the main road into the airport terminal. There is a stoplight at this intersection.

You can go into the airport if you need services: ($). If not, you cross Barlow Trail. Then, oddly enough, you are on the extension of Barlow going north, up to Country Hills Blvd/112th Avenue. Country Hills Blvd is 112th Avenue NE east of Barlow and eventually becomes Highway #564 further east. Go right (east) on Highway #564 and you are out of the city heading to any points north or northeast.

You can use this route to return too as long as it is past 6 PM. Until then, McKnight may be unpleasantly busy.

Alternative route

To avoid the long, steep 14th Street hill and possible traffic on 14th Street, you can start this route a bit more restfully. Change the first part by starting with the route described in detail under NNW Simon Valley Exit on page 63. Then you switch back to this route at 64th Avenue and 4th Street NW by going left (east) on 64th Avenue and starting to read the directions on the previous page.

Services

10th Street NW, see page 32

SW corner of Northmount Drive and 14th Street

- Fas Gas, open from 7AM to 11PM seven days a week ( )

14th Street, north of John Laurie Blvd

- Turbo Service Station: 7 AM to 11 PM weekdays and 8 AM to 10 PM weekends ( )
- North Haven Food Mart opens at 9 AM so it won't be useful for early departures ( )

Centre Street & 64th Avenue NE

- Mac's Convenience Store is easy to pull into but doesn't have bathrooms ( )

- Shell Service Station beside Mac's Convenience Store welcome you, even on a bike (🚻 ♿ 🚗)
- Esso Service Station on the north side of 64th (🚻 ♿ 🚗) Hunterview Plaza Shopping Centre a few blocks further east along 64th, on the north side, just before Deerfoot Trail.
- Canadian Tire (🚻 ♿ 🏪 ☎)
- Hunterhorn Bakery (🏪) open 8 AM to 6 PM Monday to Saturday, 10 AM to 5 PM Sunday, a wonderful International bakery with samosas for a great meal on wheels, all the regular goodies and some brand new surprises (🏪)
- A&W (🚻 ♿ 🏪 🍴)

64th Avenue east of Deerfoot Trail

- Deerfoot Mall for serious shopping, (🚻 ♿ 🏪 🍴 🍎 $)

Airport

- A&W(🚻 ♿ 🍴)
- Harvey's (🚻 ♿ 🏪 ☎)
- Tim Horton's (🚻 ♿ 🏪) open 24 hours
- Food court (♿ 🏪 ☕ 🍴)
- Calgary Convention & Visitors Bureau kiosk inside a chuckwagon on the main level
- Bank machines ($)
  - plus, in the terminal (🚻 ♿ ☎)

Drop off

The intersection of Highway #564/112 Avenue and Barlow Trail works well.

Parking

The airport Park & Jet is perfect. Even for multi-day trips your vehicle is secure and it costs just $4.95 per day. It is on the corner where Barlow Trail leaves the main entrance to the airport and turns north - 9707 Barlow Trail NE. There is a traffic light there. An alternative is Park 'N Fly, down the street at 9100 Barlow Trail NE for $5.75 per day.

Remember, however, it does mean that regardless of where you cycle to, you have to re-enter the city at the same place to pick up your vehicle.

East Exit

Total route: 14 K to 1#A, 30 K south to #22/22X
Total time: 1 1/4 hours to 2 hours
Challenges

On Memorial Drive traffic will gradually build after 8 AM on weekends and build quickly after 7 AM weekdays. Once you are past Edmonton Trail, a major artery into the downtown, you will have plenty of shoulder. Traffic on Highway #1 will build at the same time as on Memorial and it will be faster but the shoulder is wide and well surfaced. There are no difficult climbs here but you have to cross traffic exiting from Memorial Drive onto Deerfoot Trail so the lighter the traffic the easier to shoulder check, looking backwards and riding forwards as you cross these exits. Calgary has an east wind about 20% of the time so that's how often you will be heading into wind leaving this route.

Route: East Exit

This is an excellent, direct and traffic-free route early in the morning. Tenth Street NW ($) leads onto the 10th Street/Louise Bridge. Don't cross the bridge. Go left (east) onto Memorial Drive. Continue east under the Centre Street Bridge and across Edmonton Trail (stoplights). Then Memorial opens up a bit, becomes wider and faster. There is a bit of ambiguity at the Deerfoot Trail interchange where you have to keep crossing the exit lane to proceed east on Memorial but this is easy enough when there is little traffic. The grade up the east side of the river valley is comfortably gradual and Memorial carries you straight east past 44th Street NE () to 68th Street NE: (). Pretty simple. You are now 1.5 K south of Highway #1/TransCanada and 1.5 K north of Highway #1A, both of which go east.

So you have a choice. You can turn left (north) at 68th Street to get to Highway #1/TransCanada Highway /16th Avenue going east. At the time of writing, the 16th Avenue and 68th Street intersection is the last traffic light on the east edge of the city.

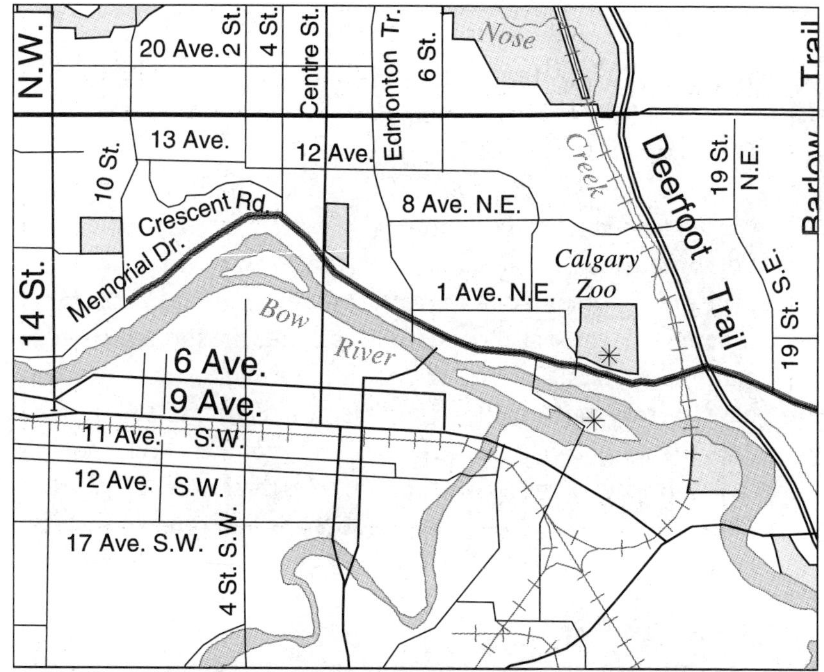

The TransCanada Highway is usually carrying major traffic and it is going fast. However it hasn't got out of bed at 7 AM so you have a head start and a wide shoulder. You are now heading due east. Lake Chestermere is 8K further along. Strathmore is about 40 K.

Late in the day there is heavy traffic pouring into the city on Highway#1/ TransCanada. And afternoon on Memorial Drive can be busy. But both roads have good shoulder and can be used for return routes if you are feeling traffic toughened.

Your second exit choice from 68th Street NE and Memorial Drive, is to go right, (south) onto 68th Street SE, which takes you down to 17th Avenue SE. Seventeenth Avenue becomes Highway #1A as it leaves the city. It also links you to the south exit through Shepard.

Watch 68th Street south of Memorial Drive. If you are riding it after the new subdivision there has woken up you will face heavy traffic. The road hasn't been upgraded to deal with the traffic volume it carries at the time of writing. The problem is compounded by the fact that there is no shoulder and a high curb – leaving you nowhere to escape to. So this strip can feel

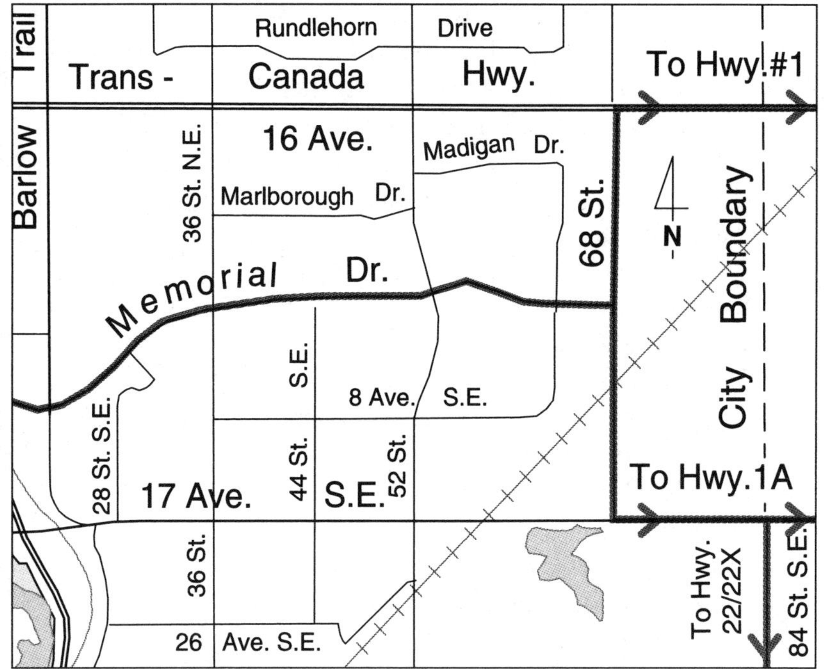

stressful when you share it with traffic. Like all others, early in the morning, it's great. And direct.

Turn left (east) onto 17th Avenue SE, which takes you beautifully out of town as it turns quickly into Highway #1A to Lake Chestermere. Lovely, curving, quiet road. Returning, you have the 68th Street problem unless it is late in the evening.

If you are going south, you also turn right (south) onto 68th Street from Memorial Drive and then left (east) onto 17th Avenue SE. You only stay on 17th Avenue SE to 84th Street SE at which point you turn right (south) again and ride all the way down to the SE corner of the city limits. On the way, 84th has curved and become 88th Street SE and that Ts at Highway 22/22X.

Both Highway #1A and 88th/84th Street through Shepard are excellent entry routes.

Alternative on cycle paths

There are bicycle paths that wind through northeast suburbs and can take you as far as about three blocks south and west of the intersection of 68th Street and Memorial Drive. Study your bike map. They are a little hard to follow because they wind around a fair amount, but they do keep you away from traffic if you are late leaving. Add extra time to exit using them.

The cycle path along the irrigation canal goes all the way to Lake Chestermere. Consider that, described on page 113 and clearly shown on your bicycle map - trailing off the map on the lower right side.

Services

10th Street NW, see page 32

Memorial Drive & 44th Avenue NE

- 7/11 store on the south side of Memorial Drive, open 24 hours ()

Memorial Drive and 68th Street NE

- Mac's Convenience Store ()

68th Street and 8th Avenue NE

- 24-hour Mac's on the east side

Chestermere

- Porter's Gas and Food Mart, () open Monday to Friday 6:30 AM to 9 PM, Saturday 7:30 AM to 9:30 PM and Sunday 8 AM to 8 PM
- Chestermere Landing Restaurant and Lounge: () there is pizza and steak 7 days a week and the dining room, serving a range of food, is open Thursday to Sunday. The dining room overlooks the lake

Drop-off

Do not try a drop-off on 68th Street NE at the entry ramp to Highway #1.There is no pull-off room. Your choice is either the convenience store parking lot on 68th Street and Memorial Drive, 68th Street and 8th Avenue or after turning onto the #1 Highway. You should then drive until you've crested the hill and see fields beyond. At that point there is room to pull off and merging traffic as all sorted out. If you go south to Highway #1A, as soon as you get to 17th Avenue SW there is wide shoulder and plenty of room for dropping people off, organize bikes and gear etc.

Parking

If you are just doing a loop to Lake Chestermere you are almost there at that point. For multi-day trips, if you take the big Highway #1, get driven east to Strathmore and negotiate with a business or resident there. And remember to plan your return route to pick up your vehicle.

S Midnapore Exit

Total route: 27.5 K to City Limits, 35 K to turnoff onto Highway #2A to Okotoks
Total time: 2 to 2 1/2 hours
Challenges

Traffic is a major consideration on this route, particularly the MacLeod Trail stretch until you pass the 22X/Marquis of Lorne overpass. After that you have a huge, well-surfaced shoulder. Headwind is rarely a problem heading south from Calgary but this does not constitute a guarantee. No steep grades.

Route: S Midnapore Exit

Leaving early matters more with this route than any other. Not only is it a bit further but the traffic you face at the last stretch can pose more of a problem than on your other exit routes. Give yourself almost 2 hours to get out of the city via this route. On weekdays the last stretch of this route will already be busy by 7 AM, on weekends, 7:30.

If you start on 10th Street NW, ($), go south across the Louise (10th Street) Bridge. Once across the bridge, the street curves right and becomes *9th Street SW*. Ninth Street Ts at 9th Avenue SW. You go left (east) onto 9th Avenue skirting what is, on the weekend, deserted downtown, to 5th Street SW. You turn right (south) onto 5th Street that takes you under the railway tracks, across 17th Avenue, south to Elbow Drive. Again the road ends and you go right (southwest).

You are now on Elbow Drive. Early on a weekend morning you can cycle all the way down Elbow Drive to Canyon Meadows Drive at the south end of the city without encountering much traffic. You come up a little rise on Elbow that keeps the Canyon Meadows Drive street sign hidden until the last minute at which point you need to go over into the left turn lane. You'll see the tall Husky Service Station sign on the southeast corner before you see the street sign ( ).

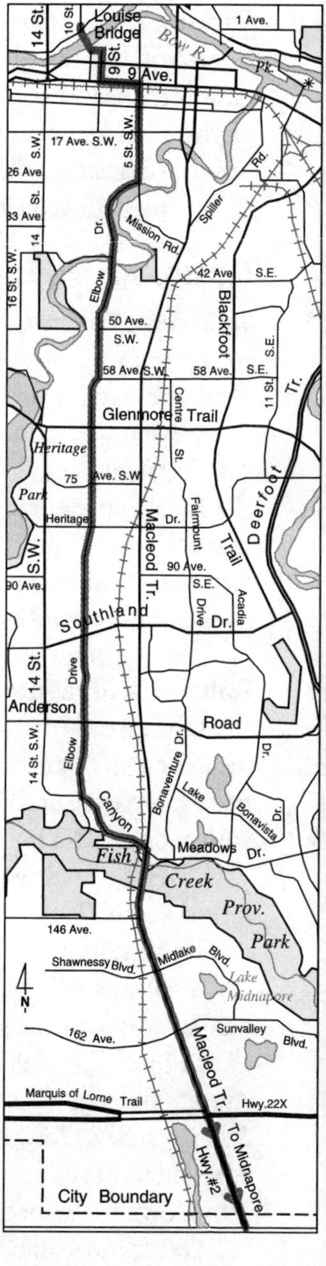

Turn left (east) onto Canyon Meadows Drive which takes you comfortably down the hill to MacLeod Trail. This puts you onto the least pleasant stretch because even early – and by then it probably isn't that early – there is traffic on this stretch of MacLeod Trail and it is travelling fast. The sign says "110 K" and they drive 130. Turn right (south) at MacLeod Trail /Highway #2. That takes you through a bedroom community called Midnapore, ($) and on to open highway. Fortunately, the high-way has a very wide shoulder within a few kilometers of passing Midnapore. You can feel yourself relax with the addition of this breathing space.

If you stick to Highway #2 for about 4 K from the city limits sign (which is about 25 K from the city centre) you can turn off onto quieter roads – always a preferable option. You need to watch carefully for your first chance to do so, which will be at Pine Creek Road. Look at the map to track this section. You will see the Pine Creek Road turnoff after crossing a lovely valley with an elegant horse ranch on your right. Just before you crest the next hill you see a small, green highway sign on your right that says De Winton. Parallel to it, on your left, placed on the highway median, a green sign says De Winton and below it Pine Creek Road. That's what you want.

Alert: Prior to that you will have passed a brown sign, on your left, that said Pine Creek Campground and indicates a turn. Don't be fooled. That isn't the turn you want.

If you go past the correct turnoff, Pine Creek Road, you get a second chance about 2 K further down Highway #2. This turnoff is called Dunbow Road and is also 242 Avenue. Go left (east) onto that if you missed Pine Creek Road.

Whether you took Pine Creek Road or Dunbow, you get to a corner where Pine Creek Road joins Dunbow Road/242 Avenue. Pine Creek Road becomes 2nd Street at this point and continues south. Take 2nd Street, heading south.

Now you are riding parallel to Highway #2 on your right. This is a little used road that, in spite of being a bit lumpy, is just fine considering that you rarely need to go over to the edge to make way for traffic. You see grass encroaching on the edges of the old pavement and have the feeling this may have been the only highway south of Calgary for years. (Did it carry DeSotos? Edsels?)

Now, it carries you and winds around and down a hill where it turns around into Highway #2A leading into Okotoks if you go right (west). If you go left it is secondary Highway #552.

Highway #2A carries you over the busy Highway #2 and then curves southwest and up a gradual incline before the big, long hill down into Okotoks. This is a wide, well-paved, wide-shouldered road. The fact that there is more local traffic is hardly noticed. This stretch feels like country. Fields around you. Pleasant cycling. If the weather is clear, a great view of the Rockies to the west.

Down the big hill into Okotoks. ($) You are on your way to wherever you wish, heading southwest. This is the least advisable return route back into Calgary. MacLeod Trail is extremely busy as the day progresses.

Alternative on cycle path

You could keep away from traffic, which will be an issue if you leave late, by using the cycle paths. It doesn't, unfortunately, eliminate the unavoidable MacLeod Trail/Highway #2 part of the exit traffic. And the cycle path route would add substantially to your time. If you choose this, use the Calgary Pathway & Bikeway Map to pick up the trail that follows the Elbow River south to Fish Creek Park. You would exit Fish Creek Park after going under the Macleod Trail overpass. Get up on the road and head south. You would still face the challenging high traffic area through Midnapore but you are near the edge of the city.

Services

10th Street NW, see page 32

Elbow Drive & Canyon Meadows Drive

- Canyon Meadows Husky Service Station with a convenience store is open at 6 AM weekdays, and 7 AM weekends. ( )

Midnapore

- 7/11 ($)
- There are several large, suburban grocery stores plus service stations and convenience stores along this strip. You can see them from the road but have to turn off to actually get to them. Your next chance for bathrooms is Okotoks.

Okotoks

- cappuccino spots ( )
- fast food, like A&W ( )
- restaurants ( )
- Ginger Room, a giant old house remodeled for classic tea: sandwiches, scones, Devonshire Cream, Sunday brunch, lunch and dinner ( ) one block east of the main intersection stoplight and one block south of Elizabeth, the main street
- Okotoks Lions Sheep River Park has 60 campsites and a picnic area and is lovely for a walk in trees, particularly in the fall ( )
- shopping centres lining Southridge ($)

- B & Bs: book ahead (🛏)
- (🍦 $)

Drop-off

Pine Creek Road, 4K south of the Calgary city limits sign. Do not turn left at the Pine Creek Campground sign. It's the next one you want.

Parking

You can probably leave your car at the drop-off point for the day. For multi-day trips I negotiate with one of the rural residents along Pine Creek Road to let you leave your vehicle on their property.

SW 45th Street Exit

Total route: 14 K
Total time: 1 1/4 hours
Challenges

The climb out of Edworthy Park is steep and long enough that it feels like work. So aim for a steady pace without going into your anaerobic zone and you'll make it. After that your climbing is done. Now you will only be bothered by traffic if it is past 8:30 AM on a weekend and only on the short Sarcee Trail stretch - - unless it's after 9 AM and then it can be busy around the shopping centres on the short Richmond Road section. On weekdays you are going against the main flow of traffic but it could be hectic on Sarcee after 7 AM.

Forty-fifth Street SW is never busy. Shoulder is great on Spruce Drive and adequate everywhere else until Sarcee where it feels scarce because traffic is travelling at highway speed. If there are strong westerlies, particularly a chinook, you'll battle all the way out on #8 after this exit.

Route: SW 45th Street Exit

Go south on 10th Street NW, (🚻 ♿ ▣ 🍦 ☕ ✕ 🍎 🍸 ⛩ 🚗 🛏 🚲 $ 👫 📞), to the stoplight at the Bow River. Go right (west) on Memorial Drive. Memorial Drive is quiet on a weekend morning and busy on weekdays after 7:30 AM but it will all be going the other way. Although you will be travelling on the same street,

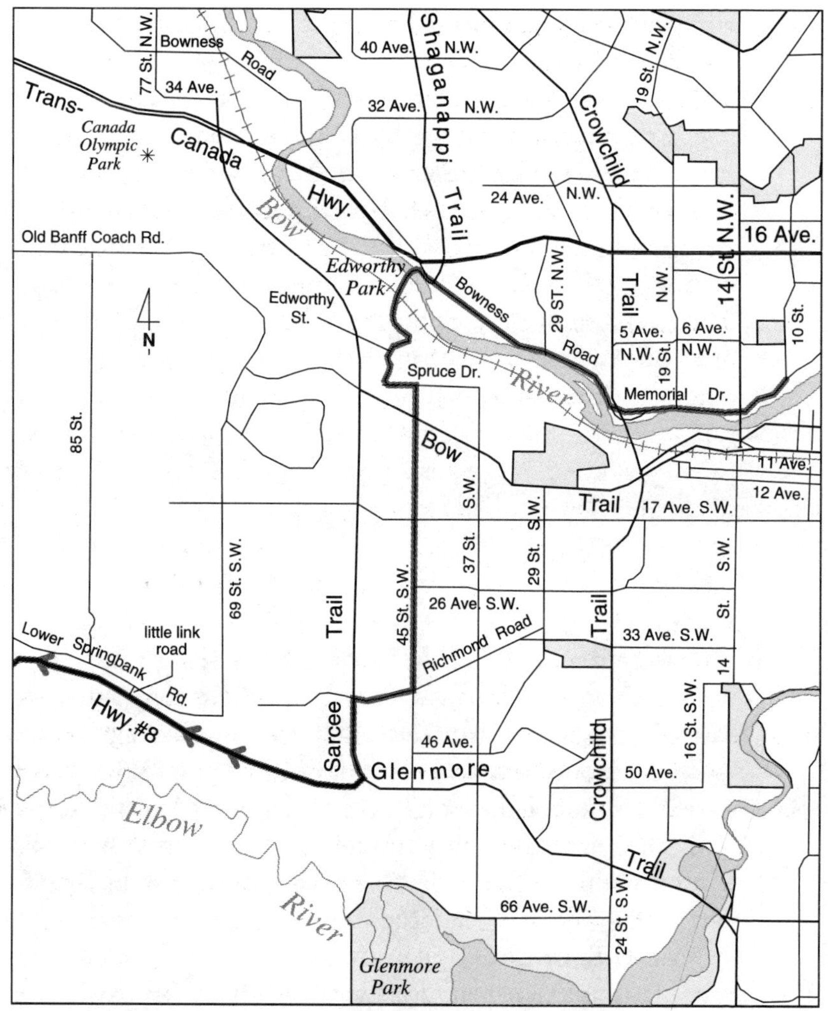

without turning off, don't be surprised to see that the name changes several times. Memorial Drive becomes Parkdale Blvd ( ) two blocks after Crowchild Trail. It then becomes 3rd Avenue ( ) for a while before it turns into Bowness Road around the Point McKay condominiums. Ignore all this and just keep to the main road. It's obvious.

Just where Shaganappi Trail (stoplights) takes off to the right, you turn left (south) into the Edworthy Park parking lot. This road is a bit rough but it is short. It is marked "Edworthy Park". The more prominent Shaganappi Trail signage is your signal to get over into the left-hand turn lane.

You can also get to this point by cycling west on the city bicycle path along the north shore of the Bow River. This is a good choice if you are late leaving and traffic is already busy.

Either way, when you get to the footbridge that crosses the River into Edworthy Park, you turn left, onto it. Once across the footbridge, follow the park trail as it goes to the left. It then curves right and takes you through the Park, across the railway tracks and up the hill into the parking lot. The Park has services in operation in the summertime: ( ).

If you chose the wonderful cycle path on the south side of the river to get this far, you enter the Edworthy Park parking lot from the east side and turn left (south) from there.

Alert: A word of caution about the south river bank cycle path. The springs on the bank above the path leave a thick sheet of ice across the trail in one spot. It often isn't melted off until well into May. Be careful.

The climb up the hill on the south side of the parking lot, Edworthy Street, is serious work. The road is smooth gravel and not busy but it is steep and you'll use all your gears and work up a sweat for the .8 K it takes to get to the top.

Once you are on top, you take the first road that crosses Edworthy, which is Spruce Drive, an elegantly wide street. Go left (east) on Spruce Drive to 45th Street SW. At 45th Street, where you'll see one of the blue and white city cycle path signs, you turn right (south). There are several services where 45th Street crosses Bow Trail: ( ). Forty-fifth Street rolls up and down through mainly residential streets. There are many school and playground zones so vehicular traffic avoids it. And the street is wide and comfortable. There are a couple of sharp dips and climbs but they are short and the road carries you painlessly down to the south end of the city and connects you with Richmond Road.

Go right (west) when you get to Richmond Road. There is a stoplight there, the first since you crossed 17th Avenue SW. The Calgary Co-op Store on Richmond Road provides services ( )

You are only on Richmond Road three or four blocks before you come to the busy intersection of Richmond Road and Sarcee Trail (going north-south). This can be intimidating but you are through it quickly. Get over into the left turn lane prior to getting to the intersection and go left (south) onto Sarcee. You only travel on this busy, fast-traffic street for 800 meters to get onto Highway #8 west.

You now have smooth sailing and are heading west. You can go southwest to Bragg Creek, page 142 or you can go northwest to Cochrane, page 123. Both have wonderful snacks, shopping and things to see.

Returning this route on a busy weekend afternoon, the heavy traffic on Sarcee may force you up on the grass until you reach the right turn bay heading into Richmond Road. It is a short distance and well worth "discretion being the better part of valor". As well, be very cautious on this strip from 4 to 6 PM on a weekday.

Services

10th Street NW, see page 32

Parkdale Blvd

- Robin's Donuts, at 3303 3rd Avenue NW, open 24 hours (🚻 ♿ 🥤)

Edworthy Park

- During the summer there are water fountains operating, washrooms available (🚻 ♿)
- During the busy part of summer weekends, (probably 11 AM to 6 PM) in good weather there is an ice cream/hot dog/cold drink vendor parked in an old bread truck in the parking lot (🥤 🍦)

45th Street & Bow Trail West

- Turbo Service Station open at 7 AM (🚻 ♿ 🥤 🚗)
- Mac's convenience food store, kitty corner to the Turbo, open 24 hours.

Richmond Road

- Calgary Co-op Store (🚻 ♿ 🥤 🍴 🍎 🚗 $) opens usual retail hours, fresh fruit, muffins, scones, nuts, trail mix, juice. Their bathrooms are easiest to access in the service station.

- Richmond Square Canadian Tire (☎)
- London Drug on the south side of Richmond Road (☎ ☎ plus film, cameras, makeup, drugs, candy, drinks)

Drop-off

You avoid the worst traffic spot on this route by being dropped off past Sarcee Trail on Highway #8. The highway has plenty of shoulder to pull off anywhere there or turn onto the little road on the right that connects to Lower Springbank Road. It is well marked.

Parking

This is another spot where you'll have to negotiate parking on the private property of a local resident along Highway #8 or Lower Springbank Road.

W Bow Trail Exit

Total route: 13 K
Total time: 1 1/4 hours
Challenges

You have to climb the same Edworthy Park hill and then a more graded climb up Bow Trail.

Route: W Bow Trail Exit

This is a good exit route if you are a bit late leaving and want to avoid the traffic around the shopping centres at Richmond Road and Sarcee Trail.

Use the SW 45th Street exit (page 51) to the top of Edworthy Street. Then, after climbing the Edworthy Park hill, you can take Spruce Drive left (east) for 100 meters, then immediately turn right (south) onto Worcester Drive. Worcester Drive curves around east and parallels Bow Trail. At that point there is just a grassy strip, 8 feet wide, between you and Bow Trail. Get off your bike and lift it over the grassy strip that separates you from Bow Trail West. Of course, if you have mastered "jumping" your bicycle over curbs, you can do that. Once over the grass, turn right (west).

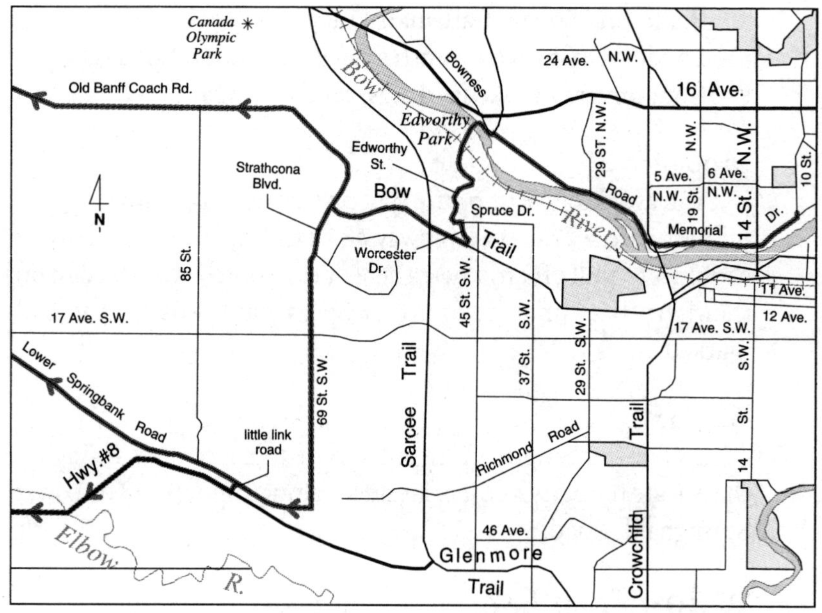

Now you are heading west on Bow Trail. Cross Sarcee Trail at the stoplight and go straight up the big hill, which is still called Bow Trail. This is a long hill but it is graded so that you can get up it by just keeping pedaling. You probably won't have to go into your lowest gear if you've been cycling a bit.

At the top you hit another stoplight and T-intersection. There is a bus shelter and bus loop in front of you that you can pull into if you want a rest or to look at maps and drink water and be pleased for making it up the hill.

Here, you will choose whether you want to exit northwest or southwest. Both eventually get you to Highway 22/22x, both are beautiful rides with manageable traffic. The northwest route has less traffic and less shoulder. The southwest route, on Highway #8, is real highway conditions: well-graded hills, wide smooth shoulder and fast traffic.

If you are aiming southwest you now go left (south) along Strathcona Blvd and that carries you past a shopping centre and service station (). The road then curves a bit more south and becomes 69th Street. This feels like the western city boundary line although it isn't because once you are past the subdivision this street feels rural. Sixty-ninth takes you down a steep hill to connect you with Highway #8. On the way you cross 17th Avenue SW. There is a four-way stop there. Seventeenth Avenue looks like another exit option going west. Don't bother taking it. It is still restricted from cyclists at the time of printing and has a horrifically steep gully, down one side and up the other. You'd have to be crazy to try it.

When you get to the bottom of the big 69th Street hill you can see Highway #8 ahead. For 1 K you ride parallel to it on Lower Springbank Road. Then you hit a little link road that joins Lower Springbank to Highway #8.

You can choose to proceed west on Highway #8 or on Lower Springbank Road. Both of them eventually get you out to Highway #22 but if you take Lower Springbank it will loop you north to connect with the road you would have taken west if you had chosen the northwest exit from the bus shelter. Lower Springbank Road turns north, becomes 7th Avenue /Springbank Road. A pretty route.

For returning, you face going up the 69 Street hill - - brutal but done by racing cyclists for training. Once you have accomplished that, Bow Trail may be busy late in the afternoon. If that doesn't bother you, this route works fine both ways.

Back at the bus shelter on Strathcona Blvd and Bow Trail you may have decided to go northwest. And at press time you can do that due to the defeat of an attempt by the Municipal District of Rockyview to close Old Banff Coach Road to cyclists. At the time we go to press this was defeated in court as discriminatory. It could be appealed by the Municipality. Local cycling groups are lobbying to ensure that you have access to this alternative. If you do, you can now turn north on Strathcona Blvd. It circles around northwest and then west, offering services on the way, (🚻 ♿ ☎) and then becomes Old Banff Coach Road. This also continues west past acreages and links to Upper Springbank Road in an increasingly rural landscape running more or less parallel to Highway #8 out to Highway #22.

It is a source of great jubilation among the cycling community that this lovely road is again open and cyclists are advised to ride this stretch, as all roads, with courtesy to vehicles. Remember it is illegal, unsafe and discourteous to ride side by side on bicycles.

Note that a friend with children says he wouldn't take his kids out this way because there isn't much shoulder. There also isn't much shoulder on 69th Street.

Services

10th Street NW, see page 32

Parkdale Blvd

- Robin's Donuts, at 3303 3rd Avenue NW, open 24 hours

Edworthy Park

- During the summer there are water fountains operating, washrooms available.
- During the busy part of summer weekends (probably 11 AM to 6 PM) in good weather there is an ice cream/hot dog/cold drink vendor parked in an old bread truck in the parking lot

Strathcona Blvd south of Bow Trail

- PetroCanada with a snack shop is open 24 hours
- IGA Grocery Store is open 9 AM to 9 PM every day of the week ($)

Strathcona Blvd north of Bow Trail

-convenience stores on the right

Drop-off

There's plenty of shoulder on the little road that links Lower Springbank Road and Highway #8. Your driver can let you off safely and turn left onto Highway #8 to get straight back into the city.

Parking

Again, negotiate with residents on Lower Springbank Road or Highway #8.

NW Crowchild Exit

Total route to city limits: 23 K
Total time to city limits: 1 1/2 hours
Challenges

Crowchild is another one of those routes that builds traffic steadily in the morning. On a weekday it is going the other way so you should be okay. On weekends this route builds a bit earlier than others. If you don't like traffic, get out of here before 7 AM on weekdays or weekends. There isn't much extra shoulder until you are past Brentwood Shopping Centre at 32nd Avenue/Charleswood. After that it improves substantially except at stoplights where it

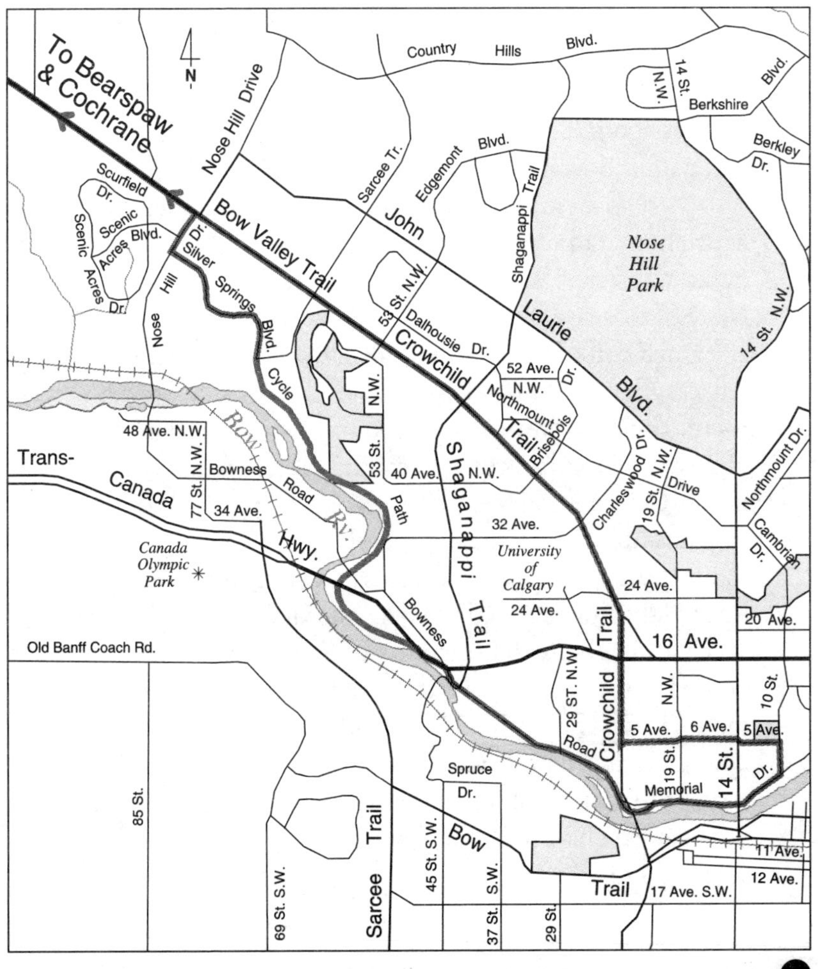

narrows until you are through. The grade is only steep in the first climb from 5th Avenue to 16 Avenue and that is quite do-able.

A word about headwinds is in order here. Calgary's prevailing winds are westerly and during a chinook, (powerful fohn winds that bring dry air rushing down the lee side of the Rockies), grinding west into the teeth of the wind can be discouraging. Good exercise but discouraging. If you have a choice and don't want headwinds, check the forecast. Also the earlier you leave the less likely you are to hit a chinook.

Route: NW Crowchild Exit

From 10th Street NW, (🚻 ♿ ⛽ 🍦 ☕ 🍴 🍎 🍸 ⛩ 🚗 🚲 $ 👪), go west on 5th Avenue NW. It takes you west to Crowchild Trail where you go right (north), (🚻 ♿ ⛽ 🚗). Go north on Crowchild and up the hill. From 5th Ave NW to the point that you cross Charleswood/32nd Avenue NW, the shoulder is limited. It gets better after that and even better yet after Nose Hill Drive.

There is a gas bar across the street from the red and white McMahon Stadium and again at Brentwood Mall (🚻 ♿ ⛽ 🍦 ☕ 🍎 🚗 $) after 10 AM, on your right at 32nd/Charleswood Drive. None of these will be open before 9 or 10 AM.

Once you are past Nose Hill Drive, where there are many services after 10 AM, (🚻 ♿ ⛽ ☕ 🍴 🍎 🚗 🛏 ⛺ $), you have more room. Then you are out in the country. This is a rolling route and often a corridor for strong prevailing westerlies, particularly later in the day. So it can feel discouraging and you will be convinced that it is uphill even when it is level.

But you are surrounded by pleasant rolling hills and can see the Rocky Mountains ahead of you. The view is enough to get you speculating about the reactions of the original settlers as they headed west in wagons. What did they think when they saw those mountains? The city limits are at 12Mile Coulee Road and about 2 K past that you pass a tiny acreage community called Bearspaw. Bearspaw Gas is a fully equipped service station (🚻 ♿ ⛽ 🚗). Past Bearspaw you have rolling highway and can head west to Cochrane, see page 123.

This isn't a preferred route for entering Calgary after a major excursion because the long hills out of Cochrane can be daunting after a day of hard riding and Crowchild will be very busy by the middle of the day.

Alternative on cycle path

To avoid the Crowchild traffic you can use the cycle path to travel along the north side of the Bow River and out to Silver Springs Drive. You'll need the Calgary Pathway and Bikeway Map to follow this route as it leaves the river at spots and makes use of roads.

Briefly, follow the north side of the Bow River cycle path west to Home Road. Go right (north) onto Home Road and cross the TransCanada Highway/Bowness Road. This is the part you'll need the map for. In order to pick up the north river bank again after an s-bend in the river you turn left off Home road at 19th Avenue NW. Nineteenth Avenue takes you two blocks west to a one-way street, 52nd Street. I break the law here and cycle the wrong way for two blocks to get up to the church parking lot on the left and through it to the path. I don't advise doing this but it does save you the steepest part of the Home Street hill.

The cycle path along this north bank of the river does have some steep hills on it but they are relatively short. At the top of one of the hills, 3.2 K from where you entered this path beside the church, there is a pathway exit to 56th Avenue/Silver Springs Blvd. Leave the path on that exit. It will dump you out close to Silver Springs Blvd and 56th Avenue NW. Get out to the road and get your bearings. You want to get onto Silver Springs Blvd going north and west, curving around up to Nose Hill Drive. This is a grand, wide street worthy of the title "boulevard".

Nose Hill Drive is busier. You go right (north). Some people pedal this stretch on the sidewalk on the east side of Nose Hill Drive to get up to Crowchild. Courtesy to pedestrians is critical.

If the left turn lane onto Crowchild Trail seems more hectic than you want to take on, you can cross at the lights with the pedestrians and then again cross going west and that puts you on the correct side of Crowchild heading west out of town.

This provides an excellent re-entry option because it gets you out of traffic. If you can get yourself back into the city as far as Crowchild, Nose Hill Drive and Silver Springs Blvd to the entrance of the cycle path, you can use the description starting on the bottom of the previous page to travel on the cycle path route the rest of the way in to the centre of the city.

Services

10th Street NW *see page 32*

Crowchild Trail & 5th Avenue NW

- Esso self-serve service station on the northeast corner,( ) open 24 hours
- Village Park Inn ( )
- There are other hotels along Crowchild, consult Travel Alberta **1- 800-661-8888**

Brentwood Shopping Mall

- full range of mall stores but none open before 10 AM ($)

Nose Hill Drive

- You could turn right (north) if you are willing to brave busy shopping centres ( ) after 10 AM.

Bearspaw

- Bearspaw Gas is fully equipped ( ), opens at 7 AM weekdays, 8 AM weekends and in summertime sometimes switches to opening at 6 AM weekdays.

Drop-off

Bearspaw Gas is well past the Calgary sprawl inching out along Crowchild and has ample space to unload your bike.

Parking

You can ask Bearspaw Gas or people at the few houses along Highway #1A past there. If you are planning an excursions past Cochrane you can park in the parking lot at the Cochrane Ranch, less than 1K west of Cochrane on Highway #1A or the Western Heritage Centre 1K north on Highway #22 from the intersection with Highway #1A.

NNW Simons Valley Exit

Total route to city limits: 21 K
Total time: 1 1/2 hours
Challenges

After the little burst of energy required for the 10th Street hill you have no problematic grades. The only place you'll hit traffic if you leave late is the initial stretch of Simons Valley Road where the shoulder is narrow. At the very latest, that traffic disappears at 144th Avenue NW.

If there's a Chinook blowing you'll experience strong crosswinds on this route once you are out of the city. If you are leaving Calgary late in the day, this is the most forgiving of all the exit routes.

Route: NNW Simons Valley Exit

This is a truly excellent cycling route out of the city north because the part of the route inside the city isn't used for cars to leave town. It's mainly residential and kind and untraveled. And once you are at the edge of the city on Simons Valley Road, there aren't many vehicles.

This route starts the same as the N Centre Street Exit so you may be familiar with much of it already. Turn to page 37 and read up to the point that you are proceeding west on Beddington Trail looking for the Centre Street North sign.

To get to Simons Valley Road you stay on Beddington Trail past the Centre Street exit. It winds a bit and becomes Country Hills Blvd. Shortly after that, you see the green sign veering you off to the right for Simons Valley Road. Simons Valley Road is narrow for 2 K where new subdivisions are being built. There is no shoulder. This little stretch can be a bit busy. But it is marked 50 K so they are only going 60. It will probably be widened eventually but you are past it soon and on open country road, Simons Valley Road.

When you get to the City Limits sign at 144th Avenue NW it feels like you have already been out of the city for some time. There you find Symons Valley Ranch, which is the way the road used to be spelled - - go figger. You are heading north.

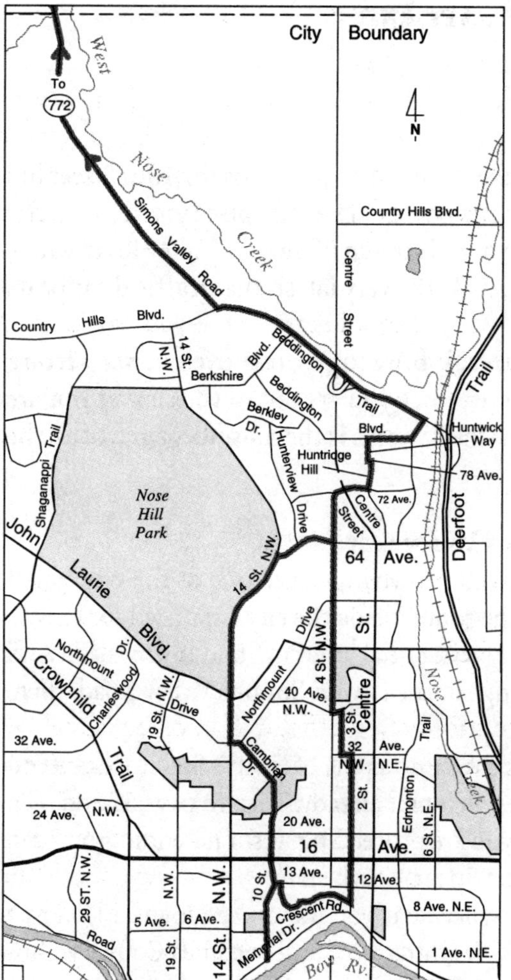

This route is also excellent for returning, with slight variation. See NNW Simons Valley Entry on page 93.

Alternate

You can begin this exit using the route described at the beginning of the NE Airport Exit, page 38 and when you reach 64th Avenue and 4th Street NW, turn right (north) and continue on the N Centre Exit page 34. To get onto Simons Valley Road, read the above exit starting at Beddington Trail and Centre Street North.

Services

Symons Valley Ranch has parking, (🚻 ♿ 🍴)

Drop off

Symons Valley Ranch has generous parking lots completely past any city traffic.

Parking

Symons Valley Ranch will probably let you park in their lot for a small fee.

Out from the train, plane or bus station

If you arrive in Calgary from out of town, the chances are it is by plane, train or bus - - the latter of which will usually take your bike "...at the discretion of the driver". All of these modes of transport are close to routes directly out of Calgary described here. The below descriptions will get you from the arrival point to an exit route.

For out of town travelers who want accommodation in the city before starting to cycle see pages 11 and 247. If you have been in transit overnight or arrive downtown in the middle of a weekday, consider a layover or a taxi to the edge of town. During July and August, if it isn't rush hour, the C-Train is another alternative. See page 33.

Exiting Calgary from the International Airport

If you arrive at Calgary's Airport this is all easy. The airport is so close to excellent city exits that it doesn't matter what time you arrive, you will not face traffic getting out. It also offers full services (🚻 ♿ ▣ 🍦 ☕ ✕ 🛏 $) and a currency exchange, payphones, a tourist information office and an on-site hotel

To cycle away from the airport, go up the elevator inside the airport terminal, taking your bike up to the departure level. The car ramp there is never as hectic as the arrivals level, which is dark and unpleasant. The departures car ramp is one way south and then curves around north and then east. Just stay on it to leave the airport. The road is wide enough for riding on the right and the traffic is never heavy. It leads you out of the airport area to a stoplight. You can see this on the NE Airport Exit map on page 38. On the corner at the stoplight there is a huge lot of parked cars: Park & Jet for long term parking.

Turn left (north) onto Barlow Trail. Don't be fooled. Barlow Trail also continues straight ahead in front of you at the stoplight. That would take you into town. Go left. Travel north on Barlow Trail to 112th Avenue NE, about 2 K.

Accessing east and northeast rides (Northeast, page 107; Chestermere, page 112; Strathmore & Langdon, page 119; Drumheller, page 162; and Acme & Carstairs, page 180) from here you go right (east) on 112th Avenue which becomes Highway #564. For Chestermere and Strathmore & Langdon rides you will go south on 68th Street NE to connect with the Highway #1 or #1A exits.

Accessing south rides (Mossleigh, page 135; Vulcan, page 149; High River & Millarville, page 169; and the Grand Tour, page 193) will still be easiest if you go north and around the outside edge of the city and pick up a south route outside. Go east on 112th Avenue NE to 68th Street NE. Turn right (south) and you can travel along the east edge of the city down to Memorial Drive. From here you can see your route on the East Exit map on page 45 and read the East Exit description on page 43. It will guide you the rest of the way out of the city.

Accessing west rides (Cochrane Triangle, page 123; Bragg Creek & Elbow Falls, page 142; High River & Millarville, page 169; and even The Grand Tour, page 193) you can go left (west) onto 112th Avenue NE/Country Hills Blvd. Again we suggest first getting out of the city and then circling around on the outside to get to the start of the ride. Country Hills Blvd Ts at Centre Street. Check the N Centre Street Exit on page 34. Turn right (north) onto Centre Street and travel up to the first main east-west road you come to: Highway #566. Again, this is a T-intersection. Go left (west) on this excellent road to Highway #772/Simon Valley Road. Go right (north) on #772. Continue north on #772 for north routes. For west and southwest routes turn left (west) off it onto Highway # 567 to get to the north/south Highway #22, about 22 K farther west. This is a nice introduction to rolling foothills and coulees - - which are river valleys cut into the prairie.

Try to avoid reaching Highway #22 the Friday afternoon of a long weekend or 4 to 6 PM any afternoon. It will be quite busy then. However it is only 9 K south to Highway #1A and then 1 K east to Cochrane. To get on a good ride from here, pick up Cochrane Triangle, starting on page 123. If you have just flown in, stay in Cochrane over night.

Services

two blocks up Coventry Drive from Country Hill Blvd

- Mohawk service station, open from 7 AM to 11PM seven days a week. ( )

Airport

- A&W( )
- Harvey's ( )
- Tim Horton's ( ) open 24 hours
- Food court ( )
- Calgary Tourist & Convention Centre kiosk inside a chuckwagon on the main level, staffed from 10 AM to 10 PM every day. They have a free City of Calgary map but not the Calgary Pathway and Bikeway Map.
- Bank machines ($)
- plus, in the terminal ( )
- Calgary Airport Hotel, ( )

Exiting Calgary from the bus depot

The bus depot has services: ( ) payphones and a wall-mounted index of accommodation for booking a place to stay. It is close enough to downtown to mean you need to plan around rush hour traffic (7 to 9 AM, 4 to 6 PM) particularly if you arrive in the morning. It is far enough away from our cycle routes that you will need instructions to get to them. However, once you get a few blocks east of the bus depot on 9th Avenue SW, you are at the hub of the city and can connect with cycle exit routes in any direction.

Ask in the bus depot how to get onto 9th Avenue going east from their exit door. It is a tricky maze of entrances, exits and side streets around the bus depot building, many of them one way. On site directions will prevent you going the wrong way.

Regardless of which way you want to be riding and which rides you want to connect with, I suggest getting to the middle of the city first to get to exits. Head left (east) on 9th Avenue SW. It carries you across the 14th Street overpass and then straight east into the downtown core. This is a major morning rush-hour artery into town.

If you are going to ride out of the city on cycle paths, you'll need to stop into Map Town for your Calgary Pathway and Bikeway Map. To do that, turn left (north) from 9th Avenue SW onto 6th Street. Ride north to 6th Avenue. Map Town is on the corner. Lock your bike to one of the signs outside and pick up your map. Then retrace your steps to 9th Avenue and go left (east) on 9th. Street numbers are well marked and you will see them count down as you travel east, getting closer to Centre Street.

For rides out to the south, (Okotoks, page 129; Mossleigh, page 135; High River & Millarville, page 169; Vulcan, page 149; and The Grand Tour, page 193) turn right (south) off 9th Avenue SW onto 5th Street SW. You will pass restaurants on the corner of 5th Street and 11th Avenue SW. These stretch out for a few blocks along 11th Avenue. They are not open early in the morning but they are open for business lunch and well into the evening – when this becomes a jumping strip nicknamed Electric Avenue.

For rides to the south when traffic is busy (weekday 3:30 to 6:30 PM, weekend 9:30AM to 6 PM) you can take the bicycle path to exit the city. It is easy to connect with it from 9th Avenue, just continue further east on 9th.

Alert: Watch for the dual right turning lanes from 9th Avenue onto 5th Street SW. You could walk across 8th with the pedestrians or get into the middle of the lane second over from the right hand curb so that you do not get cut off as you cycle through. This is a particularly tricky corner because the majority of the cars turning right will turn into the two far lanes of 5th Street, a one-way street going south.

In fact it is worth being cautious about cars coming up behind you and turning in front of you on any corner, any country. It seems to be a universal driving habit.

At Centre Street and 9th Avenue you'll see the landmark Calgary Tower, with its giant, rather ugly, concrete leg. There is a Calgary Convention & Visitors Office in the base of the Tower. They can give you help with accommodation and local events from 8:30 AM to 4:30 PM weekdays. There are also restaurants in the high-end Palliser CP Hotel, just before the Calgary Tower, and the Radisson Hotel, across the street.

Continuing east on 9th Avenue. You will notice that since crossing Centre Street the street numbers that you cross are now rising and are now called "southeast".

Continue past 5th Street SE. The railway yards are on your right. This is where 9th Avenue becomes a two-way street. Fort Calgary Historic Park is on your left and the Elbow River and bridge over it are straight ahead.

The cycle path exit you want to connect with has come from behind Fort Calgary and gone under this bridge in front of you and follows the Elbow River south. Cross the right-hand sidewalk and go down to the asphalt-paved pathway you see emerge from under the bridge.

You can use the Calgary Pathway and Bikeway Map to follow this exit south to Fish Creek Park. For the most part it is well signed with the distinctive blue and white signs but it would be frustrating to get lost. This route is sometimes scenic and quiet, sometimes close to traffic, sometimes quite isolated. It has one long, steep hill just before you enter Fish Creek Park.

Once in the Park, exit south after crossing under the MacLeod Trail overpass. Go up on the road and turn south - away from the city centre. You still have to get through the bedroom community of Midnapore, where traffic can be hectic but you are soon out on the highway. If you have the cycle path map you can weave your way through some of the residential streets to avoid some of this traffic, ($).

Turn to the S Midnapore Exit, page 47 for directions south from here.

For rides out to the north, east or west (Northwest, page 101; Northeast, page 107; Chestermere, page 112; Balzac, page 116; Strathmore & Langdon, page 119; Cochrane Triangle, page 123; Drumheller, page 162and Acme & Carstairs, page 180) from 9th Avenue you need to get north across the downtown core and the Bow River. From 9th Avenue turn left (north) onto 8th Street SW. This carries you north to the Bow River and riverbank cycle path.

As soon as you reach the end of the street and see the cycle path ahead of you, you will also see the bridge that carries the C-Train over the river, ahead to your left. The footbridge beneath that is the best way to get across the river and one block west to 10th Street, where all the rides in this guide originate and you can ride out from any of them.

Services

Bus depot

- cafeteria, payphones, accommodation guide (🚻 ♿ ☎)
  Map Town, 6th Avenue and 6th Street SW
- Calgary Pathway & Bikeway Map, The Country Key, and detailed sectional maps of the whole province

Electric Avenue: 11th Avenue between 4th and 6th Streets SW

- Restaurants and bars from The Keg to the exotic.

Centre street and Ninth Avenue

- CP Palliser Hotel and Raddison Hotels (🚻 ♿ ☎ ☕ ✕ 🛏)
- Calgary Tower revolving restaurant, expensive but has a great view and may help you get your bearings is you have a map and want to sit and collect yourself and eat and relax, (🚻 ♿ ✕). Ye it costs to go up.

MacLeod Trail/Highway #2 in Midnapore

- shopping centres with restaurants and service stations on either side of the road. You'll have to get off the highway to ge to them, (🚻 ♿ ☎ ☕ ✕ 🍎 🚗 $).

10th Street NW, see page 32

Exit Calgary from the train station

Train service from Calgary is very limited. At time of writing the only passenger service is from Great Canadian Railtour between Calgary and Vancouver. They offer package to see the Rockies in daylight. Passengers spend the night in Kamloops. These train rides are not cheap and a bicycle is only accepted if it is virtually dismantled and packed in a box. This is not practical when you arrive at the station on your bike. Their management people have indicated that their policy is open for discussion so you can try talking to them.

Their information number is 1-800-665-7245.

The Calgary train station is in the basement of the Calgary Tower. The exit routes from the bus depot, described above, work for the train station too. I will describe here how to connect with those instructions, which sound complex because you are dealing with one-way streets downtown.

There is a Calgary Convention and Visitors Bureau Office in the same building as the train station. Go up to the ground level and ask anyone for the base of the Calgary Tower.

If you are taking rides to the south (Okotoks, page 129; Mossleigh, page 135; Vulcan, page 149; or The Grand Tour, page 193) you need to circle the block to connect with the one-way streets that go in the right direction. Walk out of the train station. (The Radisson, a high-end hotel, is across the street.) Turn left and walk your bicycle on the sidewalk to the end of the block (1st Street SW.) You pass another high-end hotel, the CP Palliser, on the way. Cross 1st Street SW with the pedestrians and turn left (south) on the sidewalk and walk one block south. In both cases you are travelling against the flow of one-way vehicular traffic, hence the need to stay on the sidewalk.

First Street SW takes you under the railway tracks you just arrived on to 10th Avenue SW. Turn right (west). This road is outside the central downtown core and has a mixture of through traffic and parking traffic, but it is not heavy. Travel west, four blocks, to 5th Street SW where you connect with the S Midnapore exit on page 47. If it is a weekday during business hours you will have passed some restaurants on 10th and 11th Avenues SW.

If you prefer to get out of the city without encountering cars, turn right (east) on 9th Avenue when you come up onto street level out of the train station. Then start reading the bus exit directions on page 67, which describes passing the Calgary Tower en route to the bicycle path.

To get to north, west and northeast rides, (Northwest, page 101; Northeast, page 107; Chestermere, page 112; Balzac, page 116; Strathmore & Langdon, page 119; Cochrane Triangle, page 123; Bragg Creek & Elbow Falls Road, page142, Drumheller, page 162;

and Acme & Carstairs, page 180) you need to get north across nine blocks of the downtown core and across the Bow River.

Again walk up to street level from the train station, turn left (west) and walk, on the sidewalk, to the end of the block, to 1st Street SW. Turn right (north) and traffic-hardened cyclist can now cycle through classic downtown traffic for nine blocks. Others can walk on the sidewalk.

First Street SW stops at Riverfront Avenue. Cross Riverfront and you will see a paved pathway continuing on in the same direction, the remaining half-block to the riverbank. Go ahead to the riverbank but be careful, there are two stairs and a gate you have to get through on your bike. Once on the riverside path turn left (west) on the path and ride two blocks to Eau Claire Market (on your left) and Prince's Island Park (on your right).

Eau Claire has all the upscale services and entertainment you could possibly want (🚻 ♿ 🏪 🍦 ☕ 🍴 🍎 🍸 ⊼ $ 👪 ✆). So if you choose to stick around there for a while, it is understandable. When you are ready to get out of town, follow the same river bikepath further west. In about 1 K you will come to the C-Train bridge with a footbridge underneath it. Cross to the north side of the river on the footbridge and go one block left (west). Now you are on 10th Street where all the exit routes originate and can pick whatever you would like.

Services

Calgary Tower

- Calgary Convention & Visitors Bureau with road and accommodation information, open 8:30 AM to 4:30 PM weekdays.
- Calgary Tower Restaurant (🚻 ♿ 🍴) expensive and it costs to go up. But a great view for getting your bearings while you study a map.

Electric Avenue: 11th Avenue between 4th and 6th Streets SW

- Restaurants and bars from The Keg to the exotic.

Centre street and Ninth Avenue

- CP Palliser Hotel and Radisson Hotels (🚻 ♿ ☐ ☕ ✕ 🛏)

Eau Claire Market

- (🚻 ♿ ☐ 🍦 ☕ ✕ 🍎 🍸 ⊼ $ 👪) plus movie theatres, IMAX, foo court, entertainment indoors and out, a wading pool, convenient free standing washrooms beside the wading pool, drinking fountain, and a footbridge to Prince's Island with ducks, geese, a lagoon, lawn and trees and a place to be peacefu for a while.
- YMCA – on the west side of the Eau Claire plaza, with swimming pool, massage, cafeteria.

10th Street NW, see page 32

Oh... and By the Way...

For Camping Trips

Have the highest paved road in Canada to yourself.

The Highwood Pass, also known as Highway #40, is closed to motorized vehicles from mid-December to June 15 each year. Even after that, vehicles are few and far between because most people are unsure when it is open, where it is and where it goes to. A great situation for cyclists - and the Bighorn Sheep who's breeding grounds are protected by the closure.

You can start this spectacular ride in Bragg Creek and cycle down through Turner Valley and Black Diamond to Rivers Edge Campground, at Highway #541 just before Longview. If you did all that on a bike, it would be 105 K and a full day.

On the second day you can cycle west on Highway #541 to Highway #40/Highwood Pass and continue north to Mount Kidd Campground, 115 K.

On the third day you continue north again to the Barrier Lake Information Centre. You may want phone from there and arrange for someone to pick you up at the intersection of Highway #40 Highway #1 because the ride east on Highway #1 is not particularly pleasant.

If you camp and can arrange the drop off and pickup, this an amazing ride; physically challenging and beautiful.

Routes back into Calgary

The route choices here reflect the fact that traffic builds during the day and a steep downhill leaving the city isn't fun returning. Your familiarity with your exit route may beckon but your cycle holiday may have you returning from quite a different compass point. If you want to circle the city, outside the city limits and enter on your exit route, see page 97 for roads that will take you around the city edge. Check the variations on those exit routes, below, to be sure you adjust for traffic patterns later in the day and for topography going in the opposite direction. Then pick the city entry route that works for you.

Riding the C-Train in

Whatever mode you used to get out, the C-Train is an option for getting back in. You'll need to look at a C-Train map to determine if either the end of the line stop in the northeast or in the south will take you somewhere from which you can ride home. If necessary, phone Calgary Transit for help: 262-1000.

The location of the Anderson Station at Anderson and MacLeod Trail is not helpful during the daytime for a cyclist trying to avoid heavy traffic. However if you've been riding too long, the weather has turned bad or if you have bicycle problems it may be worth putting up with the traffic to connect with this transport. Use the SW 37th Street Entry on page 87. After turning north onto Elbow Drive, turn right at your first chance: Sacramento Dr. Sacrament takes you east to Anderson Station.

If you are catching the Whitehorn C-Train, in the northeast, you are going to be able to get to the end-of-line station with minimal traffic even during traffic peaks. Get on Highway #564 heading toward the airport, either going east or west, depending on where you are coming from. You want to be east of Barlow Trail and the airport. Go south on 68th Street NE to McKnight Blvd. At the stoplight at McKnight Blvd turn right (west) and ride along this wide, divided street to 36th Street NE. Turn left (south) onto

36th Street NE and the last C-Train station is just past 39th Avenue NE on your right.

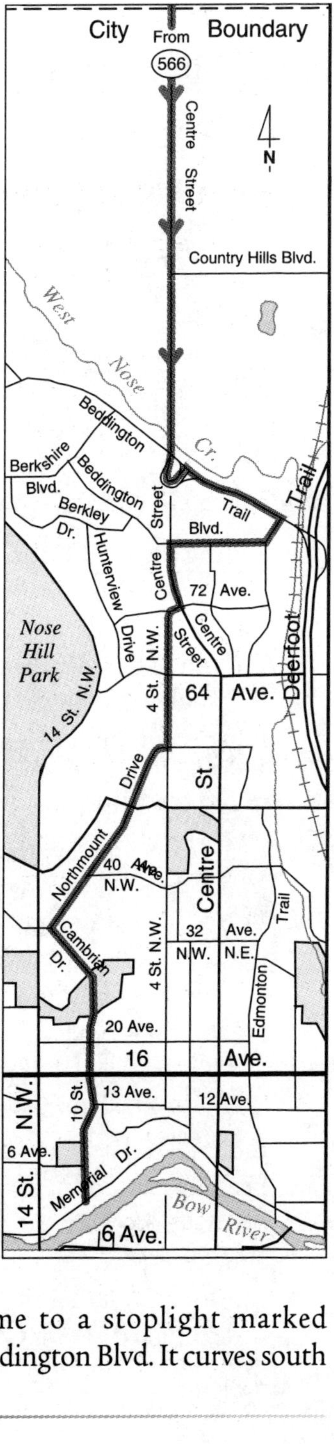

N Centre Street Entry

Total distance from city edge: 18 K
Total time: 1 hour
Challenges:

Not many. The last strip of Centre Street can be hectic before Beddington Trail and navigating onto the in-city continuation of Centre Street to head south seems counter-intuitive but is simple when you have done it once.

Route: N Centre Street Entry

Pick up this route coming back into the city from the north, northeast or even from the northwest if you have the time. Highway #566 takes you to the top of Centre Street from the northeast or northwest. Turning south onto Centre Street and go straight south from there and on into the city.

Stay on Centre Street past Country Hills Blvd on the east. Go down the hill and underneath the Beddington Trail overpass and then the only route that you can take is to curve left up onto Beddington Trail. This has you going right (southeast) onto Beddington Trail. Continue on Beddington Trail until you come to a stoplight marked "Beddington Blvd." Go right on Beddington Blvd. It curves south and then west, a wide, divided street. There is a little rise when it meets Centre Street. Go left (south) on Centre and from here you can use the NNW Simon Valley Entry and services described on page93.

NE Airport Entry

Total route: 21 K
Total time: 1 1/2 hours
Challenges

This route means minimal traffic unless you hit McKnight Blvd in the late afternoon. By evening it is quiet. And so is the rest of the route in. No difficult climbs, shoulder ranges from adequate to excellent.

Route: NE Airport Entry

You can enter almost the same NE Airport route that you took out. From 112th Avenue NE/Country Hills Blvd, turn south onto Barlow Trail. That takes you just over 2 K to the corner with a stoplight that leads to the airport terminal on your right. The airport terminal offers your first services (🚻 ♿ ☎ 🍦 ✕ 🛏 $) opportunity as you enter the city. But you won't find anywhere convenient to lock up your bike except the carpark.

To continue on into the city, cross Barlow (yes, both are Barlow) and curve around on Air Services Place. It takes you in a semicircle to McCall Way, on your left. McCall Way takes you all the way south past the airport runways to a stoplight and McKnight Blvd. Go right (west) onto McKnight and continue on McKnight until the next stoplight, about 2 K. This is Aviation Blvd. Turn right and then very soon left onto Skyline Way. This is the connector to 11th Street NE. You are now out of the most demanding traffic stretch.

Take 11th Street right (the only way it goes, which is north) down the hill to 64th Avenue NE. Sixty-fourth can be busy with shoppers, even in the evening, but they are not travelling fast. Here you have access to services too, (🚻 ♿ ☎ ✕ 🍎 🍸 🚗 $). Go left (west) onto 64th.

Travel west on 64th Street NE, across Centre Street, (where 64th becomes NW), to 4th Street NW. Again a traffic light and you want to get over into the left-hand lane to turn left (south) onto 4th Street from 64th. This route is now different from the exit route. Go south less than 1 K on 4th Street you will pick up Northmount and go right (southwest). There is a stoplight there and services ($). Northmount meanders around and takes you comfortably down the hill to Cambrian Drive, which turns into 10th Street NW after you turn left (southeast) on it. Again, some limited services here, ( )

Left (southeast) along Cambrian, through Confederation Park, down 10th Street to home - - and Calgary's LaLa Land ($).

You can exit the city this route too but the climb up Northmount is steep.

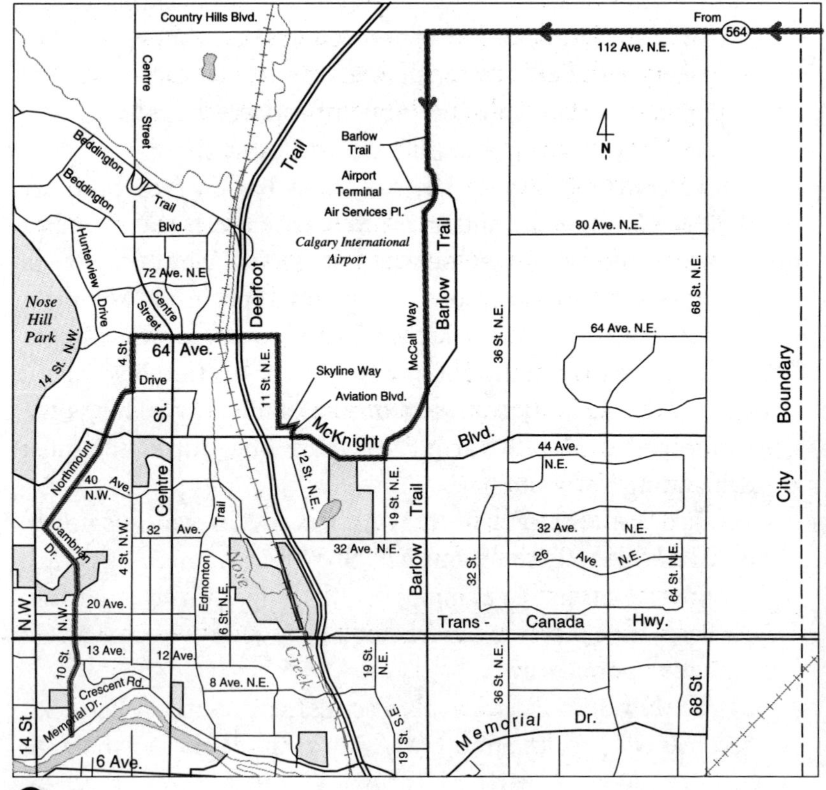

Services

Airport

- A&W ( )
- Harvey's ( )
- Tim Horton's ( ) open 24 hours
- Food court ( )
- Calgary Convention and Visitors Bureau kiosk inside a Chuckwagon, would you believe, on the main level, open 10 AM to 10 PM daily
- Bank machines ($)
- plus, in the terminal ( )

64th Avenue east of Deerfoot Trail

- Deerfoot Mall for access to a range of ($)

Hunterview Plaza Shopping Centre a few blocks further west along 64th, on the north side

- Canadian Tire ( )
- Hunterhorn Bakery ( ) open 8 AM to 6 PM Monday to Saturday, 10 AM to 5 PM Sunday, a wonderful International bakery with food you can pick up to warm for dinner, all the regular goodies and some brand new surprises
- A&W ( )

Centre Street & 64th Avenue NE

- Mac's Convenience Store is hard to get to from this direction you would have to cross at the stoplight. It doesn't have bathrooms ( )
- Shell Service Station beside Mac's Convenience Store welcomes you, even on a bike ( )
- Esso Service Station on the north side of the street, easy to pull into, ( )

4th Street & Northmount

- Shell Service Station: ( ) on the southwest corner, open 7 AM to 11 PM seven days a week
- Safeway grocery store ( )
- Bank of Commerce (CIBC), on the east side of 4th, has two bank machines ($)
- A string of ($) in the strip mall

Scattered along Northmount

- (🚻 ⊛ ▣)

Northmount and Cambrian

- small shopping centre (▣ ♨ 🚗)

10th Street NW, see page 32

East Entry

Total route: from Highway #22/22x and 88th Street SE to city centre: 29.5 K, from #1A, 14 K

Total time: 1 1/2 to 2 hours

Challenges

Traffic wise this is feast or famine. No traffic on 88th/84th Street but as soon as you hit 17th Avenue SE traffic mounts block by block and is heavy during late afternoons. Highway #22/222x can be busy on weekends until the evening. Seventeenth Avenue SE quiets down right after dinner and is amazingly quiet weekend evenings. No problematic grades.

Route: East Entry

Highway 22/22X, which is also called Marquis of Lorne Trail, traverses the south end of the city. From there you can easily connect with 88th Street SE at the southeast city limits. Eighty-eighth/84th Street is very quiet. This is an excellent route back into the city. In fact, even if approaching the city from the southwest, along 22/22x, if you have time you may want to cycle the extra 17 K from 37th Street SW, (your other southern entry option) to 88th Street SE.

If you do so, you'll pass Spruce Meadows and then go over the Highway #2 overpass - at which point #22/22x starts being called Marquis of Lorne Trail. You'll then pass Fish Creek Park and the turnoff to Highway #2 north/Deerfoot - at which point 22/22x seems to stop being called Marquis of Lorne Trail. Bicycles are prohibited on Deerfoot Trail. Once most of the vehicular traffic takes that turnoff, #22/22x is carrying very light traffic.

Eighty-eighth Street is well marked when you are travelling east on Highway #22/22X: a big green sign on your right says 88 Street and Shepard. Also, on your right, you'll see the green City Limits

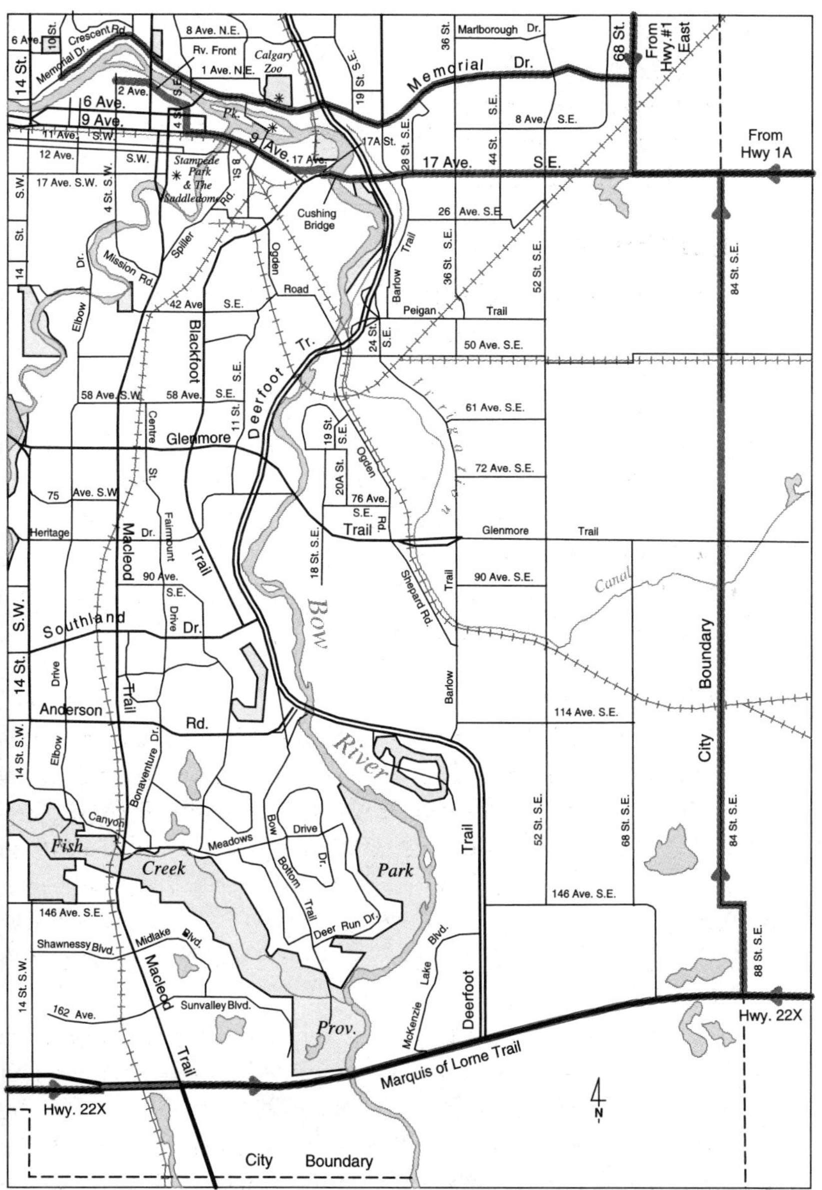

sign. That, plus the standard little city street corner sign, looking a bit forlorn out in the middle of nowhere, is all you get if you are cycling west. So you have to watch for it. It is small. But there is nothing else around it, standing on its little pole.

Turn north on 88th Street SE and you can go 15 K north to 17th Avenue SE. Soon after getting onto 88th, the number changes to 84th after a big S curve. You feel very much out in the country on this road. You see marshes, ponds, ducks, red-winged blackbirds standing sideways on reed stalks and even some pens of sheep, not common in cattle country. You can see the tiny downtown core off in the future like the Emerald City.

You go in past Shepard, a non-town known primarily for its car races. Sometimes as you cycle by you can hear the cars roaring on the track and the waves of cheering from the grandstands. It seems a bit incongruous on your bicycle. This is your first chance for a convenience store, ( ). You cross Glenmore Trail, which extends a long way east out of the city.

Eighty-fourth takes you to 17th Avenue SE. Seventeenth Avenue becomes Highway #1A to your right. You turn left (west) to get back into the city. This takes you into the heart of Forest Lawn where cars are king and drivers are young and inexperienced but it is DIRECT. And there are wide lanes so you are not crowded against the curb.

If you are continuing in on 17th Avenue SE, skip to bottom of next page page.

If you prefer Memorial Drive for the last stretch in, you can turn off 17th Avenue SE at 68th Street SE. Go right (north) and it will take you up to Memorial Drive then left (west) onto Memorial. When you do this, you'll find services at Memorial and 68th Street E ( ). Turn Left (west) onto Memorial and continue heading west down into the river valley, across Deerfoot Trail and past the Zoo. Memorial is also busy in the afternoon but you have sufficient shoulder. It is only a noticeable problem past the Zoo and big, brick General Hospital where the two right hand lanes of traffic swing off to the right to take the flyover to downtown. At that point you need to get across those two lanes of exiting traffic to continue west on Memorial. Be careful. Stop and wait if you need to. Traffic is fast in this one spot as vehicles accelerate to curve up onto the flyover.

As an alternative, to avoid this, you can take the overpass at the Zoo, immediately after you have crossed the Deerfoot Trail interchange, two sets of lights that you can't miss. Then you see wrought iron birds and animals decorating the overpass crossing the road ahead of you.

Turn into the right exit lane and up onto the Zoo overpass. Turn left (south) onto the overpass. That takes you across Memorial Drive. Then you have to become a pedestrian because you will not be able to go where you want on the road. It is one way - - toward you. So, go up on the sidewalk on your right at the end of the overpass. At the T-intersection light, cross to the south side of the ramp with the pedestrian signal. Once across, go up on the south sidewalk. Turn right (west) and walk down the sidewalk. This takes you down a short hill where you still face on-coming, one-way traffic but you have two options off to your left.

You can get to the Zoo by going left and crossing the Zoo Bridge onto Zoo Island. You would then follow the road as it curves left to the Zoo entrance.

If you want to continue travelling west toward 10th Street NW and the centre of the city, cross the traffic coming across the Zoo Bridge and go up on the paved cycle/foot path that extends in front of you along the river. This off-road option is worth serious consideration. You are not missing anything pretty on the roadway and you are safer and can get quite directly to Eau Claire or 10th Street NW on this stretch of cycle path.

Meanwhile, back at 68th Street and 17th Avenue SE. If you stick with 17th Avenue to get back into the city, you ride west along 17th Avenue into increasingly dense traffic but if it is after supper it is much quieter than during the daytime. Even the cruisers in Forest Lawn eat dinner. There are a string of services on either side of you: (Nm ⊛ ▣ ✕ 🚗 $).

Eventually the road curves a bit southwest and down a hill past the entry ramp to Deerfoot Trail, the big north-south throughway. This is tricky for about 1 K. You want to pay attention here and get out of this traffic quickly. You stay on 17th, Avenue, which is about to turn into Blackfoot Trail, and you ride up the Deerfoot Trail overpass and then you get off your bicycle, unless you know how to jump the curb with it. Either way, get up on the sidewalk on the right. You are on the north side of 17th Avenue SE/ Blackfoot Trail.

Stay with the sidewalk to cross the Bow River on the Cushing Bridge, ahead of you here. There is little lane space for a bicycle on the bridge traffic lanes and a sign that says cyclists have to dismount and use the sidewalk. So use it.

I didn't once, before I had seen the sign, and it was a hair-raising few seconds as I pedaled like crazy across there. Cars were honking, which was unnerving. It felt as if a pack of animals were at my heels.

Once across the bridge you stay on the sidewalk to the first intersection: – 17A Street SE – at which point you have to make a funny little switch to get onto 9th Avenue SE. Turn right onto 17A. You ride a brief 10 meters to 17th Avenue SE onto which you turn left (sort of southwest). This gradually angles southwest, away from Blackfoot, which you just left. Seventeenth Avenue links you up to 9th Avenue SE in about three blocks. Trust me. You are now immediately away from heavy, fast traffic and will feel yourself relax.

Ninth Avenue from 6PM on is a quiet, lovely road with a few cars and the ambience of old Calgary shops. This neighbourhood offers the invitation to stroll and kind of services you find on 10th Street NW ($).

Stay on 9th Avenue SE across the Elbow River at Fort Calgary and you are now at the east edge of downtown. At this point you can turn right onto the bicycle path that goes behind Fort Calgary or continue cycling on streets by continuing west on 9th Avenue until it becomes one-way (against you) at 4th Street. Turn right (north) onto 4th Street SE, which takes you five blocks north to the Bow River. Now you have a choice. You can follow Riverfront Street left (west) to the Eau Claire Market (you can't miss it, Riverfront goes right into it) and jog north half a block and enter the Eau Claire outdoor parking lot on the north side of the complex.

Or you can get onto the cycle path as soon as you get to the river and travel that leisurely river-view route to Eau Claire. Either way you end up at Eau Claire.

This gives you a chance, as you savour your victorious re-entry (with an ice cream?) to see what the rest of Calgary is doing outdoors. It feels like they are the audience for your triumphant return. Then you can travel the river cycle path further west or whatever direction you need for the last leg back home.

You can also use either Memorial Drive or 17th Avenue SE when you are entering via Highway #1A, or Highway #1. From Highway #1A, stay on 1A/17th Avenue SE and, when you get to 17th Avenue and 68th Street, choose to continue in either on 17th Avenue SE or go north on 68th to Memorial Drive, bottom of page 80.

Entering from Highway #1, turn south at the big, double-turning bay onto 68th Street NE and go south to Memorial Drive. That's where you choose to either go right and continue in on Memorial (page 80) or continue further down 68th Street to 17th Avenue SE where you turn right (west) onto 17th Avenue (page 81). If you choose the latter just be warned that 68th Street between Memorial and 17th Avenue SE can be very busy and the lanes are narrow, there is no shoulder and the curb is high. This will eventually be improved.

You can exit the city via 9th Avenue and 17th Avenue SE but Memorial is much prettier so if both are early-morning-quiet, Memorial wins.

Services

17th Avenue SE

- rows and rows of stores and the Calgary Co-op Store ($)
- restaurants, with a growing number of East Indian, Thai and Chinese options, ()

68th Street and 8th Avenue NE

- 24-hour Mac's on the east side

Memorial Drive & 68th Street E

- Mac's Convenience Store ()

Memorial Drive and 44th Street NE

- 7/11 store on the south side of Memorial Drive just before 44th, open 24 hours (), tricky to reach riding west

Memorial Drive & 36th Street NE

- Food court in Franklin Mall, north side of road, ($)

Memorial Drive & 23rd Street NE

- Swiss Chalet for an economical chicken meal, (🚻 ♿ 🍴), north side of Memorial - - but it won't be open early if departing this way

Chestermere

- Porter's Gas and Food Mart, (🚻 ♿ ☎ 🚗) open Monday to Friday 6:30 AM to 9 PM, Saturday 7:30 AM to 9:30 PM and Sunday 8 AM to 8 PM
- Chestermere Landing Restaurant and Lounge: (🚻 ♿ 🍴) pizza and steak 7 days a week and the dining room, overlooking the lake, is open Thursday to Sunday.

9th Avenue SE

- Cross House Garden Café (two blocks north toward the Zoo bridge, 1240 8th Avenue SE) in a beautifully restored old mansion has a huge garden with outdoor patio and George would never turn away a weathered cyclists. This is high-end eating, (🚻 ♿ 🍴)
- Dragon Pearl Restaurant where Chinese food is excellent and the atmosphere is unassuming,(🚻 ♿ 🍴)
- Dean House, just before the bridge crossing the Elbow River is another lovely, old historic residence where tea and snacks are served during the daytime, (🚻 ♿ ☎ 🍴)

Eau Claire

- Eau Claire Market, between 2nd and 3rd Streets SW, on the south bank of the Bow River offers luxury pleasure galore: (🚻 ♿ ☎ 🍦 ☕ 🍴 🚲 🍸 ⛱ $ 👪 ☎). You can lie around on the grass, watch outdoor or indoor entertainment, eat ice cream chosen from dozens of flavours, go the full-meal-deal in the food court or lovely restaurants. You have high-end shopping, a wading pool to cool your feet and even movie theatres and IMAX. And bathrooms. The YMCA and their swimming pool, massage and cafeteria is on the west side of the courtyard.

10th Street, see page 32

SW 37th Street Entry

Total route: from 22/22X, 22 K
Total time: 2 hours
Challenges

Because this is a heavily traveled route, this is a demanding entry ride during any summer daylight hours. It is particularly hectic in the afternoons. If it is a weekend, traffic quiets down when you reach downtown. The fact is that there is no other southwest route back into Calgary. So if you have time consider continuing to the southeast where you can get quite close to the city on 88th/84th Street SE before hitting traffic, see page 78.

Thirty-seventh Street SW has limited shoulder and steady traffic from the minute you turn off Highway #22/22X. You also have a steep climb up from Nose Creek.

Anderson Road can be busy but it has wide shoulders. Elbow is busy until evening but the traffic isn't that fast. Fourth Street is chaos in the afternoon but quieter in the evening although the sidewalks will be jumping with the social scene on a hot summer evening. Downtown is quiet on the weekends.

It would be unusual to experience wind problems on this route.

Route: SW 37th Street Entry

In spite of its traffic challenges, this it is a good route to know about. It may offer your best option, time-wise, if you are returning from the SW and going to be staying in the southwest part of the city, or if you are late.

Thirty-seventh Street SW (which becomes Highway #773 south of 22/22x) meets 22/22X on the crest of a slight hill. Highway #22/22x is divided by a wide, grass median at this point so you have a safe place to sit and wait for an opening to cross the on-coming traffic

You are now going north on 37th Street SW, which takes a little eastern jog and then goes down a steep hill to cross Fish Creek on a narrow, single lane wooden bridge – that is budgeted for upgrade. This stretch of 37th is narrow with little shoulder and there can be quite a bit of traffic. The good news, however, is that it is heavily

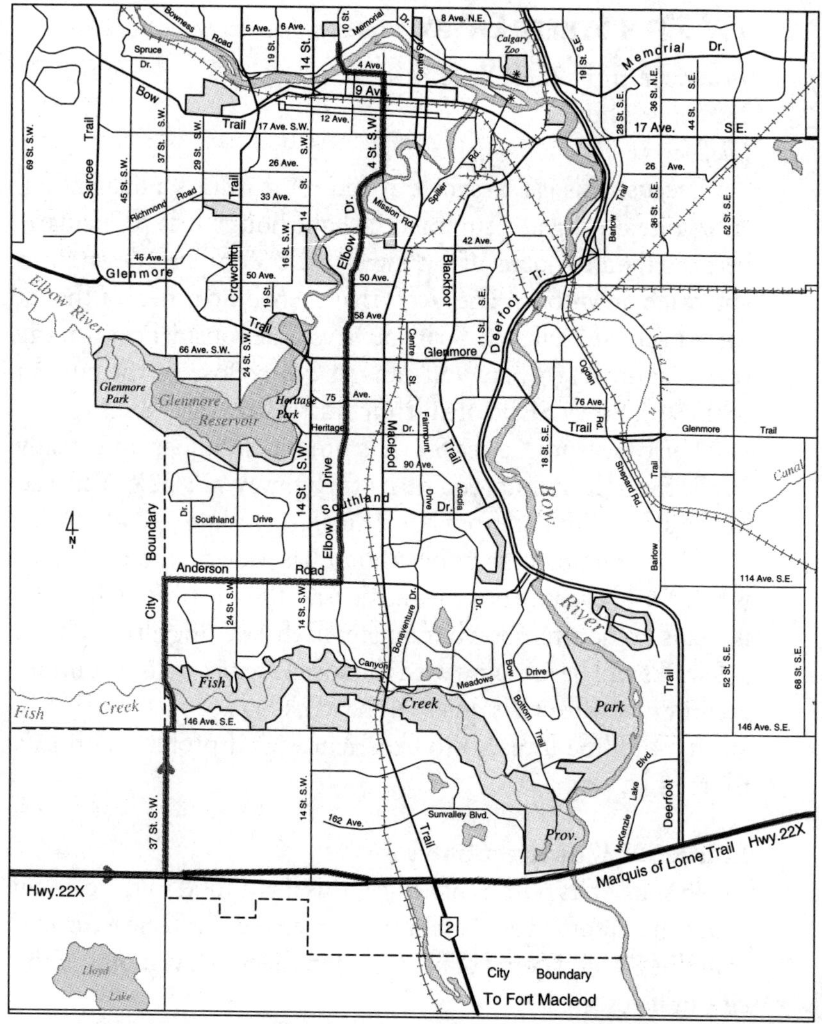

used by cyclists so the traffic seems to be used to sharing the road.

After crossing the bridge, you go up the hill, a bit of a grind. Stay on 37th to Anderson Road, which is puny at its western end but quickly becomes the wide, divided corridor we know and love. Stay on Anderson east to Elbow Drive. You hit services in strip shopping centres along Anderson and again along Elbow Drive, (🚻 ♿ ⛽ ✕ 🍎 🚗 $).

To get onto Elbow Drive from Anderson you have to get across two lanes of fast traffic to turn left (north). However the traffic seems to come in bunches so you should find an opening. Stay with Elbow Drive as it curves around and eventually turns east and crosses 4th Street SW, (🚻 ♿ ☎ 🍦 ☕ 🍴). Go left (north) on 4th Street to downtown. Downtown Calgary gets very quiet in the evening so traffic will be light and you may have trouble finding a store or restaurant that is open.

Once you are downtown, continue north on 4th Street to 4th Avenue SW. Turn left (west) there and cross the 10th Street (Louise) Bridge to get to 10th Street NW.

Services

Anderson Road strip malls

- (🚻 ♿ ☎ 🍦 ☕ 🍴 🍎 🚗 $)

Elbow and Anderson

- 24-hour 7/11convenience store just south of Anderson on Elbow.
- grocery stores and convenience stores on either side of Elbow from time to time

4th Street SW

- rich choice of restaurants(🚻 ♿ ☎ 🍴) Greek, ribs, health and trendy

10th Street NW, see page 32

W Highway #8 Entry

Total route: 14 K

Total time: 1 1/2 hours

Challenges

Most of this route is excellent except a short stretch on Sarcee Trail. Richmond Road is busy in the afternoons and you have to cross two lanes of traffic to turn left onto 45th Street SW but the traffic isn't fast and seems to cluster.

It you turn in Lower Springbank Road and ride up the 69th Street hill you have a serious climb.

Route: W Highway #8 Entry

Coming back into Calgary on Highway #8 takes you to 69th Street SW or to 45th Street SW via Richmond Road.

If you choose the 69th Street hill, take the Lower Springbank Road turnoff on the left just past the city limits sign on Highway #8. You may have to stop on the shoulder to get a safe time to cross the traffic. That puts you onto the little link road for 20 meters and then you turn right onto Lower Springbank Road, which ends in less than 1K. At the end, turn left and up the hill on 69th Street SW. This is a very challenging hill. I never come back this way but racing cyclists do it for a workout.

Sixty-ninth becomes Strathcona Blvd, carries you past a shopping centre with your first services (

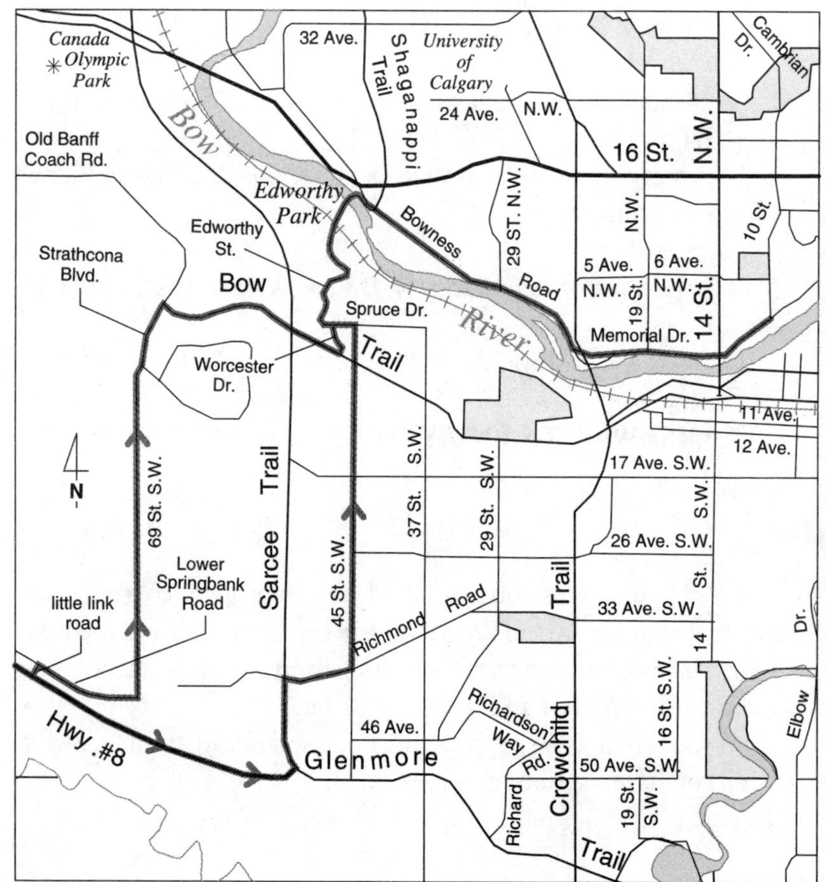

☎). Then you go downhill to the stoplight and intersection with Bow Trail. Go right (east) onto Bow Trail, down the hill, across Sarcee Trail (stoplights) and down to 45th Street SW where you again have stoplights and go left, (now north), (🚻 ♿ ⛽ 🚗 🚲 $ ☎).

Forty-fifth takes you to Spruce Drive, a lovely, quiet, street with generous grass right-of-way on either side. Turn left (west) onto Spruce Drive and just past an A-frame church, curve right (north) down the gravel Edworthy Park hill on Edworthy Street.

At the bottom, in the parking lot, you may still be able to catch snacks from the bread truck. Now you have a choice of two bicycle paths or the road. The bicycle path on the south shore of the Bow River starts at the east side of the Edworthy Park parking lot, just before the railway tracks. It is well marked and paved. You'll probably see people coming and going on it. But in May a short stretch of it may still have ice on it - - hard though that may be to believe. This path carries you east to the 14th Street NW Bridge, the 10th Street bridge, Eau Claire, downtown and points east.

Or you can go north through the path in Edworthy Park around to the footbridge, cross the river on the footbridge and immediately turn right for the cycle path on the north side of the river. If it is busy, which it can be, take your time and be careful.

As you come off the footbridge if you feel the smart thing to do would be to sun yourself on a river-view patio and drink fancy cappuccinos and eat carrot cake, turn left and go 400 meters to the Flying Bear - on the ground floor of a multi-story medical building. Just pull up on the grass and enter their patio entrance.

The fastest way of all your last leg alternatives, is to come off the north end of the Edworthy Park Footbridge, cross the parking lot on your right, take the short gravel road from the parking lot to Memorial Drive and turn right onto Memorial Drive.

This is a 50 K per hour section but it can be busy and the shoulder is narrow. If you are unhappy with the traffic, turn left at any of the cross streets with a stoplight and continue east on one of the roads more-or-less parallel to Memorial. Be advised, however, that the street grid in this area is at an odd angle and you may have to snake your way through a bit. Also, plan for the fact that the only road on which you can cross Crowchild Trail to continue east is 5th

Avenue NW. That is a comfortable street to ride all the way east to 10th Street.

If you want to avoid the steep 69th Street hill and are ready to face the heavy traffic on Sarcee Trail, Highway #8 will T right into Sarcee Trail at a stoplight. You go left (north) on Sarcee but have little shoulder for 200 meters until a turnoff lane opens to your right. Traffic whips around that corner fast and if you have a gusty crosswind and are tired you may want to walk that short stretch along the grassy boulevard. Whether you walk or ride it, once you turn left onto Sarcee, stick close to the right curb until you can get over into the right turn bay. If it is 4 to 6 PM on a weekday, be particularly careful on this stretch.

Go right (east) at your first chance - - which is Richmond Road. In the afternoon the traffic can be busy on Richmond Road too but it isn't so fast. Be careful. You have full services on Richmond Road, ($).

You then need to keep checking your shoulder to look for a chance to cross the traffic coming from behind you to get over into the left hand turning lane at 45th Street SW. There is a stoplight here. But as soon as you are on 45th Street you are down to no traffic.

You go through school and playground zones, past parks where you can sit and finish your snacks, record your impressions or lie on the grass. Forty-fifth Street crosses 17th Avenue and then Bow Trail at stoplights. Bow Trail has services ($).

You continue north on 45th Street SW to Spruce Drive, which is a wide, lovely street. Now go back to page 91 to get the rest of the route in.

Services

Strathcona Blvd - $

- PetroCanada with a snack shop is open 24 hours ( )
- IGA Grocery store is open 9 AM to 9 PM every day of the week, full range of groceries, deli, and fresh fruit
- specialty shops, drugstore, liquor store, ( )
- high-end Italian restaurant with an outdoor patio ( )

45th Street & Bow Trail

- Turbo Service Station, opens at 7 AM (🚻 ♿ ☐ 🚗)
- Mac's Convenience Food Store kitty corner to the Turbo, open 24 hours, (🚻 ♿ ☐)

Richmond Road

- London Drug on the south side of the road (☐) and candy, cold drinks, drugs, cameras, film and makeup
- Calgary Co-op Store is across the street so will be harder to get to (🚻 ♿ ☐ 🍎 🚗 $) - if you feel like braving shoppers.

Edworthy Park south parking lot

- During the busy part of summer weekends (probably 11 AM to 6 PM) in good weather, there is an ice cream/hot dog/cold drink vendor parked in an old bread truck in the parking lot (☐ 🍦)

Edworthy Park

- During the summer (🚻 ♿)

Edworthy Park north parking lot

- kiosk (🍦)

800 meters west of the Edworthy Park footbridge, north end

- Flying Bear Coffee Den (🚻 ♿ ☐ 🍦 ☕)

Parkdale Blvd

- MacKay's Cochrane Ice Cream (🍦)
- Robin's Donuts, at 3303 3rd Avenue NW, open 24 hours (🚻 ♿ ☐)

10th Street NW, see page 32

NNW Simons Valley Entry

Total route from the city limits to the centre of the city: 21 K

Total time: 1 1/2 hours

Challenges

Even in the bustle of Saturday afternoon shopping, traffic is not a problem on this entry route. You will see traffic thicken as Simons Valley Road nears the suburbs. And you don't have much shoulder. So it is tight for 2 K. But as soon as you turn onto Country Hills Blvd/Beddington Trail you have substantial shoulder.

Your most hectic task is crossing traffic on Berkshire Blvd to turn left onto Beddington Blvd. But there are plenty of breaks in the traffic and you shouldn't have trouble if you look early for a chance to ride across to the substantial left turn lane. You have plenty of room on Centre Street and even around the shopping centres on 4th Street. Then the route has a downhill tendency most of the way.

Route: NNW Simons Valley Entry

This is the best all-around entry route. From Symon's Valley Ranch/144th Avenue NW, which is the city boundary, (b w s r) you cycle through pretty country with nice rock outcroppings on the hills around you. Suddenly there are suburbs and traffic. After 2 K of busy traffic you get to a T-intersection: Country Hills Blvd. There is a stoplight there.

Go left (east) on Country Hills Blvd, which immediately curves southeast and becomes Beddington Trail. From this point you want to get onto Centre Street heading south but it doesn't connect directly with this road so you need to follow kind of a convoluted route. It is well marked, but not logical.

As you approach the first traffic light since turning onto Country Hills Blvd, you'll see a sign on your right To Centre Street South. Follow its directions to go right (west) onto Berkshire Blvd. After turning, you get another sign To Centre Street South just to re-assure you that this will work. Go left (south) at the first stoplight on Berkshire, which puts you on Beddington Blvd. After several traffic lights, Berkshire eventually takes you around to Centre Street.

Centre Street is well marked and there is a large shopping centre up the hill on your left, and your first services, ($). You may not want to bother with these however, because you have to go uphill and away from you direction of travel to get to them and there will be many opportunities ahead.

The first light you get to, heading south on Centre, is at 72nd Avenue NE to the left and 4th Street NW if you go right. It's the same street, called different things depending on the direction that you go. If you go right (west) it immediately curves around to a

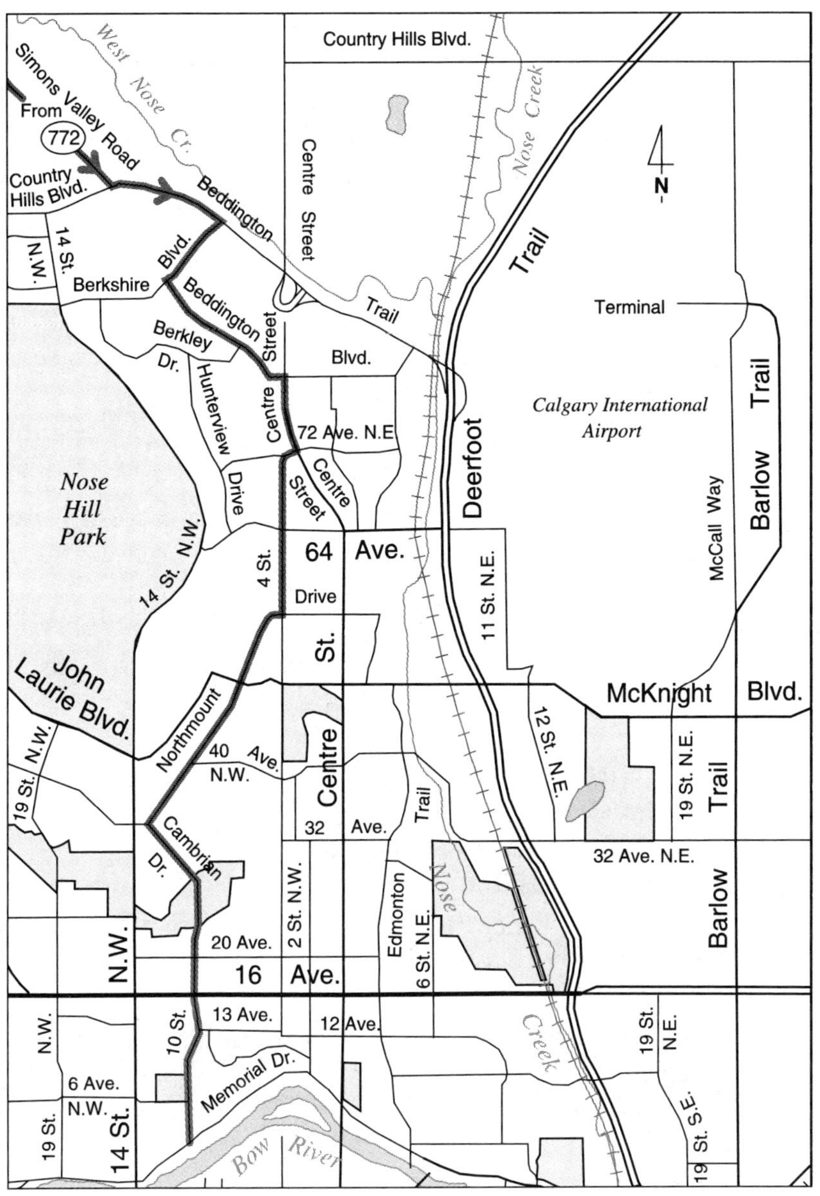

southerly direction. Go right (west and then south) onto 4th Street, where you will find services, (🚻 ♿ ▪ ✆) on your left.

Fourth Street NW is a wide street and never very busy. You can ride comfortably here. Northmount Blvd also curves right immediately after you turn onto it. So again, go right (west then south) onto Northmount, ($). Northmount has even lighter traffic and curves comfortably down to a T-intersection where it continues to the right as Northmount Blvd but you go left onto Cambrian Drive, ($).

When you go left (east) on Cambrian you pass through Confederation Park and the street is renamed 10th Street NW. Down the hill to the river, which is only busy in morning rush hour and you are painlessly back into the centre of the city.

You can leave the city on this route as well but the first uphill on Northmount is quite steep. The variation NNW Simons Valley Exit is easier because it avoids busy roads and steep hills.

Services

- Syman's Valley Ranch has a restaurant that faces the highway and opens for lunch. It is dark and attracts a bar crowd but you can get essentials, ().

Centre Street & Beddington Blvd

- Calgary Co-op Shopping Centre and cluster of little malls (b w s r g ss c/Nm $)

4th Street & 72

- Zellars ()

4th Street & 68th Avenue

- 7/11 Convenience Store () open 24 hours.

4th Street & Northmount

- Shell Service Station: (), southwest corner, open 7 AM to 11 PM seven days a week
- Safeway grocery store ()
- Bank of Commerce (CIBC) in east side strip mall has two bank machines ($)

Scattered along Northmount

- ()

Northmount and Cambrian

- small shopping centre ($)

10th Street NW, see page 32

Cycling back to the Calgary Airport, bus depot or train station

When you depart Calgary at the end of your visit the same way you arrived - - plane, train or bus - it is easiest to retrace the steps you took to leave. The best description in the world is never as good as a familiar route that you have cycled already. Enjoy a relaxed return on the back of your own experience. Just remember that traffic into the city will be busy 7 to 9 AM on weekdays and 10 AM to 6PM on weekends. Check the entry route here for possible variations on the route you exited that will help with traffic and hills.

If you are finishing a multi-day cycle trip in another quadrant of the city to which you exited, you can find outside-of-the-city roads to virtually travel all the way around the city and get back to your original exit without coping with city traffic or navigation:

- east boundary – 84th/88th Street SE and 68th Street NE, linked with a brief east-west jog at Highway #1A/17th Avenue SE;
- north boundary along Highway #566 east of Simons Valley Road and #567 west of there, linked along Simons Valley Road;
- or within the city, Crowchild Trail and Country Hills Blvd which has a gap in it that you need to fill by going north on Centre Street until you get to the Country Hills Blvd completion
- west boundary along Highway #22/22x and
- south boundary, Highway #22/22x – the Highway turns.

Using these highways you can circle around outside the city to any route you want, given the time. The exit and entry route maps show you how to connect with these.

For cyclists leaving Southern Alberta a different way than they arrived (i.e. arrived by bus, are leaving by plane) we include some detailed directions on getting to the airport, bus depot and train station.

Re-entering Calgary to fly out of the airport

The airport is the quickest, easiest, most hassle free location to cycle back to and depart Calgary. Wherever your cycling trip ends, around the Calgary perimeter, you are best to reach the airport via 112th Avenue/Country Hills Blvd/Highway #564.

From the northeast, go west on Highway #564 to Barlow Trail. Turn left (south) and ride to the stoplight. The airport terminal is on your right. Turn right (west) and follow the clear signage to the upper, departure ramp.

From Highway #566 in the northwest, you turn south onto Centre Street, then left (east) on Country Hills Blvd to Barlow Trail. The only services are two blocks north of Country Hills Blvd ( ). Country Hills Blvd takes you all the way east to Barlow Trail where you go right (south) down to the stoplight. The airport is on your right and the exit ramp route is clearly marked. The airport has services too: ($)

If you are coming from the south, west, northwest or east, use the highway routes above to circle around to Highway #564 or 566.

Services

two blocks up Coventry Drive from Country Hill Blvd

- Mohawk service station, open from 7 AM to 11PM seven days a week. ( )

Airport

- A&W( )
- Harvey's ( )
- Tim Horton's ( ) open 24 hours
- Food court ( )
- Calgary Tourist & Convention Centre kiosk inside a chuckwagon on the main level
- Bank machines ($)
- plus, in the terminal ( )
- Calgary Airport Hotel ( ) and swimming pool

Re-entering Calgary to depart via the train station

Calgary's train station is the centre point of the city, in the base of the Calgary Tower on Centre Street and 9th Avenue South. It is not a pleasant place to cycle to during weekdays - especially 7AM to 9 AM. Oddly enough, Calgary's downtown core is quiet any time on the weekends, but getting through the suburban ring between 10 AM and 6 PM on weekends can be hectic.

All the Routes back into Calgary, starting page 75, will bring you into the middle of the city. Pick the one that works from your location. From 10th Street NW, where all those routes take you, the simplest route is to ride your bike south across the 10th Street (Louise) Bridge, at the foot of 10th Street. Stay on the same road as it curves south and continue until it Ts at 9th Avenue SW. Go left (east) at the T and take 9th Avenue to the base of the landmark, Calgary Tower. It ain't pretty but it's big. The train station is in the basement of the building attached to the tower.

Alert: If you take this route, just be careful when proceeding east along 9th Avenue at 5th Street SW. There are dual turn lanes there and cars will turn right into you. Either cross with the pedestrians or get into the middle of the second lane over from the right to proceed through.

Services

Calgary Tower

- Revolving restaurant at the top, expensive but fun view
- ( )

CP Palliser Hotel and Radisson

- Both are high end hotels with full amenities ( ) plus business services, exercise room etc

Re-entering Calgary to depart via the bus depot

You face the same challenges and work with the same options as the train station cyclist, until 6th Avenue SW. Cross the Bow River on the 10th Street (Louise) Bridge, stay with the street as it curves south until 6th Avenue SW. Turn right (west) onto 6th Avenue. It is a one-way street and is busy 4 PM to 6 PM.

Sixth Avenue goes underneath the approach to the next-over river crossing, 14th Street Bridge. As you approach that you need to look carefully to avoid getting caught by traffic taking Bow Trail west. Avoid the fork closest to the river on your right. Get over on the left curb early but be careful that you don't get swept up and over the 14th Street Bridge, which you don't want.

Instead, get across the traffic and into the quieter slow lane that says "14th Street SW " and shows another sign: "Bus depot". (850 16th Street SW) Follow the signage into the bus depot - - a two-story dark brown brick building with a ramp up the side for vehicular parking. Just go to the ground level main doors on the west side because that's where you will be taking your bike and buying your ticket. Toilets, cafeteria, payphones are inside. The bus station is clean and well lighted.

If you don't realize it, you can book a particular seat on the bus - - such as the up-front one beside the driver seat - - if you go in and buy your ticket up to two weeks ahead of departure.

Services

Bus depot

-cafeteria, (🚻 ♿ ☎)

Goodbye

Thank you for being our guest. Thank you for bringing your bicycle to Southern Alberta and enjoying a healthy holiday adventure. We sincerely hope our guidebook has been helpful.

Please write, fax or e-mail any updates, comments or suggestions for change. We will post notice of new routes being added to our Southern Alberta guide on our homepage as well as maintain a list of other destinations around the world where we can help you enjoy a holiday on a bicycle.

Homepage: www.monday.ab.ca
Email: monday@ nucleus.com
Fax: 403 283-5983

City exploring

City cycle trips are a good way to open the season or get used to a new city. They give your crotch a chance to adjust to being on a bicycle seat - the big issue. They also give you a chance to regain your confidence that you do know how to ride a bicycle and that you can get up a hill and that you are ready to be cycling in the country.

These are two circle routes because circles are satisfying. Both the northwest and northeast offer roads that make an easy loop. The south doesn't have roads that easily and comfortably do that within the city so exploring there works better outside the side and falls into multi-day trips. Enjoy the variety and exercise and acclimatization of the Northwest and Northeast circuits.

You could do either of these rides the opposite direction but the Northwest one would present you with a long period of climbing from the river up Nose Hill Drive to Country Hills Blvd.

Northwest

Highlights

This trip is a great season's opener if you have a bicycle seat that you can adjust to fairly quickly. It offers up and down hills, Bowness Park and all its play options, open fields and ice cream shops. If you have just arrived in Calgary it is a chance to look around the city, get used to your bike and get a sense of the city exits. If you start or end at 10th Street NW you have excellent shopping, people watching, restaurants, snacks and even a repertory movie theatre.

Challenges

All the climbs are well graded. Some are long but manageable. You will have some traffic in stretches, depending on the time of day but the shoulder is adequate relative to the speed of traffic. Even with a westerly wind, you are somewhat protected by the topography in some of the stretches when you are heading west.

Total distance: about 48 K
Total cycle time: Half day or a summer evening that stays light late
Route: Northwest

Because this is just a half-day run, you can leave any time but you'll encounter less traffic the earlier you go. It may also be quiet in the evening, which if you like evening cycling, is feasible with the long-light summer days of Calgary in June and early July. Another window is in the middle of a weekday, after morning rush-hour timing the whole ride to fall between 9 AM and 2:30 PM.

You start on the exit route called NNW Simons Valley, page63.

Follow that route up to Beddington Trail and curve around north and then west to where Beddington Trail changes name to

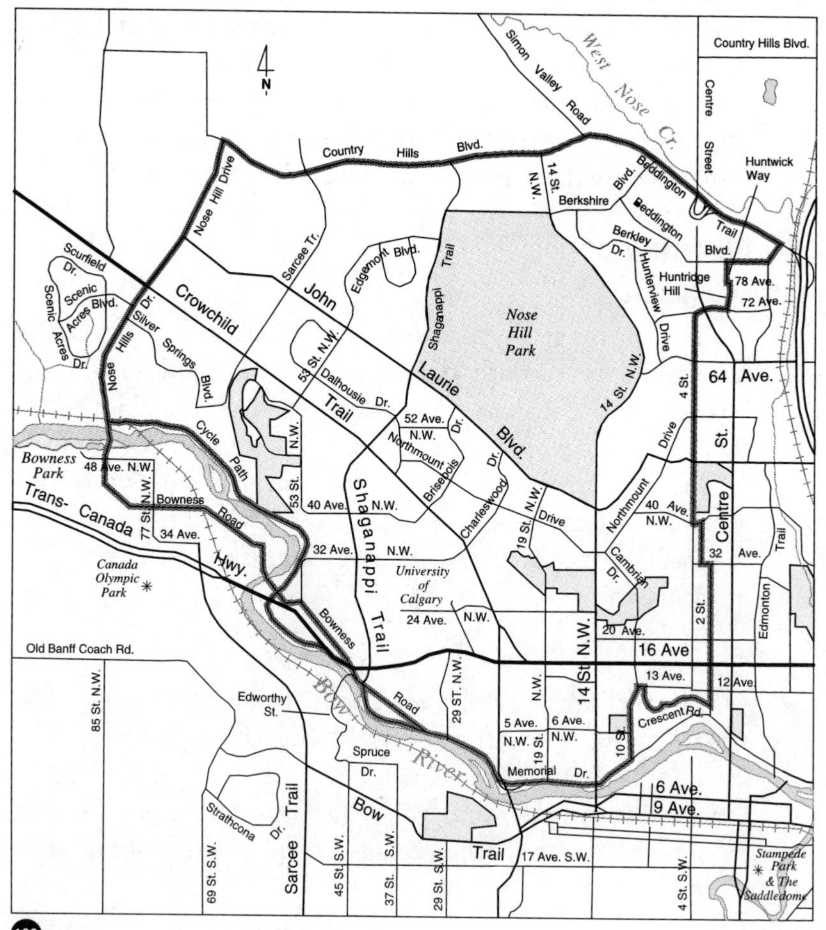

Country Hills Blvd. Then, instead of going right (north) onto Simons Valley Road, stay on Country Hills Blvd, which is part of a planned ring road that will go around the northwest quadrant of the city.

Although you are on a large artery, the shoulder is generous and you will feel comfortable with the traffic. The new section of Country Hills Blvd will carry you around the top of the city to Nose Hill Drive. Some of this feels quite out-in-the-country. By the time you reach Nose Hill you are in the top northwest corner of Calgary with only a bit of suburb creeping out beyond. Nose Hill Drive takes you south straight down into the Bow River Valley along the west edge of the city. It is all downhill after which you cross the Bow River and start your southeastern return leg.

From the last services you passed on 4th Street & 68th Avenue NW you won't hit any more until hectic Crowfoot Shopping Centre, on the slope of Nose Hill Drive just before Crowchild Trail. There are shoppers here and shoppers are never good news for a cyclist. They are rushed, harried and operating on autopilot. But you are through them after a couple of K. And if you want things, you can pull in, ($). The road may continue to be a bit hectic from Crowfoot south until you cross Silver Springs Blvd, where there are more services, ( ). Then traffic quiets down and Nose Hill turns down to the River.

At the bottom of the hill you have some choices. You can cross the river and ride along Bowness Road to Memorial Drive and back into the middle of the city. Or you can hit the bike path and travel, away from traffic, along the north river cycle path back toward the city centre. Or you can go in to Bowness Park to play.

If Bowness Park wins, cross the river and immediately turn right (west) off the sidewalk, down the kid-worn pathway right into the park. Or if that feels uncomfortable, cycle on to the 48th Avenue intersection (stoplight), ( ) go right (west) along 48th about four blocks to the Bowness Park entrance sign on your right. Turn in there.

If cycle path is your choice, take the path that leaves Nose Hill Drive to your right just before the bridge. It circles under the bridge approach and carries you east, on the north side of the Bow

River. This is a secluded cycle path with no cars around, few other users, wonderful views and interesting variety. This is a beautiful long path. If you haven't done it before, do it. But be warned: there are some challenging hills and one short murderous climb that you may want to walk. You can easily cycle this stretch of the pathway without the cycle map because as long as you stay on the path you can't go wrong. The place you need the map is navigating the link from this stretch of riverside pathway to the next, along roads.

The cycle path dumps you out at a church on 52nd Street NW. Go right (south) on 52nd to your first opportunity to turn left, which is probably 19th Avenue NW. Go left (southeast) to Home Road, one long block. Turn right again, (south) onto Home Road and follow it all the way down to the river. You cross the TransCanada Highway doing this but once past those stoplights traffic drops right off. There are good on-road cycle path signs most of the way.

This little street stretch gets you past an S-bend in the river. The alternative, which keeps you closer to the river, is being expanded and you can test that instead. To do so, go straight down 52nd to the bottom, Bowness Road. Turn right, away from the city centre, and follow the cycle path signs that take you off the path to your right and underneath the bridge ahead of you and onto the cycle path heading eventually east. It will wind you around a bit but eventually bring you to the same spot at the river pathway you would reach using Home Road.

If you have chosen to stay on Bowness Road and wind through Bowness to Memorial Drive, just go straight ahead on Bowness Road, along which are a string of service outlets: ( ). You will notice some of the white and blue cycle paths signs giving you alternatives as you travel along Bowness Road and if you have a cycle path map you may want to try some of them out. If you more or less stay with Bowness Road it crosses under the TransCanada Highway and joins the western end of Memorial Drive, also known as Parkdale Blvd.

You are now at the intersection where Shaganappi Trail joins Memorial Drive as well and the cycle path provides the option of crossing the river to Edworthy Park. For this last leg into the middle of the city along the river you can stay on the road, Memorial Drive, or get on the north river cycle path or cross at the Edworthy Park Footbridge to the delightful cycle path along the south shore.

Along this central stretch, the cycle paths, particularly the one on the north bank, can be very busy on warm-weather Sunday afternoons. You are sharing the path with many and varied enthusiasts. Watch for strollers, puppies, rollerbladers, kids with training wheels and high-speed cyclists who haven't yet learned the joys of riding out of town. One of the most unnerving pathway users is the in-line skater who's long, gliding strides go right into your lane. Together all this can be frustrating after being on the open road. Just be forewarned.

You can use the W Highway #8 directions, page 89, to get from here to 10th Street NW.

Services

This route offers a cornucopia of eating and loafing delights, but they are all at the beginning and end of the ride. It means you can give yourself treats, refill questionable tires, do errands, get to bathrooms and generally test things out at the beginning of the season or as you adjust to Calgary and recover from jet lag.

10th Street NW, see page 32

Nose Hill Drive just before crossing Crowchild Trail

- Calgary Co-op Store ($)
- several fast food outlets if you feel like braving the automobile flurry ()

Nose Hill Drive/Bowness Road & 48th Avenue SW

- Bowmont Food Store () open 8 AM to 10 PM seven days a week
- Bowness Park ()

Bowness Road

- several convenience stores, fast foods and service stations in strip malls scattered along the road

Bowness Road and Home Road

- fast food outlets, restaurants and a shopping centre, KFC, DQ ( )
- Safeway ( )
- Several service stations ( )

West of Edworthy Park footbridge (4411 16th Avenue NW)

- The Flying Bear Coffee Den, whether you arrive by the river path or Bowness Road (called 16th Avenue here), offers a beautiful river-view patio and access right off the cycle path. It is on the ground floor of a glass and brick MediCentre building, ( ).

Parkdale Blvd at Parkdale Crescent NW

- MacKay's Ice Cream ( ), does not offer a nice spot to sit and enjoy but offers a dizzy range of flavours of hard ice cream, very popular.

Additional excursions

- Errands: There are enough shops on this route that you could actually do some of your errands as you go.

- Bowness Park: In this huge park on an island, you can lie on the grass, feed ducks, rent a canoe or paddle boat, eat a picnic, buy a picnic, ride the kiddy rides, watch kiddies riding the kiddy rides, ride the miniature train, watch other people riding the miniature train, buy junk food, suntan or sleep, have a barbecue – you name it.

- Old sandstone school: You can stop briefly at the historic old sandstone school on 44 Avenue and Bowness Road, sit on the steps, sun yourself and eat a snack.

- Edworthy Park: The Park has firepits, plenty of trees and proximity to the Bow River. This is a shady park.

Reflections

Feeling like a lizard on a rock, I'm off the bike, mid-ride, sunning myself on the front steps of an old sandstone school. The early spring sun is just starting to feel as if it has some warmth in it. Wonderful memories of all the sun I have ever soaked up. Thinking about all the generations of children living their schoolyard dramas there.

- The Flying Bear Coffee Den: You can stop at this superb, pathside patio for loafing, gloating, de-briefing, sunning and actual eating.

Northeast

Highlights

This route provides a chance to explore other routes in and out of Calgary and get around the edge without being far from options to return. A good route for the I'm-not-sure-how-far-I-want-to-go rider. If you are a Zoo fancier, it takes you there, eventually.

Total distance: 48 K
Total time: Half day or summer evening
Challenges

This is a comfortable ride. You are climbing on your way out and generally downhill on your way back. If the exit stretch of Centre Street North is busy it is a bit tiresome but it doesn't last long. Sixty-eighth Street NE and stretches of Memorial Drive will be busy in the afternoon and get quieter into evening.

Route: Northeast

If you want to avoid heavy traffic, depart before 7 AM or after 7 PM. You could also try this circuit on a weekday immediately after morning rush hour and returning before 11:30 AM. After that Memorial Drive will be busy for the rest of the day.

Take the N Centre Street Exit, page 34. Stay on this route all the way out to Country Hills Blvd where you turn right (east). This road is wider than it needs to be for the current load being carried, which hints of further development to come. But right now it's you and space. So enjoy the leisurely stretch. There are no stores on the road but if you turn left (north) up Coventry Drive and go two blocks up the hill there is a Mohawk Service Station ().

Back on Country Hills Blvd, once you pass the golf course and cross Nose Creek the road narrows as it goes up and over Highway #2/Deerfoot Trail (just where it shouldn't go narrow!) and approaches the north end of Barlow Trail.

You can cross Barlow and then do a little city-edge exploring weaving back and forth on the streets you cross. You can explore by turning right (south) on 36th Street NE and then, explore streets off 80th Avenue. You start back into the city centre at 68th Street NE. It's your last chance to circle back short of going out to 116th Street, beyond the city boundary. Then you are limited to returning on Highway #1.

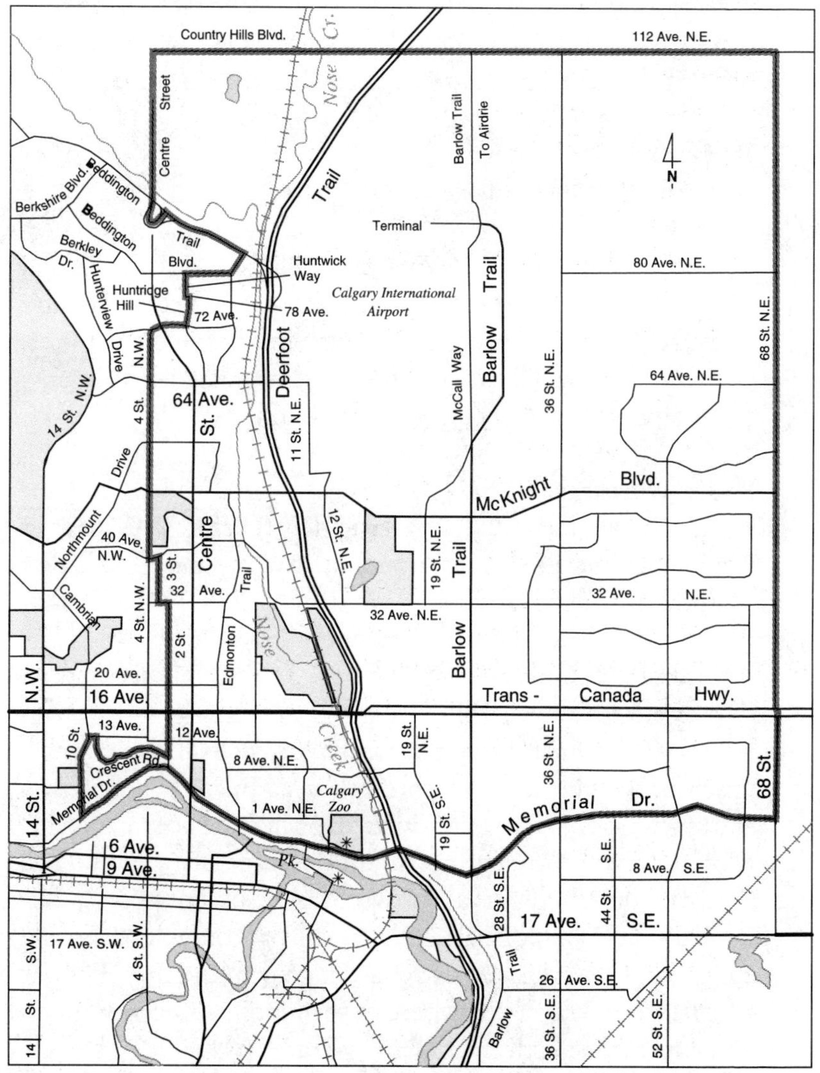

If you take 68th Street from its north end it is very pleasant up there and only gets busy as you get into the city and the new suburbs that are still underserviced by roads. Sunday afternoon developers' open houses with all the coloured flags flapping hopefully can result in heavy traffic - - a rough go on a bicycle. If it is early or evening you won't have that problem. Stay on 68th Street NE to Memorial Drive. Then follow the East Entry directions, starting on page 80.

Services

10th Street NW, see page 32

Airport, south on Barlow Trail

- A&W ()
- Harvey's ()
- Tim Horton's () open 24 hours
- Food court ()
- Calgary Convention and Visitors Bureau kiosk inside a Chuckwagon, would you believe, on the main level, open 10 AM to 10 PM daily
- Bank machines ($)
- plus, in the terminal ()

Additional excursions

- Airdrie: You can go north on Barlow Trail and explore further out in the country. Eventually that extension from Barlow, north of the airport, gets to Airdrie parallel to Highway #2. It is quite chewed up but has virtually no traffic and is kind of fun. It feels as if you are travelling on one of the original roads and can prompt pleasant musings about the nature of time. The residential and retail part of Airdrie is on the west side of Highway #2 - - so you'll need to cross on the underpass you hit at the south end of town or the overpass at the north end of town to get into parts that are pleasant to cruise around. From the minute you turn north onto the Barlow extension you are in the country. Services abound in Airdrie: ($).
- The Zoo: It is pleasant to poke around the Calgary Zoo, which has some excellent, humane and natural animal habitats that

take some of the sadness out of a zoo. Plus there are magnificent flower gardens. If you want to wait out a storm, the giant botanical gardens are a peaceful way to pass some time. See page 82.

Oh... and By the Way...

World Famous Mountain Rides

The annual Golden Triangle Ride (Castle Mountain, Radium, Golden, Banff) managed every year by The Elbow Valley Cycle Club is considered one of the three or four best cycle rides in the world.

The Icefields Parkway ride from Jasper to Banff holds the rarified distinction of being one of the top two rides in the whole world.

Both of these rides involve serious mountain climbs and long days, yet the world class scenery and the draw of the challenge bring enthusiasts back year after year.

Contact Calgary's active Elbow Valley Cycle Club for information on groups doing these rides or a chance to talk to someone who has done one: (403) 283-BIKE (283-2453).

Oh... and Another Thing...

100 Miles of Tailwind

It's a one way ride so you need a lift to start or pickup at the end. But it is almost guaranteed that you will have tailwinds all the way. You also have nine conveniently placed towns and services (🚻 ♿ ⛽) spaced along the route. Start in Lethbridge where Highway #3 leaves the city in the southeast. Travel Highway #3 to Medicine Hat. You get 168 K of feeling smart, strong and fast!

DAY TRIPS

Day trips are a chance to get out of the city, have a mini-holiday, do some exploring, get some exercise and be an adventurer - all without prior arrangements. For a few hours you are seeing and dealing with completely different things from your average day. Your habitual tasks and worries are far away. You return refreshed and feeling like you have been gone for much longer.

Your day trips don't need much planning. Think about wind direction and whether you want to face it heading out or coming back – and then be philosophical if it changes. Think about your city re-entry point so that you don't get trapped out there with a rush hour between you and home. Think about whether you want to explore new ground or retrace an old favourite.

Is there someone you want to visit as you cycle? An errand you want to do? Do you want a scenic picnic spot in the middle? The planning is your first step into adventure. But the beauty of a day trip is that you don't need to do much planning. You don't book accommodation, buy food or pack anything special. If your necessities (bike tools, sunscreen, rain gear and medical kit) are always packed and ready, you can wake up on a sunny morning and decide at that moment to forget about whatever else you had planned - - you are heading out.

From that moment it usually takes about an hour to be on your bike riding off. Think about where you want to go. Call the weather office and find out about wind direction and temperature changes. Put on sunscreen. Dress and gather backup clothes, raingear, journal, and pens. Pick your tapes if you want to cycle with a walkman. (This is a highly contentious practice. Do it at your own risk.) Eat first or just pack all your food. Load your water. Check that you have your bike lock, key, compass, reading glasses (if you need them) basic medical kit (see page 229) I.D., cash, a credit card, anything that matters to you. Get on your bike and go.

Think of a day trip being about the equivalent of one hour by car on the highway once you are outside the city. It will vary with wind and your conditioning and how long you want to be on the bicycle but this gives you a yardstick for planning your route. Thirteen hours on a bicycle is too long for most people. Less than six hours feels like a short day with plenty of time for other things - - once you are used to your bike seat. Seven to nine hours feels optimal. You want to find this out about yourself.

The Chestermere and Balzac trips can be cycled in half a day. Strathmore/Langdon is a full day. Together, these rides give you a cross-section of what Southern Alberta has to offer: foothills, prairie, river valleys, isolation, quality roads, variable winds and probably different kinds of weather.

Away you go - - day trips ahead.

Chestermere Loop

Highlights

A popular and comfortable circuit that provides choices in amount of traffic. Lake Chestermere is not good for swimming but it is good for watching wind surfing, small boat sailing and water skiing. The restaurant is a possible destination and with summer evenings that stay light late, you could cycle out for dinner on the deck over the lake and cycle back in the evening.

If you use the wonderful city cycle path extension that follows the little-known irrigation canal for the trip out or back, you have protection from traffic (but not wind) and some delightful and odd things to see. This is a fun path that delivers industry, ducks, a golf course, a canoe club, the underside of Deerfoot Trail – which is BladeRunner weird, and - - if you are lucky, miniature radio-controlled airplanes flying from a tiny aerodrome on a hill above the path. You also see the dangerous Bow River weir where water is extracted for the irrigation canal system, the Zoo and amazing peacefulness in the middle of the city. You must ride the irrigation canal route sometime. The surface of this path is rough until south of 17th Avenue SE and the best of any in the city after that.

Great ride for kids if they like being around water.

Challenges: This is an easy, short and mostly flat ride. The catch: if a strong Chinook blows in you will struggle against it all the way home.
Total distance: The loop ranges from 62 K to 40 K from the city centre and back, depending on the specific route you take.
Cycle time: is 4 to 6 hours, again depending on route and where you start from in the city.

Route: Chestermere Lake

The widest loop is to leave or return on the East Highway #1 Exit, page 43, and do the opposite leg on the bicycle path along the irrigation canal. Down the middle is the East Highway #1A Exit, page 43 & 45, which you can use for either leg. Highway #1A is definitely the shortest, most direct of these three routes.

Highway #1 east to Lake Chestermere gives you an immediate prairie feeling after cresting the first hill east of the city. You won't find visual drama unless the weather is performing dramatically but you have a chance to test cycling on a major highway and exploring service options on the exit route. They are all listed in the Exit East Highway #1 on page 46. There is nothing after that until you come to Chestermere.

If you go out on Highway #1A you enjoy quiet, gently rolling road east of the city limits. It is peaceful and lovely but all too short before you arrive at Lake Chestermere. This is a road that gives you a taste for more country cycling.

If you come back on Highway #1A and 17th Avenue SE or start in on #1A and jog north to Memorial Drive, you scout additional services and traffic patterns. Again, the services outlined with the East Entry route, page 80, outline them all.

The City cycle map only shows the irrigation canal route to the southeast edge of the city but at that point you can't get lost because there is just you and the canal until you get spilled out on the road at Lake Chestermere. So you mainly need a cycle map to see where you will enter the pathway system within the city and to ensure that you connect with the right pathway going east. When you have the map, look at the lower right hand side to find the spot that the irrigation canal pathway goes off the map. Then, just trace the pathways backwards from there to the spot you want to get on or off the path.

If you use the cycle path for either your trip out or back, watch for the tiny airplanes, or more appropriately listen for them. You have to walk your bike across 50th Avenue SE. That is

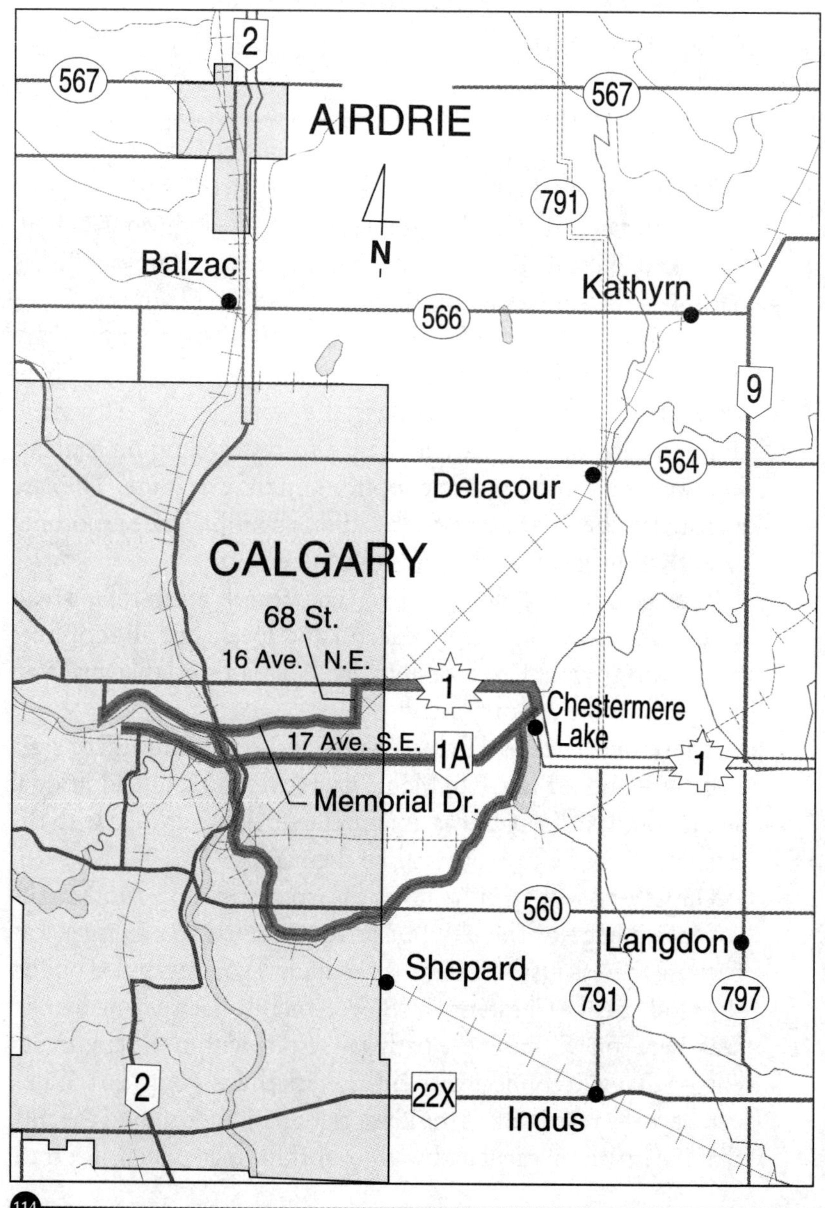

when you can start to listen for the airplanes that, if they are flying, would be over the hill up on your left. The path will curve around the base of that hill so keep an eye open. It stops at the south end of the lake with a road on your left that goes up the west shore and connects with Highway #1A.

From the three route options, pick what appeals to you. Go out and back on the same one if you want. This is a day to just pedal for pleasure.

Services

See 10th Street NW, page 32

See services listed with the exit and entry routes you choose

Alert: for all routes

- No services between city limits and Lake Chestermere
- The only place to access services from the bicycle path route is on Glenmore Trail where you walk along the sidewalk, west, for half a block, cross the street and walk half a block east again. There is a small strip mall on the way with a Dairy Queen ( ) soft ice cream, hamburgers, hotdogs, chips and coffee as well as the Glenmore Inn for alcohol and full restaurant service.

Chestermere

- Porter's Gas and Food Mart, ( ) open Monday to Friday 6:30 AM to 9 PM, Saturday 7:30 AM to 9:30 PM and Sunday 8 AM to 8 PM
- Chestermere Landing Restaurant and Lounge: ( ) pizza and steak 7 days a week and the dining room, overlooking the lake, is open Thursday to Sunday.

Additional excursions

- Dinner at the Chestermere Landing Restaurant ( ): You can plan your Chestermere ride around going out for dinner overlooking the lake on a summer evening that stays light late. Then you have a leisurely pedal back in the quiet of a summer evening when 17th Avenue SW isn't busy.

- Sailboarding: You can rent a sailboard at Chestermere and switch outdoor modes.

- Exploring Highway #1 further east: You can explore as far as Strathmore, page 119, or just cruise up and down the paved secondary roads either side of the highway.

- A picnic: You can take your own picnic and settle on a pleasant vantage point beside the Lake.

- Eau Claire: At this urban market you can indulge in a huge number of upscale culinary delights: cappuccino, wine, Tex-Mex treats, ice cream cones and gourmet ready-for-oven meats to take home, pop in the oven and deliver fabulous, restaurant-caliber food with ease. You can also wade in the kiddy pool and sit on the steps there watching the wonders of water play. On a light-late summer evening, you can take in an early movie in the multi-plex theatres or the wonderful IMAX. See page 86.

- Errands: You can cross items off your list while you cruise in and out to Chestermere. Shops and services on 17th Avenue SE and Memorial Drive NW cover a wide range of needs.

Balzac

Highlights

A wonderful, comfortable, low-stress ride in rolling hills and beautiful farmland. And Balzac provides a couple of delightful amusements - - in the middle of no-where. A pleasant, un-assuming little ride. A personal favorite.

Challenges: Not. Traffic is minimal once out of Calgary and hills are short and gently rolling. Headwind will only be a problem in a strong westerly.
Total distance: the loop is about 55 K
Total time: 4 to 6 hours cycle time depending on your pace and where you start out in Calgary.

Route: Balzac

Take the East Highway #1 Exit, page 43, so try to leave early enough to beat the traffic. This means you are out of the city before 9 AM on weekends and before 6:30 AM on weekdays or between rush hours on a weekday with the whole trip falling between 9 AM and 3 PM. Stay on Highway #1 just past the city limits sign. Then turn left (north) onto 116th Street NE. There's a sign and it is paved. This is a practically unused road, with prairie all around. You pass through the equivalent of a one-horse town- -one house and store/service station- -in Conrich.

You can shorten this trip and leave out some of the good parts by turning left (west) onto Highway #564 and back into town via the NE Airport Entry, page77. This has given you a tiny taste of prairie, some bike acclimatization and a nice bit of exercise. Better yet, continue north on 116th Street to Highway #566 where you go left (west). This is an excellent, open, rolling road with good shoulder and rare vehicles.

It carries you on an overpass across the busy north-south Highway #2. You can stop and look down and savour the pleasures of being on a bicycle versus in a whizzing car, hell-bent for destination. And there, across the highway is - - Balzac.

Balzac is a grain elevator; a flourishing, huge nursery; café/store/service station combo; church; four houses and a railway track. Balzac is a delightful little sleeper. When you pull yourself away from Balzac continue west on Highway #566. A bit hilly-ER but beautiful with Rocky Mountains in the distance.

Again you can shorten your ride by turning left (south) onto Highway #782/Centre Street and re-entering Calgary via N Centre Street Entry, detail and map page 76. But if you aren't tired or the weather hasn't turned questionable, you can add a pleasant 1/2 hour to your ride by continuing west to Highway #772/Simons Valley Road. Then return on NNW Simons Valley Entry, page 93.

Services

Conrich Store (🚻 🚲 ⛽ 🚗)

Balzac Store (🚻 🚲 ⛽ 🍴 🚗 📞)

Long weekends

...that beginning-a-long-weekend-hippie-Dippy-I-love-you-all feeling for everyone who passes. Everyone is happy. Perfect long-weekend weather: hot, sunny, bit of breeze. The boats are in tow. The kids have games. We're all heading' out. Three days of play.

Additional excursions

- Plant shop: If you need an important, but small, plant you can get it at the nursery in Balzac and cycle it home.

- Lunch or dinner in Airdrie: If you turn north on #772 to Highway #567 and then go right (east) you can enjoy the small scale, pleasant little town of Airdrie, or have lunch or dinner there before heading home.

- Find new paved roads: If you weave in and out any of the roads you cross you can check for newly paved surfaces that provide additional options.

Strathmore and Langdon

Total distance: over 130 K from city centre back to city centre
Total cycle time: This is a long one-day ride particularly if you hit westerly headbands returning.

Highlights

This is an extension - a substantial extension - to the Chestermere Lake one-day trip. This is not a dramatic route. It is a chance to pedal meditatively, get exercise and explore two pleasant prairie towns. This is a day to practice the joys of the process rather than the attainment of the goal and to look at prairies versus foothills.

Challenges

It is long. It may test your distance limits if you are not used to a long day. And if you hit a strong westerly (Chinook) and, worse yet, cooler weather, on your way back, you'll feel like you have really worked on this ride. And of course you'll feel the proportionate amount of pride.

Route: Strathmore & Langdon

Leave on the East Exit to Highway #1, on page 43. Once you are on Highway #1/TransCanada Highway it is a straight run east out to Strathmore apart from the s-curve at Lake Chestermere, which provides (🚻 ♿ ⛽ ✕ 🚗). The highway traffic will be steady and it will be fast and there will be trucks. But the shoulder is huge and flawless. It is an easy highway-acclimatization road. If you have a tailwind you'll zip along quickly as you are also going gradually downhill. You'll feel smart and strong and think now you've got this cycling aced. Watch it. The return ride will be harder work.

There is nothing but fields between Lake Chestermere and Strathmore. You get a taste of the big-sky-country look that Southern Alberta's boost about.

Strathmore is right on the intersection of Highway #1 and #817. This intersection is the only stoplight on the TransCanada Highway between Calgary and Medicine Hat. The town is pleasant and small, a bedroom community to Calgary. The residential

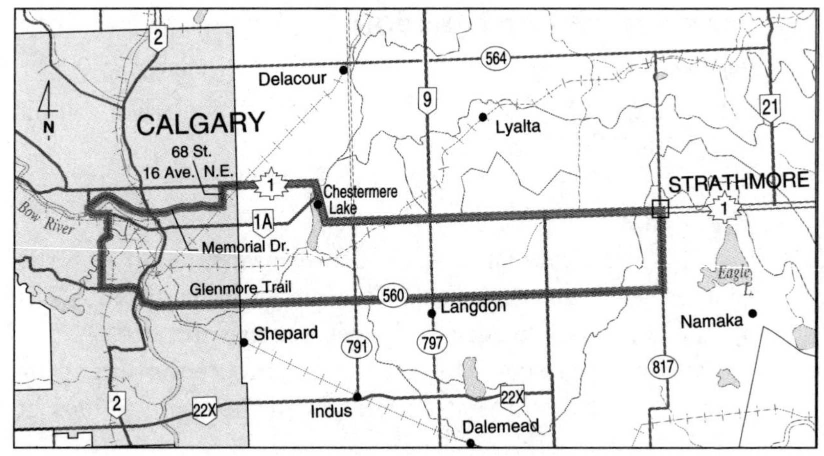

architecture indicates most significant growth was in the 70s and you will see some surprisingly good architecture in provincial government buildings. There are full services, (🚻 ♿ ⛽ 🍦 ☕ ✕ 🍎 🍸 🛒 🚗 🛏 $).

When you are finished in Strathmore, go south on Highway #817. This stretch can be a bit discouraging on a weekend morning while you get a taste of ranch living. Horse trailers, one after another, are hauled past. The road is a bit rough and there is no shoulder. So if a horse trailer is passing you and one is coming from the other direction, it won't give you much room.

But it isn't long before you hit Glenmore Trail/Highway #560 and can turn right (west). This is a great road. Almost zero traffic out this far from Calgary, straight, gently rolling with plenty of room. The aggregate is a bit coarse until you cross Highway #797 but it is consistent - not patched. You just need to pedal. No decisions, no diversionary swerves, just look around at open fields, skies, Rocks in the distance.

At Highway #797 you can turn south 800 meters to Langdon for services (🚻 ⛽). The washrooms are in a park outhouse unless a new service station/convenience store has been built as part of the new development of a Langdon suburb. Older Langdon, with a preference for country-sized larger yards, has a pleasant, restful feeling.

Back on #560/Glenmore you continue west on smoother aggregate, more like city paving and it feels welcome after the prior vibration that you probably stopped noticing. This lovely road continues to be fairly deserted, not only of cars but of stores and farmhouses as well, until you reach the city boundary at 84th Street SE. Take that route to return into Calgary, East Entry on page 80.

Services

Chestermere

- Porter's Gas and Food Mart, () open Monday to Friday 6:30 AM to 9 PM, Saturday 7:30 AM to 9:30 PM and Sunday 8 AM to 8 PM.
- Chestermere Landing Restaurant and Lounge: () there is pizza and steak seven days a week and the dining room, with a range of food is open Thursday to Sunday. The dining room overlooks the lake.

Strathmore

- Convenience store ()
- Grocery store, regular retail hours

Langdon

- Grocery store ()

Additional excursions

- Town exploring: If you like exploring towns, Strathmore and Langdon are small enough to cover thoroughly and provide an interesting contrast to each other. You can plan a picnic in either one or a restaurant meal in Strathmore.
- Pick fruit: There are pick-your-own fruit/vegetable businesses off #560/Glenmore Trail. Watch for signs. Most are somewhat off the highway but could be rewarding, particularly if you planned your excursion around them.

- Stay in Strathmore: If you want to turn this into a two-day trip, there is accommodation in Strathmore. This is not an endorsement, just information:

King Edward Hotel - 403 934-3262
Leroy's Motel - 403 934-3534
Strathmore Hotel - 403 934-3155
Wheatland Country Inn - 403 934-4000

Oh... and By the Way II...

The Other Golden Triangle

The famous Golden Triangle ride has a desert knock-off starting in Medicine Hat.

- Day One: ride northwest 105 K to Brooks on Highway #1 . Camp at the Tillibrook Campground, near Brooks - an excellent campground with showers.
- Day Two: ride south 124 K on the quieter Highway #36 to Taber and camp at the campground by the river.
- Day Three: pushed by a tailwind, ride the 127 K back to Medicine Hat on Highway #3.

A Desert Triangle!

Multi-day trips

Some of these rides can be cycled quickly, in one to three days, but offer enough delightful holiday diversions to be worth additional days if you have the time. It won't be long before you notice that getting in and out of cities is the least attractive part of cycling. That's when getting out and staying out gains appeal.

Multi-day trips present more planning options that are only limited by finding places you can stay and roads that are paved. It is fun to sit for a summer evening phoning B & Bs and putting your route together as you book accommodation. You can't be casual about this on the prairies. The distances are too great between places to stay and during the summer many towns have reunions or weddings that take up all the accommodation available for miles around.

Indulge your preferences. Are you after good weather? The southeast part of the province tends to be hotter and dryer. New places? Go beyond your coloured in routes. Open prairie? Go east. Short riding days with interesting towns to explore at the end of the day? Pick your route with that in mind. Isolation? Amazingly easy in Southern Alberta. Read about the trips ahead. Think about your preferences and the time you have. Consider the Rides to Try, on page 23. Then try some of the below. Change them to suit your preferences. These just get you started.

Cochrane Triangle

Highlights

This circuit is popular with cyclists so you may see many of them. It is a substantial ride, but you are never more than 1 1/2 hours from population centres. The roads are excellent and you get a gorgeous view of the foothills and Rocks from Highway #22. MacKay's Cochrane Ice Cream, delightful shops and the possible addition of Cochrane Ranch or The Western Heritage Centre give this ride serious kid appeal.

Challenges

This is a long one-day ride and if it is your first jaunt out of the city limits may feel too ambitious. But if you have worked your way up to it and pedal patiently you won't have any trouble. It is a lot of pedaling but the roads are good.

Traffic is also manageable except in the short stretch (800 M) between the end of Highway #8 and Richmond Road when you are returning and pedaling along Sarcee Trail. Crossing traffic on Richmond Road to turn left onto 45th Street SW during the afternoon can be hectic but it is easier than you think. If Memorial Drive is busy, you can turn off it.

Total distance: 109 K

Total cycle time: 3/4 day or a full day trip and worth extending to two days with an overnight in Cochrane. It takes approximately 7 hours of fairly straight cycling during a day or part of a day plus an evening.

Route: Cochrane Triangle

Take the NW Crowchild Trail Exit, page 59. At the city limits you have 18 K more to get to Cochrane. You cycle past Bearspaw, an acreage, bedroom community, and eventually to the infamous Cochrane Hill. You have three choices getting down the hill into Cochrane.

First, you can stay on the highway and take the huge long hill (2 K that feels like 5) down. If you like to keep good control, you will be riding your brakes all the way down. Watch for loose gravel on the shoulder. You may want to stop to do justice to the truly spectacular valley on your left and the hang gliders coming down the hill above you on your right - if there are already afternoon thermals. You'll also see an interesting house dug into the brow of the hill that must get a world class view up the valley.

Your second choice is to take Retreat Road that you come to before the hill, where it goes off to the right. It takes you through some pleasantly treed countryside and down a very steep hill that you don't want to try coming back up. If you take Retreat Road you enter Cochrane on the north side of the highway, on a smaller hill above town. You'll be beside the high school. This road is gravel in the odd spot but good quality surface and easy to ride down on.

Or you can pick the third option of turning left at the top of the big hill and getting onto Glen Eagles Drive through a new subdivision below the highway. It lands you back on the highway

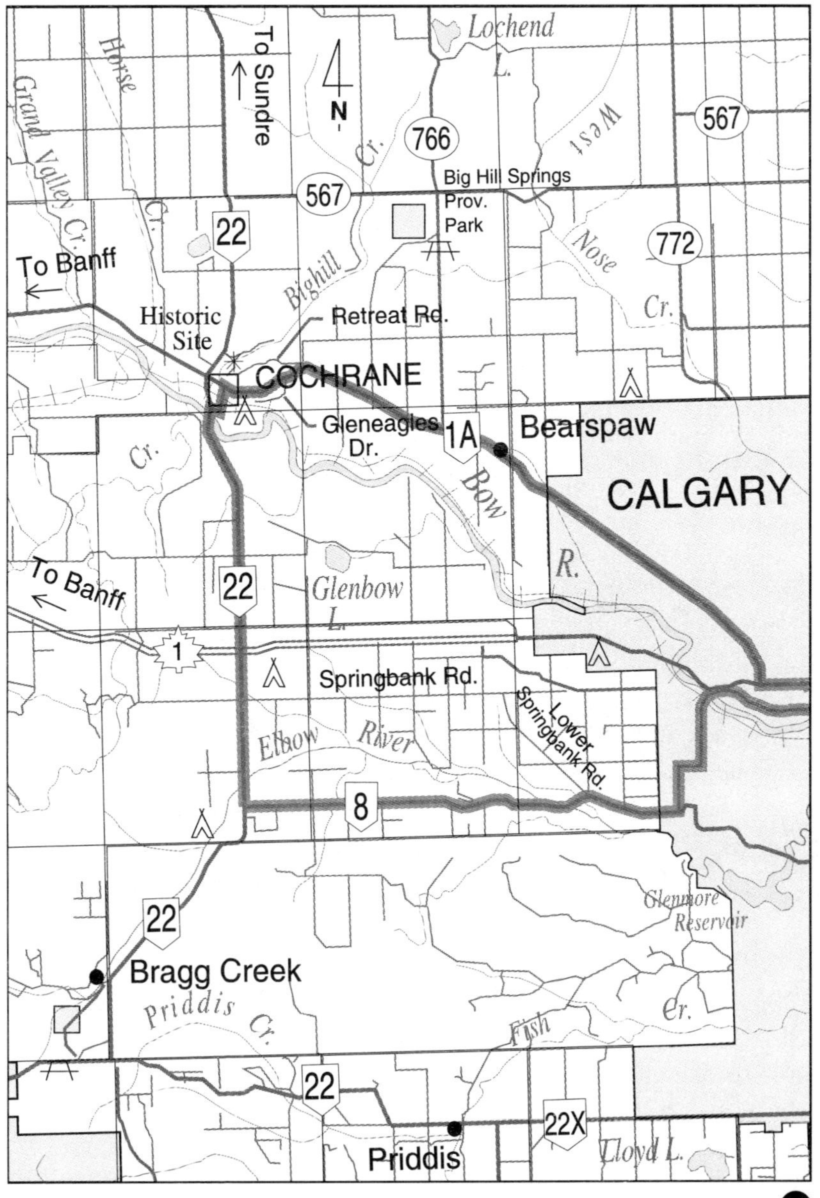

at the bottom of the hill, having curved your way down in a more leisurely way.

There is plenty to do in Cochrane: (🚻 ♿ ▣ 🍦 ☕ 🍴 🍎 🍸 ⛩ 🚗 🛏 $ 👪 📞). Turn left off the highway at any intersection to get down to First Street, the main street, which parallels the highway.

Whether or not you stay overnight in Cochrane, you eventually connect with Highway #22 for the next leg of your triangle. To avoid the hectic four-way stop west of town where Highway #1A crosses Highway #22, get on either 5th Avenue or River Avenue while you are still in town, and go south. Both of these streets cross the railroad tracks and carry you down to Griffin Road along the river. Turn right (west) onto Griffin Road, which takes you to Highway #22. Turn left (south) onto Highway #22, which immediately takes you across the Bow River. You are out of Cochrane and travelling the west leg of your triangle.

Once you are up the south side of the river valley – a long but well graded climb - you are on a particularly good road with a wide, smooth shoulder. Rolling hills. The Rocks off to the west. Really feels like foothills country. Feels like excellent cycling. Nicely graded hills, limited traffic and a bit of a downgrade tendency once out of the valley that makes you feel strong and capable. You will enjoy this for 20 K.

Then you see Highway #8, T-ing into Highway #22 ahead and below you, off to your left. It is well marked and you can't miss it. You go left onto Highway #8 so you are now heading east, leg three back into Calgary. You still have a substantial ride ahead of you, about 34 K, and quite a bit is up hill. But it is well graded and the shoulder is wide all the way in. In fact the shoulder is wider than a traffic lane and in excellent condition.

This is a stretch where you can play around with your cycling rhythm, or cadence, as the racers call it. You will see other people cycling here. Like the Cochrane run, this is a popular route.

Use the W Highway #8 Entry on page 89.

Services:

Bearspaw

- Bearspaw Gas opens at 7 AM weekdays, 8 AM weekends and sometimes 6 AM weekdays in the summertime, ( ).

Cochrane

- Tourist Information Centre, 932-6810 or the Town Office, 932-2075
- MacKay's Cochrane Ice Cream cones have long been a favourite excursion from Calgary, by car, and are now being done by cyclists, ( ).
- Many outlets for coffee and desserts ( )
- Wonderful Chinese restaurant west of town with tall glass walls that give a sitting-outside feeling, ( )
- Café de la Sport, the best Italian restaurant from Calgary pulled up roots and moved to Cochrane so you can enjoy it there. Very popular, so go early or reserve to avoid disappointment, ( ).
- There is a quiet spot for your picnic lunch at the tourist information log cabin. Turn left onto First Avenue West, the first Cochrane street that you reach at the bottom of the big hill. You can't miss it. The cabin is in the middle of a large, grassy lot. There's a lovely front porch with wooden outdoor furniture on it. It is rarely open but when it is the staff are friendly. It shelters you from sun, wind, rain and feels like home, ( ).
- B& Bs abound in Cochrane. Book ahead. If you want to explore Cochrane on foot, get one in the town, ( ).
- New Best Western Motel and complex just beside the Highway as you enter town, ( ).
- Scattered throughout Cochrane, ($) and antiques and crafts.

  Alert: There are no more services until you hit the Calgary Co-op on Richmond Road, back in the city, unless you extend your trip on into Bragg Creek on Highway #22.

Additional excursions

- Cochrane shopping: There is plenty of antique, craft and fun shopping in Cochrane, This town has become very tourisitic yet maintains a genuinely friendly, old prairie atmosphere and is the perfect scale for walking around.
- Picnics and history: Whether you take your own picnic from home or buy it in Cochrane you can spend it at the historical Cochrane Ranch, less than 1K west of Cochrane on Highway #1A. This is the site of the first large-scale cattle ranch established in the region in 1881, 932-2902. Also the Western Heritage Centre, north 2 K on Highway #22, offers interactive exhibits and gives visitors a chance to try their hand at rodeo sports, 932-3514, website: www.whcs.com.
- Add Bragg Creek: Pedaling on to Bragg Creek you get more snacking, cappuccino-ing, sitting around on a picnic table, eating ice cream and fresh bakery goodies. There is also a full grocery store, antique stores and hiking there. If you stay overnight in Bragg Creek you'll have time to explore west of Bragg Creek to Elbow Falls, the ice caves, and up to Little Elbow campsite. To do this, look to page 142 on the Bragg Creek ride.

A lesson in body temperature management

The forecast was for 7 to 10 degrees C. Heading out for a day ride the west wind was gusting so strongly that I had to pedal ***down*** *the legendary Cochrane Hill. Contrary to the forecast, the day wasn't getting warmer. The wind wasn't decreasing in strength.*

When turning onto the third leg of the Cochrane triangle trip, the phrase "temperature plummeting", came to mind. There was a low and heavy cloud ceiling. It felt like I would bump my head against it. It was shipping along fast, at right angles to my direction of travel. I was freezing.

Now snow was blowing horizontally. After being blown off the road onto the grass for the second time I realized that it wasn't just because I wasn't paying attention. I was so cold I was having trouble controlling the bicycle in the crosswind. So I walked the bike for a while until the road curved around a bit and the wind wasn't quite so flat on sideways. Over

- Ambitious NW destinations: From Cochrane, you have access to northwest destinations: Sundre to the north, or Canmore and Banff to the west further along Highway #1A or Highway #1.

Okotoks

Highlights

This is a beautiful ride with excellent, little-used roads and truly lovely scenery. Okotoks offers useful services for those passing through and an excellent variety of poking-around options for those staying over, including The Big Rock.

Challenges: There are some real climbs here, particularly when climbing back out of Okotoks but all are graded well and have excellent surface.
Total distances: 135 K
Total cycling time: this is a generous one-day ride and a leisurely two-day. Riding time is about 10 hrs if you take pictures and enjoy the view.

and over asking: Why doesn't someone stop and say, "No-one should be out here in this. Get in the car. No, don't worry, we'll load your bicycle. And here's a mug of hot chocolate." Where is this family of rescuers?

When I finally staggered in my door, late afternoon, my hands were so weak I struggled 15 minutes to remove my velcro ankle straps. I sipped hot soup while I gradually pealed off my clothes. I knew that if I got into a warm bathtub too soon my skin would burn. I was realizing that what I had was hypothermia.

It was will power that had kept me going and I'm pleased I can draw on that. I also know that this was a dangerous situation and now I watch for conditions that would cause it and take action early. This lesson stays with me and has been useful in subsequent cycle trips.

On Monday people make conversation with: "Did you see that freak snowstorm on Sunday?" Aha.

Daily breakdown

Two day trip

Day one: Calgary to Okotoks through Millarville about 90 K

Day two: Okotoks back to Calgary via #2A and #2 45 K

Route: Okotoks

Exit Calgary on S Midnapore, page 47, or East through Shepard, page 43. Whatever route you choose get going west on Highway #22/22X which is called Marquis of Lorne where it crosses MacLeod Trail/Highway #2 south.

Highway #22/22x does an odd thing at 208th Street. It both continues straight ahead as Highway 22 and goes left as an alternative name to 208th Street. Go left (south) onto #22/208th

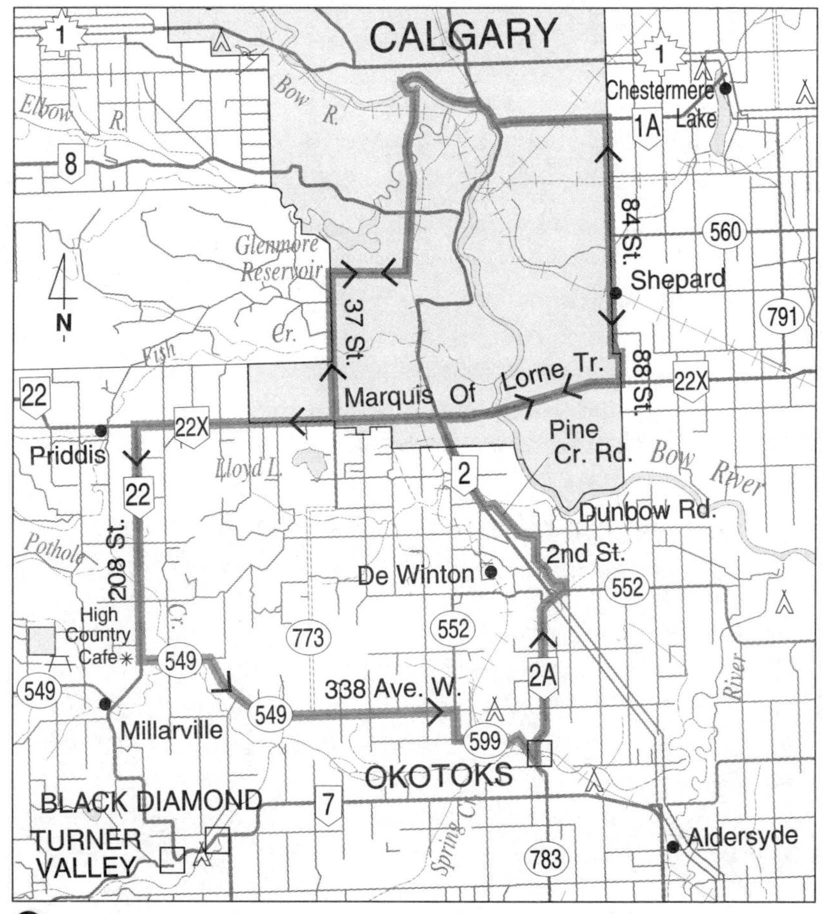

Street. The road is good and traffic moderate unless it is a Saturday morning between mid June and September 20th when the Millarville Farmers' Market is open. This has become popular and the road will be busy until you are past it.

After about 12 K Highway #549 joins into #22 from the left. The little High Country Café is on a slight rise on your right, (🚻 ♿ ✂). Turn left (east) onto Highway #549. Shortly after that you pass the Millarville Market so you are out of the market-bound traffic. Watch for tiny Millarville Church, a tiny 100-year-old building uniquely constructed of upright spruce logs. You will also see many prize horses grazing along this route. Then #549 curves south in a big arc and becomes renamed 338 Avenue West. This stops at the T-intersection with Highway #552.

Turn right (south) onto #552, which eventually curves east again and is once more renamed: #599. It is more confusing to read than ride. From here you ride down into the little-used west entrance to Okotoks. It is a lovely, tree-lined stretch and gives you the optimal first impressions of old Okotoks.

Whether you cycle back to Calgary after a pit stop or after a well-worthwhile layover to explore the town, you will start your cycle back to Calgary by cycling north on Highway #2A up the big hill. This is a long climb. Conserve yourself. Don't rush to the top. Steady will get you there.

In fact, once you establish a deep breathing/pedaling rhythm you'll notice you don't get any more tired as you continue climbing. As your fitness improves, you can climb more challenging hills without leaving your aerobic zone. This prevents the muscle burn and rapid fatigue to exhaustion that comes from anaerobic work. Some points to ponder as you cycle out of Okotoks. If your bike gear ratio, condition or cycle style push you into anaerobic zone, just keep stopping, sipping your water, walking your bike for a while.

Stay on Highway #2A to go over the Highway #2 overpass. Then take the first left onto 242nd Avenue and another climb - - but not nearly as long. 242 Avenue curves you around to 2nd Street and parallels Highway #2. After it crosses Dunbow Road it is called Pine Creek Road. Stay on it until it dumps you onto Highway #2 with an unceremonious flick.

Then you are stuck continuing north on Highway #2 until the Marquis of Lorne/Highway 22/22X exit about 6 K. Take this exit. On a sunny weekend afternoon the next stretch of Highway # 22/22X will be busy from the Deerfoot Trail turnoff in the east to the 37th Street SW turnoff in the SW. But the shoulder is wide.

Go left (west) on Marquis of Lorne if you want the SW 37th Street Entry to Calgary, page 87. This is the appropriate choice if you are staying in the far southwest part of Calgary. Go right (east) on Marquis of Lorne to get to the East Entry, page 80, if you are in the east, or north, or close to the Bow River anywhere along its length.

Services

Millarville

- High Country Café, renowned for homemade food and popular with the locals – tiny inside area, generous number of umbrella'd picnic tables outside. This is your last chance until Okotoks, ( ).

Okotoks

- Town Office, 938-4404
- Cappuccino spots ( )
- Fast food, like A&W ( )
- Restaurants ( )
- Ginger Room, a giant old house remodeled for classic tea: sandwiches, scones, Devonshire cream, as well as Sunday Brunch, lunch and dinner, ( ) one block east of the main intersection stoplight, one block south on Riverside Street.
- Okotoks Lions Sheep River Park has 60 campsites and a picnic area and is lovely for a walk in trees, particularly in the fall, ( ).
- B & Bs: book ahead ( )

Lake Sicome in Fish Creek Park

- Full Coney Island style refreshments ( )

Additional excursions

- Millarville: If you add 3 K extra to your ride you get to the town of Millarville for a look at houses built by the weekend country set, an amazingly good country general store. It is just 3 K further to Five Point Creek B&B to sleep over, even on the spur of the moment.

- Millarville Farmers' Market: You can fit in a quick shopping spree, right on Highway #549 on Saturday mornings.

- Big Rock: South of Okotoks you'll find the renowned Big Rock, an isolated gigantic - - well- - rock, sitting in the middle of prairie. 18,000 tons of what geologists call an erratic. The largest erratic in North America. They speculate that 10,000 years ago glaciers carried it there, partly because this one has the same quartzite composition as that found at Mount Edith Cavell in Jasper National Park. You'll want to ride your bike to Big Rock, it is 10 K west of Okotoks – which means Big Rock in Blackfoot - on Highway #7.

- Fun shopping in Okotoks: Okotoks is a comfortable scale for shopping and poking around in craft shops and coffee spots. Buying postcards, gifts, and stuff (👫).

- Explore old Okotoks houses: This is well worth the time if you like architecture or gardens. The first cross-street at the bottom of the Highway #2A hill in Okotoks is Elma Street. It runs parallel to and one block north of the main street, Elizabeth. Elma Street has some charming houses and creative gardens. Great for inspiration or photos.

- A swim at Lake Sicome in Fish Creek Park: You can see Lake Sicome from Highway #22/22X heading east. You may be able to scramble down the hill with your bike or you may have to lock it to the back of the guardrail and go down without. When crowded, this park offers as good people watching as you'd find anywhere.

Carried away

This absurd marathon ride began innocently with the urge to explore. "Hmmm, where shall I go today? Check the map for routes that aren't red yet. Oh look, there's Mossleigh. Right there on the map. Wonder what Mossleigh looks like? And I can get there on paved roads. Let's go to Mossleigh today."

I have twelve hours to tool around by myself, explore Mossleigh and be back in time for dancing. As the day warmed I gradually shed layers and added sunscreen, exposing more skin. Snacks by the road, stopping to write in my journal, feeling that this is perfect. Wind not an issue.

It is 1 PM. I've been on the bike for hours; I reach the junction where I start back after I tack on the extra nine K to get to Mossleigh. The highway sign tells me 86 K back to Calgary. Eighty-six K is usually a decent day's ride all by itself. Hmmm. And that lies between me and home. I decided in spite of Mossleigh inspiring the trip to begin with that I would forget about exploring Mossleigh. The additional 9 K & 9 K to Mossleigh and back would take us from the ridiculous to the sublime. It would have to be left for another day.

Fortunately I am finding the situation funny. And, having never really measured a journey before, I know I'm finally going to know if I can pedal more than 160 K in a day. This is going to be a grinding push and now the sun has gone in and the wind has come up from - guess where - the west! I'm being philosophical about timing. I'll get there when I get there, but the headwind — as they always are — is discouraging

So I push. Increasingly, everything hurts.

I plot my city entry route carefully knowing that this huge day of riding has left me a bit fragile to take on too much traffic but my priority is still short and direct. I finished on will power. Wherever I was, I just kept plotting the details of my next leg so that I could keep making the most efficient choices every turn.

When I finally made it to my house I could hardly carry my bike up the stairs to the porch. Dancing? I climbed into bed and was asleep by 8:30.

Mossleigh

Highlights

Quiet, untraveled highway, Wyndam-Carseland Park a peaceful rest beside the river and outdoor snacks. If you have camping gear along, kids could enjoy a day of fishing and loafing on the deck and mucking about in the water at Wyndam-Carsland Park.

Challenges

This is difficult to do in one day unless you have incredible stamina or cycle fast. But the whole route is very nice cycling and worth giving two days. Unfortunately there is no place near the middle to stay so you have to chop a bit off the beginning or the end. The Wyndam-Carsland Park hill is your biggest challenge. Steady, well graded and just long.

Total distance: about 200 K round trip from the city centre.
Total time: This is a two-day trip unless you want to start at 5:30 AM and cycle into the evening– a long time to be on a bike

Daily breakdown:

Two day, long first, short second

Day one: Calgary-Mossleigh-Strathmore: 156 K
Day two: Strathmore to Calgary: about 50K

Two day, short first, long second

Day one: Calgary to Okotoks: 45 K
Day two: Okotoks-Mossleigh-Calgary: 155 K

Route: Mossleigh

If you are doing this in one day, leave as soon as it is light and this is talking mid-summer when it is light early. Accept that you will be cycling into the evening. This is a day trip to prove that you can do it. Once you've done this ride in a day you won't feel you need to prove that again.

The pressure is off a bit on a two day but not as much as if there were a place to stay somewhere near the middle of this ride. Just leave early enough to get out of town before "they" wake up: 7 AM

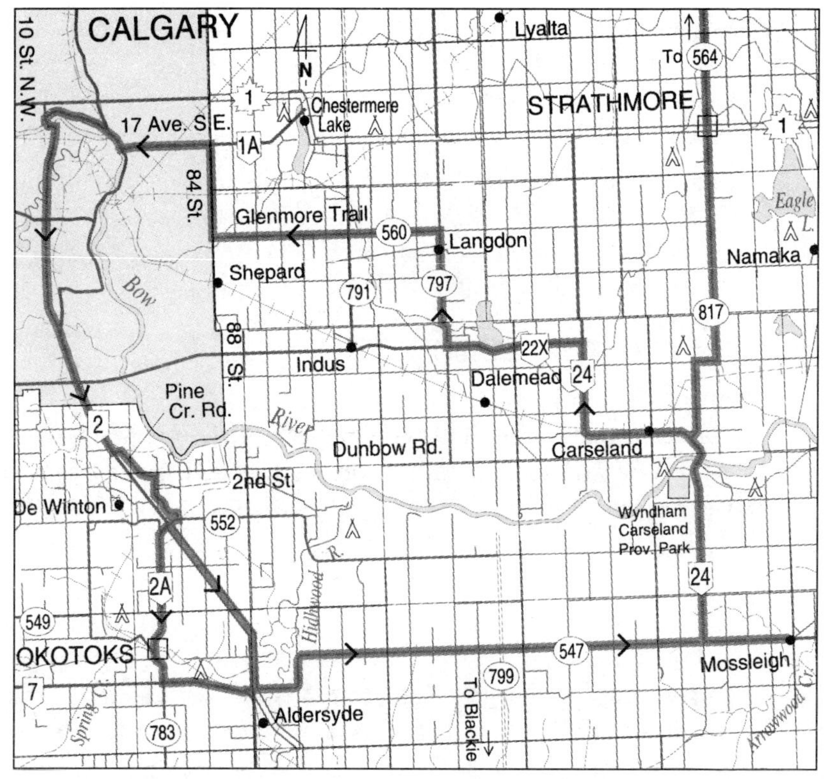

at the latest. Take the S Midnapore Exit, page 47 all the way down to Highway #2A.

You could then take Highway #2A to Okotoks and #7 east from Okotoks to connect with #547 at Highway #2, if you want to stay away from traffic on this first stretch. If you are trying to save time, stay on the big #2 Highway south all the way to Aldersyde turnoff - 27.5 K from the centre of the city.

You will see a service station on the highway where #2 meets #547, (🚻 ♿ ⛽ 🚗). Turn left (east) onto Highway #547. This is a beautiful road. Paved, quiet, rolling. The aggregate can be rough in spots but the shoulder is wide. Lovely farmland. A keeper route. You can enjoy Southern Alberta cycling at it's finest on this road. It is well graded, has little traffic and rolling fields of crops around you.

In the early spring, the fields have pale, silvery-blond stubble and seem to be the source of light on a grey day. The vast, wide swathing equipment used in contemporary farming has left its footprint. And in contrast, grey and hollow in the middle of a field, a deserted wooden house, weathered to brittle. The beauty of each season is a peaceful antidote to city life.

You'll drive past Glady's United Church on the left and shortly after that St. Thomas Anglican Church, about the size of a privy, in the middle of a field on your right. Tiny cemetery. Nothing else around. You can imagine a congregation, huddled against the elements.

Twenty-two K from Aldersyde Highway #547 intersects with #24. You are 9 K west of Mossleigh on Highway #24. You have just arrived at the third leg of your ride triangle.

If you want to explore Mossleigh you'll add a little leg out of the corner of your triangle. Go right (east) on #24, the 9 K to get to Mossleigh. Mossleigh is small and a bit odd, a tiny collection of buildings beside the highway. It has streets laid out like a real town but many of the blocks are empty and at most they have three or four houses. There's nowhere to stay. Why is it here? After you explore Mossleigh, ( ) you just get back on the highway and head west again where you came from, returning the 9 K to the Highway #547/24 intersection.

Out of Mossleigh you immediately face a long climb but from the top you can look east and see a long way across prairie. This is one place that there seems truth to the claim that the continent slopes downhill from the Rocky Mountains to the east coast. A great, tilted shelf.

It is 86 K back to Calgary from the Highway #24/547 junction. Highway #24 isn't as good as #547. The shoulder is very chewed up on some stretches. There is more traffic, but not so much that you have to pay attention to every inch of road. There are almost few trucks. Vehicles passing you have room to swing out into the other lane because there is rarely on-coming traffic at the same time.

This continues to be pretty, rolling farmland and some uncultivated grazing prairie. The highway drops down into the Bow River Valley at Wyndam-Carseland Park, with lovely trees and a spot to rest and snack, ( ). The hill climbing back out again seems daunting from the bottom but it is well graded and quite do-able.

If you want to stay overnight in Strathmore and shorten this day by 50 K, go straight north on #24, which becomes #817, to Strathmore and get accommodation there, ($). If you do that, return to Calgary the next morning by going further north on #817 to Highway #564. Then left (west) and into town the NE Airport Entry route, page 77.

If you follow Highway #24 shortly after the park, you get to Carsland. Carsland has 200 houses, a general store, a sports arena, a school, a gas station and bar and a ball diamond, ( ). When you cruise the Carsland suburbs you find a boldly designed new school: brick with peak-roofed modules, bright yellow trim, a red tile roof and big windows. It is wonderful.

Leaving Carsland you go straight west and then north on Highway #24. It curves around to meet Highway #22x. If you are racing back to Calgary in one day, turn left (west) onto Highway #22x, from #24. This is a flawless new highway: beautifully engineered, with wide shoulders and new pavement. There isn't much traffic for the quality of road, just what you want in cycling. A pleasure.

When you get to Highway #797, turn right (north) and take it up through Langdon, ( ). This is also a good highway with even less traffic so you can do plenty of gazing around and soaking in country atmosphere. Langdon houses, about 30 of them, are a bit spread out and have a nice feeling and in the summertime residents stand on their lawns and chat to each other.

As soon as you head north again, out of Langdon, you hit Highway #560, which is the extension of Glenmore Trail. This is good quality road; it goes all the way east to Highway #817. It also offers a wide shoulder, good surface conditions and, on this stretch, not too much traffic.

You go west on Glenmore as far as 88th/84th Street SE. It gets extremely busy and industrial and truck-ie as you get into town so you turn off here. It is about 20 K to the city centre from the Glenmore/84 Street intersection. So turn right (north) at 84th to get to 17th Avenue SE and back in through Forest Lawn on the East Entry, page 80.

Services

Aldersyde

- Esso ()

Okotoks

- Shell Snack Shop ()
- Cappuccino shops along Elizabeth Street ()
- OK Convenience Store on Southridge ()
- Range of service stations, such as Esso, on Southridge ()
- Range of fast food restaurants like A&W off Southridge ()
- Several grocery stores, such as IGA, on Southridge ()
- Ginger Room, a giant old house remodeled for classic tea: sandwiches, scones, Devonshire cream, plus Sunday Brunch, lunch, and dinner, () one block east of the stoplight, one block south on Riverside Street
- Okotoks Lions Sheep River Park has 60 campsites and a picnic area and is lovely for a walk in trees, particularly in the fall ()
- B & Bs: book ahead (), The Croft B&B, 938-2951, if they are full they will know of others

Mossleigh

- Service station/snack shop with a limited range ()

Wyndham-Carsland Provincial Park

- Single store with essentials () and with a beautiful spot to rest and well maintained outdoor toilets () and the all-important ice cream. They have a huge deck with sun and shade to enjoy your snack and rest for a while.

Carsland

- all-purpose store you can pick up chips, nuts, beer, cold drinks, cookies and candy, ()
- Arena ()

Strathmore

- Convenience store (🚻 ♿ ☎ 🍎 🚗)
- Grocery store
- Accommodation, but not an endorsement:
  King Edward Hotel – 403 934-3262
  Leroy's Motel – 403 934-3534
  Strathmore Hotel – 403 934-3155
  Wheatland Country Inn – 403 934-4000

Langdon

- Langdon general store. When I was last there this was the only store. It had a crabby owner (♿ ☎ 🍎).There is talk of a new subdivision in Langdon with plans to bring in another convenience store and service station.
- town park (🚻) on the north edge of town, chemical toilets.

The Cowboys meet the Indians in Carsland

The Anglo team has pretty, trim little wives to cheer them. They are settled into lawn chairs with their feet up on coolers. Pony tails, shorts, suntops, tans, manicured fingernails, and earrings. They also have a couple of guy fans with big, tanned beer bellies under which their shorts are precariously slung, held up by – what? They have plenty of cans of cooled beer and they have ball lingo:

"Push ball, push ball!"

"Make him work for it!"

"Come on baby!" (over and over)

"You KNOW how to do it!"

"Keep 'm hurten'!" (yelled)

All of these repeated tirelessly.

The Native team is still arriving even though the game has started. They have uniforms too but the captain, or someone, keeps asking everyone on the team as they pull into the parking lot if they have kneepads. He does this by pointing at his knee while he raises his leg in front of him.

The answer is always the same. They each shake their head and proceed to get out of their car, get the kids and woman out, amble over and sit in the dugout. They don't rush and they don't seem to need briefing on what is going on. They just sit down and are then part of the game. No one tells them the score and they don't ask.

Chestermere

- Porter's Gas and Food Mart, (🚻 ♿ ⛽ 🚗) open Monday to Friday 6:30 AM to 9 PM, Saturday 7:30 AM to 9:30 PM and Sunday 8 AM to 8 PM.
- Chestermere Landing Restaurant and Lounge: (🚻 ♿ 🍴) there is pizza and steak seven days a week and the dining room, overlooking the lake, is open Thursday to Sunday, with a range of food

Additional Excursions

- Check Blackie: Riding east along Highway #547, you pass Highway #799 to Blackie, which I haven't ridden but it looks paved and would be worth exploring.

Their cheerleaders are two kinds of women: the one's that have gained weight and the one's who are still skinny. And they don't have coolers and lawn chairs. They have kids. And they spend most of their time telling their kids to stop doing things: stop hitting the bleachers with sticks (yeah we have real wooden bleachers here) stop putting dirt in their mouths, stop eating candy, stop taking candy from the other kids. Kids get told to sit down and be quiet a lot, which is what they don't do.

The game trend is already established. The "Indians" don't hit enough, run fast enough, catch enough to hold their own with the cowboys but they stay pretty loose about it all.

And it is a white player who, after the heady triumph of a home run, settles into the other team's dugout before he figures out he's in the wrong place, much to the amusement of the crowd. Smirk and amble good-naturedly across the infield while the game waits. Cheers. Guffaws.

Try and catch the white cheerleaders and their sport-smart railing and the loopy casualness of the natives, so native, the players so removed from it, the mom's so obsessed with their kids not acting like native kids, and the game trying to be a real baseball game AND IT IS.

So if you want just about the best entertainment there is around, cycle out to Carsland to take in a baseball game there some summer afternoon.

- Staying over at Wyndham-Carsland Provincial Park: This park is isolated from neighbourhood convenience stores and television. Instead it has a river, fishing, camping, horseshoes, snacks and a huge deck offering sun and shade, lying dangling your feet in the river, hiking and doing nothing. If camping suits you this would break up this long ride much closer to the middle.

- Explore Dalmead: You can take in tiny Dalmead, just past Carsland. You still leave Carsland going straight west but when #24 takes a sharp right-angle turn north you divert toward an archetypal, evil looking industrial complex looming out of the landscape belching something into the air and standing alone doing heaven only knows what. It is straight west of you when Highway #24 turns north. Go straight west and then you jog north on a gravel road to tiny Dalmead. Dalmead can't even afford to oil its streets let alone pave them. So it is dusty and rough but something worth seeing. There is a small general store/post office/hub and a handful of houses, (Ⓢ ▣ ⚙). After cruising downtown Dalmead you can continue west on their gravel main street and pick up #797 north to reconnect you to #22X.

Bragg Creek and Elbow Falls Road

Highlights

Wonderful open ride, all the eating and shopping delights of Bragg Creek. Scenery that draws people from around the world and the possible addition of Elbow Falls and the bizarre ice caves.

Kids would find a lot to entertain them on this ride: great treats in Bragg Creek, the awesome ice caves, Elbows Falls for clambering around and a picnic.

Challenges

The climb out of Edworthy Park is challenging but do-able. After that, traffic at Richmond Road and Sarcee Trail can be busy if it is after 9 AM when you are leaving Calgary. If you extend the trip to include Elbow Falls Road, you have a long climb to the summit.

The shoulder is narrow in some sections of Highway #22/22X going east. 17th Avenue SE can be busy in the afternoon coming back in. If strong winds are blowing from any direction they are going to be in your face or pushing you sideways on some part of this trip. But the other legs will be better.

Total distance: 14 K from city centre to Highway #8 city limits,
44 K to Bragg Creek
Loop to Bragg Creek and back, Highway #8 both ways, 116K
Loop to Bragg Creek via #8 and back to Calgary via 22/22x and E Shepard Entry, 147 K

Total cycle time: This is a full day's ride, without the optional addition, whichever route you choose.

Daily breakdowns

Two day trip

Calgary to Bragg Creek 58 K
Bragg Creek back to Calgary 58 K (Highway #8), 74 K (SW 37t Street), 89 K (East, Shepard Entry)

Three day trip

Calgary to Bragg Creek 58 K
Bragg Creek to Little Elbow Campground and back to Bragg Creek, about 60 K
Back to Calgary 58 K (Highway #8), 74 K (SW 37th Street), 89 K (East Shepard Entry)

Route: Bragg Creek & Elbow Falls Road

This is at least a full day's jaunt so leave early unless you like returning in the evening. The middle of the three-day option, going west on Highway #66 can be as short or long as you want depending on when you turn around and go back to Bragg Creek.

Take the W Bow Trail Exit, page 55. Once you are on Highway #8 you have wide, clear shoulder all the way out to Bragg Creek. You have well-graded hills, the Rockies in front of you, and maybe a headwind. You could vary this by going out on Lower Springbank Road, 105th Street and Springbank Road to parallel Highway #8 out to Highway #22/22X, or by going west on Old Banff Coach Road, both on page 57.

These are big vista roads. You'll see falcons hunting, creeks that swell to lakes during spring run-off – and along Highway #8, other cyclists. Highway #22 into Bragg Creek, from the junction with Highway #8 (11 K) has been upgraded to an excellent wide shoulder - a marvelous improvement to this extremely popular cycle route.

Even if you are doing the whole ride in one day, you'll probably stop into the Bragg Creek Village for a rest and refreshments. Then, you can turn around and come back the same way (#8) or expand your exploring on a great circle route by going further south and take the next leg of Highway #22/22x back toward Calgary. Note that this is one of those highways that meanders a bit, changes direction, changes name, ceases to exist and then re-appears.

If you are going to also ride Highway #66 up toward the Little Elbow Campground along Elbow Falls Road, you'll probably want an extra day. A word of explanation is called for about that ride. West of Bragg Creek, Highway #22/222X is called Highway #66. It goes past the entrance to the ice caves parking lot, the start of many hiking trails, lovely Elbow Falls and continues west as Elbow Falls Road. There is a great iron barrier across the road just after

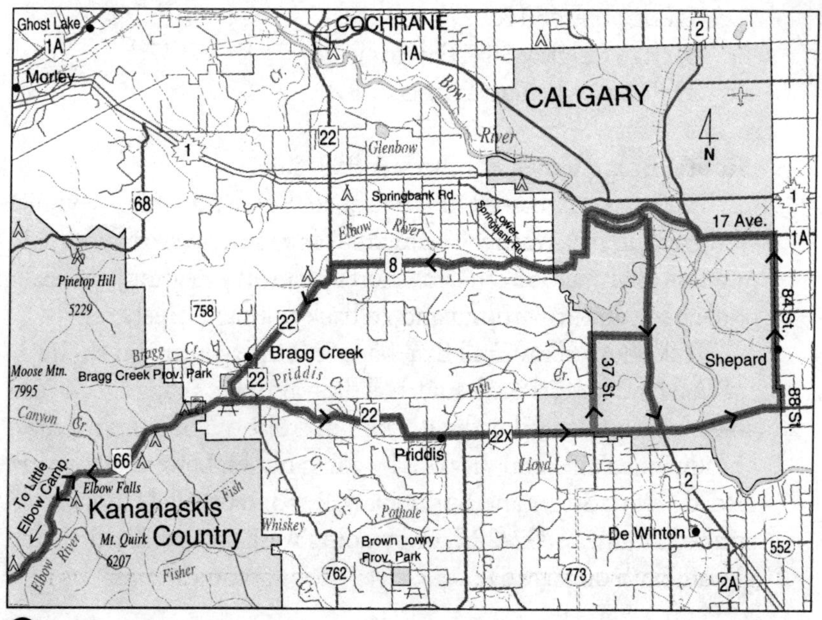

the Elbow Falls parking lot entrance. This road is closed off December 1st to May 15th so if you get out there early you have it to yourself – a great thrill. Even when the highway is open there is very little traffic because the paving only continues to one small campground and picnic area, about 10 K further along. After that you are on dirt road and hiking trails.

There are two ways you can get from Bragg Creek to Highway #66. The little, winding, connector, Highway #758 route, is hilly and has some sharp turns. You'll notice on the map that it is just a wider loop to Highway #/66/22. You exit the east side of Bragg Creek Shopping Centre parking lot and go one-half block south and turn right (southwest). That puts you on Highway #758 that curves out of town west. You get to see some of the lovely homes in old Bragg Creek and a couple of residential antique stores. The light volume of traffic on this road needs to be treated with caution. Visibility is limited in spots and it is smart to listen carefully for traffic you can't see yet. The road climbs up past a campground entrance and then turns south to connect with Highway #66, 1.6 K west of the more direct route on Highway #22. The total loop is about 5 K.

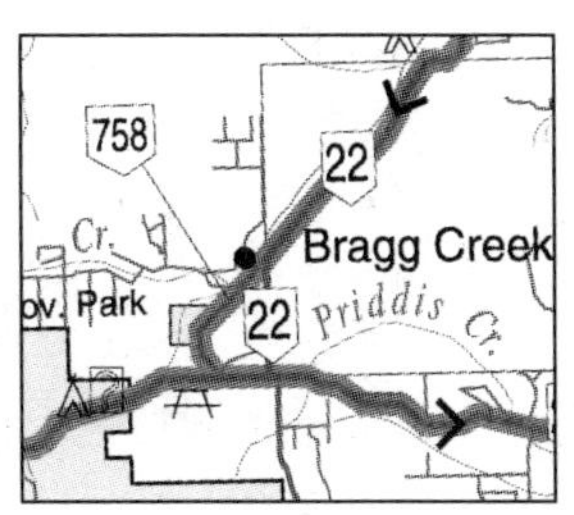

The more direct road, truly as the crow flies, just over 3 K, is a continuation of Highway #22 on which you rode into town. To get back onto it you also leave the shopping centre at the east side and take that half-block south but at that point you continue south straight up a hill. This crow-flies link has received a much-needed upgrade too. In about 3 K you get to beautiful Highway #22 off to your left and #66 off to your right.

Elbows Falls is about 22 K southwest of Bragg Creek. The shoulder is wide, the road surface is excellent, the terrain is rolling and gradually uphill - - you are heading into the Rockies.

Shortly after Elbow Falls you pass the barrier and no more traffic if the road is closed and very little if it is open. This is when you begin to see a serious climb, at least 3 K of uphill going up about 550 vertical feet. (The Ranger's topographical map was is

The serious cyclists

In Bragg Creek you will be around real cyclists who fly out there in small, intense swarms on racing machines that don't have baskets on the front and don't even have fenders. And the cyclists aren't pedaling in time to Walkmans. They have high tech cowcatchers on the front of their bicycles so they can lean their forearms on them and receive maximum aerodynamic advantage of some sort.

Their clothes do that for them too. Skin tight lycra body suits and helmets that are pointed at the back. And shoes that lock onto the pedals so that every muscle in their body can contribute to pedaling ("...the upstroke, the upstroke Marg, you aren't making use of the upstroke..."). Yeah that's right I'm not. I kinda like moving my foot around on the pedal so that when my legs, crotch or feet get tired or my feet feel tingly I can shift my position.

Anyway, out in Bragg Creek these cyclists do things like hold water bottles up in the air above their faces and squirt water at themselves and into their mouths and laugh and walk funny in their cycling shoes and eat hunks of bread out of a whole loaf they hold in one hand. All very camaraderie.

feet.) Well graded but definitely up. A great workout because you know you can walk a stretch or turn around any time you want.

From the summit, the road goes downhill about 3 K to the valley where Little Elbow Campground and the picnic grounds are sited. It is more of the same: excellent roads, Rocky Mountain views that are worth just standing and gazing at quietly - - and silence.

When you return to Bragg Creek remember you will get back more quickly than it took you to get up there. So don't think you need to turn around when your time is half used up. You will come whizzing back.

If you stay in a Bragg Creek B&B overnight you have time to ride the Elbow Falls Road, check out Elbow Falls and even the ice caves if you want and explore this delightful Bragg Creek. Antique and craft browsing are excellent. It feels like a joy just to walk around in the magnificent Rocky Mountain forest town.

On your return, Highway #22/22X going east offers lovely, peaceful riding until Priddis, wide shoulder, amazing scenery and light traffic. This is Canadian Rocky country without serious hills, and of course the trend is now downhill when you are going east. After Priddis, which mainly identifies itself with its golf course, the shoulder disappears. It is still four lane divided and the hills are well graded but you sometimes have cars passing you fast right next to you.

Your first entrance option into Calgary is the only entrance from the southwest: SW 37th Street, page 87. Not my favourite. Narrow, a steep hill down and up again to get over Fish Creek and then you face all the vehicular suburbanites on Anderson Road and Elbow Drive. It is manageable but if you have the time it is worth going on to the East Entry through Shepard, which borders the east side of the city, page 80.

Services

Bragg Creek

- Shopping Centre (🚻 ♿ 🏧 🍦 ☕ 🍴 🍎 🛒 🚗 🛏 ⛺ 👫 📞) There is a small grassy plot in the middle of the shopping centre with picnic tables and a couple of trees surrounded by every kind of snack or meal experience you could want. You'll share it with people who have driven out in cars, trucks, motorcycles as well as bicycles to just sit in that little patch of grass and eat good snacks before they go home again.
- Bragg Greek Steak Pit, a lovely, high-end restaurant with the traditional beef, baked potatoes, caesar salad done very well. And their timber and riverstone interior feeds the romantic image of dinner in the Rockies. You would probably want to dress a bit for that, (🚻 ♿ 🍴).
- Bragg Creek Provincial Park (🚻 ♿ 🛒 ⛺) 2 K west of Bragg Creek on Highway #758

Elbow Falls

- Park (🚻 ♿ 🛒) On a warm, Sunday afternoon this park will have attracted a huge number of Calgarians who park along the road and settle into the trees along the river to cook their picnics, drink beer, give the kids a bit of glorious outdoors. And it is glorious and fun and funny to watch. So fight the misanthrope in yourself and have a look. Traffic to here will not make a problem for you.

- Summit on Elbow Falls Road: If you make it to the top of that hill you can picnic there, probably in solitude. (⛼)
- Little Elbow Campground and picnic area, (🚻 ♿ ⛼ ⛺)

Priddis

- General Store and service station, 2 K south of Highway #22 at the sign, (🏪 🚲)

Nothing else until you are back into the city.

Additional excursions

- Go to the ice caves: You have to see these to believe them. It is worth cycling out to Bragg Creek and spending a night there just to position yourself to cycle to the ice caves parking lot and climb up to have a look. There are no signs at the turn-off, because the Park Warden considers this to be a dangerous place and will not publicize it. Proceed at your own risk. The parking lot is about 10 K west of Bragg Creek and you'll see the road in to the parking lot on your right when going west at the bottom of a dip. There is a creek beside it.

There are also no signs in the parking lot so you need detailed instructions or someone with you who has been there before. You can sort of see cave openings above you but there are several caves so follow other people or ask.

From the parking lot, you hike about 1 K on a trail before starting to scramble up the mountainside scree. In case you don't know about scree, it is loose rock that has come to rest after sliding down the mountainside. It is, by definition, unstable. Once you scramble up you'll be amazed how cold it is in there, even on the hottest day outside. And just as astounding, the floor of ice is frozen in a big wave. If you have a flashlight, or better yet, miner's helmet with a light, you can advance quite far on the ice, into the cave, if you crouch or scramble on your belly and inch forward. It gives you a new appreciation of what goes on under the earth's crust.

Coming back down the scree is difficult and, if your legs are feeling strong, best pulled of if you imitate one of the young guys skiing down it sideways. You face sideways to the drop, plant your feet apart and jump sideways landing further down the hill. This loosens the scree you land on and it slides down under you, carrying you down with it. You ride it down. When it stops or slows down or the spirit moves you, you jump sideways again and slide down some more.

When you stand at the mouth of the ice cave and contemplate doing this, your heart will freeze. However when you ponder the alternative of inching yourself down, possibly on your behind, it seems worth an experiment. Easiest if you see someone doing it and can imitate them. You will do better with this than you think, but we emphasize that this whole endeavor is considered dangerous. Balance that with the fact that I was a cautious woman in her mid-forties when I first went up there following a strong, young, fearless teenaged male. It was hard work and scary - - and a wonderful adventure.

- Hike: You can ride to hiking spots along Highway #66, lock up your bike and change to that other bimodal pass-time: walking.
- Priddis: You can explore Priddis, which is really just one general store and then spread out acreages, most of them only accessible on gravel roads. The turn off is well marked.
- Shepard car races: You can stop and see the car races at Shepard, which you pass entering Calgary on 88th/84th Street SE. This might get a reluctant teenager to come along.

VULCAN

Highlights

Wonderful, untraveled roads with beautiful prairie vistas. Rolling fields from horizon to horizon. Out in Vulcan you find a Noah's Ark B & B with a menagerie of animals you can pet, pick up and watch enjoying themselves. Science information stops beside the highway, the chance to catch a Carsland softball game and Wyndham-Carsland Park.

Children who like animals would enjoy the Prairie Past B & B, and a day of wading and fishing in the river at Wyndham-Carsland Park would be a pleasure for kids of all ages.

Challenges

This is not a hard ride apart from the fact that it requires long days to complete in two days. There are coulees and rolling hills, some steep, some long but all are well graded. Wind can be an issue. The shoulder is adequate except for small stretches on Highway #24.

Total distance: 245 K
Total time: 2 to 3 days.

Daily breakdowns

Two day trip

Calgary city limits to Vulcan: 124 K.
Vulcan (actually your B & B, which is outside Vulcan) to Calgary: 121 K.

Three day trip

Calgary to High River 60 K
High River to Vulcan 66 K, High River to B&B past Vulcan 74 K
Vulcan B&B to Calgary 121K

Route: Vulcan

If you are getting to Vulcan in one day, it will be a long day. So leave before traffic builds or else face traffic and accept that you will be pedaling into the evening. Take the S Midnapore Exit, page47 or, if you leave when traffic is heavy, take the East Exit and then turn south onto 84th/88th Street SE, page 43. If you take the latter, turn right (west) on Highway 22X/Marquis of Lorne Way and then south on Highway #2 South.

Both of these will have you going south on Highway #2. The S Midnapore map and directions, page 48, will get you all the way down to the Highway #2A bypass into Okotoks, (). You can linger there or you can go straight through town and up the other side of the valley on Southridge. This winds you out of town to a four-way stop sign. You can then choose to take either Highway #2A, heading off to your left, or

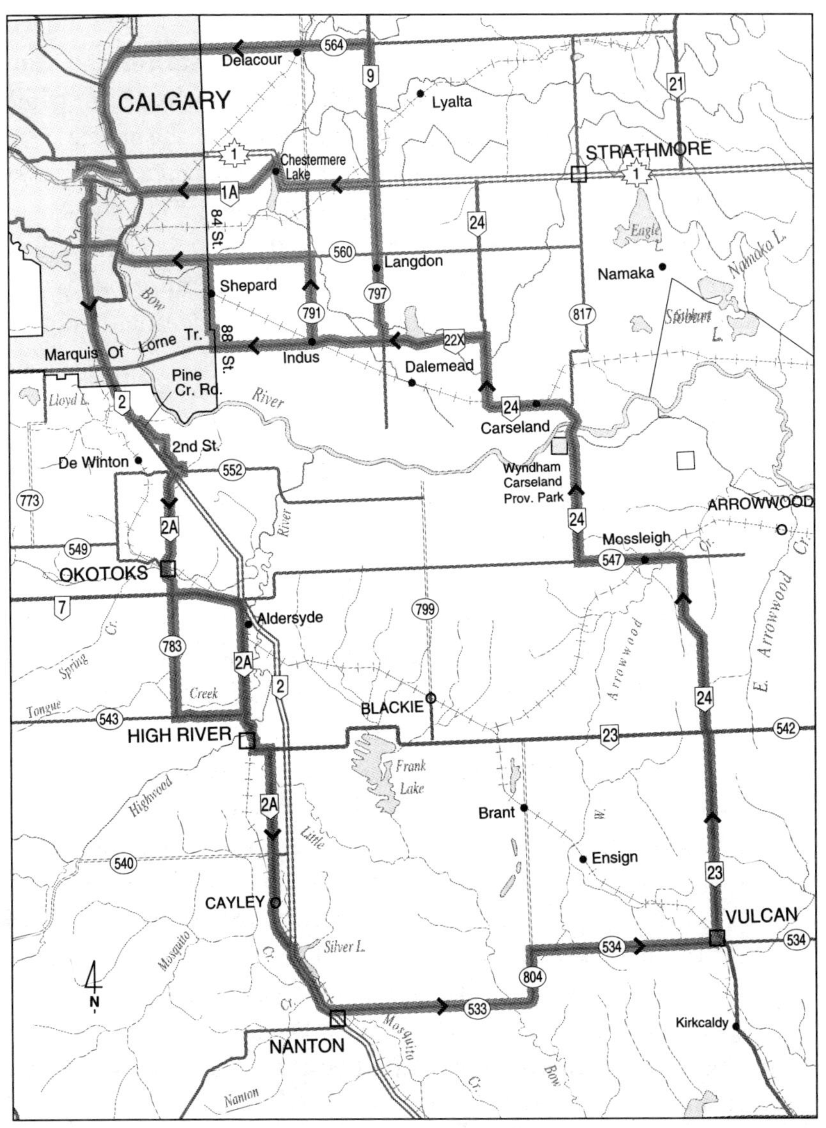

Highway #783, going straight ahead. Both of them will take you to High River with minimal traffic.

Highway #2A is restful, mostly flat and goes straight into High River. If you take #2A you don't need any other instructions until you get to High River. The road will get you there.

Highway #783 is a nice road. Not busy. It is mostly a gradual rise until it is half way to Highway #543. At that high point you see prairie dropping away to the south and east and sky forever. It feels as if you could squirt your water bottle all the way to Toronto. And in the west you'll see the Rockies. You can tell why people come from all over the world to see them rising out of the prairie.

Then it is a gradual downhill ride until you hit a steep sided coulee just before the road meets up with Highway #543. If you have taken this road, you then turn left (east) onto #543, also called Tongue Creek Road, which has a nice pastoral coulee in it as you cross Tongue Creek. Its rolling hills are all manageable. Highway #543 joins Highway #2A just north of High River.

On Highway #2A you pass the infamous River Roadhouse and cross the river into town. It is easy to get through High River quickly but it offers some nice town browsing if you want to take the time, ( ). Even if you don't spend the night in High River, it is worth cruising by the magnificent B & B on 3rd Street called Travelers' Respite. There is also a large junk store downtown with a mountain of old tools and a bit of everything else – like vintage prairie 1930's wringers for old washing machines. The town is pleasant to walk around in and has a large, well-treed park for picnics in the southwest corner.

You have entered town on Highway #2A. Traffic is light, even mid-day on a Saturday. Cross 3rd Avenue, one of the main commercial streets, at the stop sign. There is a sign right ahead of you that indicates that Highway #2A continues straight ahead. You proceed south about 5 blocks to 12th Avenue SE which borders the south end of town.

Once across town, 12th Avenue and Centre Street, you now see a sign indicating how to reconnect with and continue south on Highway #2A. It has an arrow that points left (east) and also says #2 and #23 East. You go left (east) on 12th Avenue SE. You will pass the High River Recreation Centre on your left. Make use of the cycle path on the north side of the road because it is in good condition and there is little shoulder for riding on the south side.

You pick up Highway #2A again, which is seems to be incorrectly marked #23 – but not very well. Highway #23 actually goes east from here, across Highway #2 and links with #24, which you will be on the next day. So watch this. The other end of the southbound street marked #23/2A, the end that goes into town, is on your left and a bit further ahead. It is marked 11th Avenue SE – but is also hard to see. If you go east as far as the big, Highway #2, you've gone too far.

Take Highway #2A right (south). This stretch of #2A is virtually untraveled. Open fields, rolling road, peaceful. You'll see High River's tiny little airport and you'll probably see sheep, which is unusual in cattle country. The surface is old and a bit patched but because there is zero traffic you can meander anywhere you want on the road to pick the good parts. This, again, is one of those special roads for wonderful biking.

Sixteen K south of High River you pass Cayley on your left, (). Cayley is tiny. A village losing village status and becoming a hamlet. It is so small you find it hard to imagine why it is there. It does have its own grain elevator with Cayley painted on it. And it has made the effort to be like a real town with real street signs and real stop signs. On a warm summer afternoon you have a feeling that people there feel depressed and abandoned and without options.

It is like a tiny cosmos of Canadian society and architecture. People must all know each other. They all know who is "house proud" and who isn't. They know the families that never get their act together. It has a classic, gothic United Church of Canada: tiny, white clapboard church with a square steeple in its own churchyard. Houses represent every architectural period of Canadian prairie development:

20's - tiny, wooden cottages in huge yards, sprouting organic porches, sheds leaning against them;

40's - modest wartime houses;

50's - affluent, optimistic, post-war houses with solid concrete foundations and L-shaped living-room-dining-rooms with wood paneling and built in china cabinets and poured concrete walkways and well-established perennial gardens against pastel siding;

70's - homes with stained-brown wood siding, large living room picture windows, wrought iron railings up the concrete steps, split levels and bi-levels.

Some of these houses are well kept, loved, fussed over, and some overgrown. And sprouting off the corner of the "old town": a mobile-home suburb.

Cayley is also the geodesic dome capital of Alberta. As you approach Cayley from the north you see farms and farm outbuilding geodesic domes and a house that is dome-ish. Did a family get dome-enthusiastic? Did a dome salesman blow through and take the town by storm?

A while past Cayley, you are forced to use super slab, Highway #2 for 8 K but it has a wide shoulder, is four-lane divided, with an expansive median. The traffic isn't as heavy as when it was pouring out of Calgary and you are only on it for 8 K to Nanton.

Nanton is a substantial town with one way streets. It has everything: ($) a flea market, golf club, churches galore, antique stores, farm equipment, aviation museum and probably a curling arena. Nanton figured out the economic advantage of antiquizing its old downtown years ago. Some of the lovely old buildings have been restored as part of an Alberta Heritage funding project.

Inside Nanton, you will pick up Highway #533 to Vulcan without any trouble. There is a sign pointing left about half way through the town. From here on, the journey is a treat to cycle. The sign leaving Nanton says 43K to Vulcan. You are going east out of Nanton.

Highway #533 can be rough, particularly along the shoulder, but it is very little traveled for the quality of road. This means you can ride where the cars would because there won't be many of them. Occasionally you hit spots where the road is freshly tarred with rough new aggregate in it. In those rough places, you can ride along the shoulder, where the aggregate has been pushed into the road on hot days and the hardened tar on top rides as smooth as glass.

After #533 has carried you more or less straight east about half way it curves left (north) and becomes Highway #804.You turn left with it. Continue north on #804 until it crosses Highway #534. Turn right (east) onto #534 and that carries you in a straight line to the south edge of Vulcan.

On much of the Nanton/Vulcan stretch of highway, particularly on #804, you will see fields of grain for miles. When you crest the hills you see weather systems around you and the patchwork of different crops between you and the horizon. There are spots on this highway that the road rolls steeply, giving the sensation of being on a rolling sea. In the trough, you can't see far but what you do see is waves of grain up around you. Then you ride up to the crest before surfing down to the next trough. A lovely feeling.

In the middle of nowhere, west of Vulcan, there is a science stop of interest with a sign explaining a giant bald dome that collects and transmits weather data back to Calgary. The sign goes on to ask questions about weather. Fun for students of science – whatever their age.

From Highway #534 there is little evidence of Vulcan except for trees and a big welcome-to-Vulcan sign. Turn in (left) there. Vulcan is a substantial town, ($). All the pleasures of town life: golf course, shops, Trisha's Pantry, pay phone, IGA grocery store, library, Vulcan Advocate – and teenagers wondering around in pairs looking for entertainment and videos.

If you cruise around a bit in Vulcan you'll find a delightful town. Bigger than many prairie towns, not as big as High River, Vulcan has real streets and real houses, again a nice microcosm of styles and periods. The unusually wide streets give it a stately feeling.

There is a lovely big old, brick place - a mansion, an estate. In a company town this was where the company owner lived. What happened when his kids went to school with the employees' kids? Fell in love with the grocery store clerk? Or worse yet, fell for the quiet kid from that scabby family that lives in each town? Then what kinds of scenes were acted out behind the iron gate and the brick walls?

Once you have connected with the main street, which isn't hard because it is quite grand, with a raised sidewalk down the middle, you just stay on that main street, heading northeast. Eventually it takes you out to the northeast edge of town and a T-intersection at Highway #23. My suggested B & B is out of town and north 8.5 K on Highway #23/24.

Turn left (north) onto #23/24 leaving Vulcan. It was late in the day when I did it and I was tired so it took me a good half-hour to reach the turnoff for the Prairie Past B & B. Watch carefully, the turnoff is easy to miss. The sign is small and it is on the other side of the highway. Then you go left (west) onto a gravel road with no evidence of anything you want to go to and no houses in sight.

The first time that I booked into the Prairie Past B & B, the owner warned me that nothing had been done with the outside and it was looking rundown with lots of junk in the yard. She encouraged me not to worry because the inside was all updated and clean and nice. I must admit that as I pulled up and saw no signage on this tiny dogpatch, I groaned inside and asked "What have I got myself into now?"

Well I had got myself into one of the most wonderful B & B experiences I have had in Alberta. Twenty-seven kittens, romping in the yard. Twenty-seven, can you imagine? How can you get to them all? These kittens believed they had it all together. They charged at the trunks of bushes, climbed up a bit, fell back, pranced sideways at each other and the dogs, chased feathers floating by, jumping into the air swatting nothing with their ineffectual paws. They crouched in the grass gathering power in their tiny back legs and charged at a post then, being distracted by another kitten, jumped straight up into the air and landing with an arched back and full rage until they noticed a flower bobbing in the wind that required their attention. Kittenhood. Kitten heaven. Kitten cornucopia. All of them were happy to be picked up and cuddled and stroked and then sent off again to conquer the world.

The white ducks were in charge of the whole yard and waddled around pulling over gladiolus and making a racket. The dogs made no pretense at guarding anything. They were interested in being pals. The cashmere goats and their babies were usually out of their pen doing what goats do so well, eating everything and being obnoxious. The lack of self-doubt in the tiny, soft babies was touching. And llamas.

How can you touch them all at once? Stay tired? How can you have your bath? Go to bed? You've landed in a petting zoo. And the pets are in animal heaven where you are allowed in.

The inside of this tiny, ramshackle old farmhouse is beautiful. The owners have refinished it all themselves. And the wooden floors are like glass. They are dark, slightly reddish wood that even wood experts are having trouble identifying. The house is furnished with 1930's and 40's period furniture that works perfectly. The comfortable guest bedroom leans a bit more to Victorian with a big bed and nightstand. The bathroom has gone for the contemporary comforts of a deep whirlpool bathtub. And that is a little bit of okay after a day on the bike.

Like most B& B owners, the hosts don't like to be called for breakfast before 8 AM and if you are biking long days you'll probably sleep till then anyway, even if you are a died-hard morning person.

Breakfast, once the goat that was bleating a distress was looked after, was amazing. Eggs, bacon, tons of it. Toast. Fruit. Homemade jam. Accept the fact that you'll eat lots and it will carry you a long way. It's part of the deal and it is wonderful.

This is always a time of conflict, when you find out the stories of the B & B owner and feel like lingering but you are also keen to get on the road. These people had a photo of the original homestead that had burned down around 1900. Her grandfather had come out and built the house for the bride he was bringing from the east. When he went back to get her, she had died. So he married another woman quickly and brought her home. She turned out to be very cold and their life together miserable.

Two generations later, this was a second marriage for both the B&B owners. They created the new blended family of both their children plus an additional teenager from a hopeless situation. Likewise people from town dropped off the dogs and cats that they didn't want. The couple turned nothing away and as a result lived a big, messy, happy, loving and caring kind of life. Their children are all grown now and have children of their own and bring their problems back home and are greeted with open arms and loving support. It creates a feeling of acceptance, live and let live and generosity that feels very nice to be part of while you are there.

They suggested I stick around and visit and that they would drive me into Calgary later. How can you have it all – the bike ride and the visiting? I knew that there was no accommodation in either Mossleigh or Carsland so without camping gear for Wyndham-Carsland Park, I had to make it back to Calgary. I left and forgot the sundress that I use as a dressing gown. The owner raced after me in her pickup to return it.

If you stayed the night in Prairie Past B & B, you are already well out of Vulcan when you are getting back on the road in the morning. And then you simply cycle the almost 2 K back to Highway #23/24 and are on your way.

Travelling back toward Calgary you are going north away from Vulcan on Highway #23. This is busier highway than the ones you were on the previous day but has a wide shoulder that is in flawless shape. It goes north, straight as an arrow, and then curves west just before the intersection with Highway #542. There is a lone service station at the intersection: ( ). At this point, Highway #23 goes west to High River and the same road going east is called #542. You continue north across Highway #542 through rolling prairie on what is now called Highway #24. No difficult hills.

You start this stretch with brand new, smooth, beautiful, highway with wide shoulder. Then you hit rough shoulder then it gets good again. That's cycle: the rough, the smooth, the unknown.

All along Highway #23 and #24 you'll see plenty of watch-able wildlife: birds, ducks, and gophers - which biologists call Richardson ground squirrels. When you are on the crest of hills, like in an airplane, you can see towns dotted around on the landscape below you and weathered wood farm buildings close up. You find science stops of interest that are designed for kids but always taught me something new and are a nice excuse to drink, snack and gaze.

Highway #24 turns and curves you west right in front of Mossleigh and is called Highway #547 along that stretch. Mossleigh is tiny and, like Cayley, a bit odd, ( ). There are kind of streets but they aren't paved and some square blocks have no houses on them. Feels a bit haphazard.

When you've cycled up the big hill west of Mossleigh, stop and get off your bike at the top and look to the east, behind you. You get a panoramic view of prairie forever. Again, you feel like you could see all the way to the Great Lakes if it weren't for the haze.

After Mossleigh the highway turns north again and once more is called #24. At that point you are 18 K from Carsland. Highway signs there also tell you that it is 86 K to Calgary.

Shortly after this, you drop into the valley home of Wyndham-Carsland Provincial Park, (🚻 ♿ ▣ ⚲ ☕ ⛩ ⛺). Up the big, curved hill on the other side is a bit of a grind but manageable.

The east-west stretch around Carsland (#24) feels same-old-same-old but Carsland itself is a bit of a sleeper, (🚻 ♿ ▣ ☕). It has a large Native population and delivers all the Kinsella-esque scenarios that the Native culture offers. If you can, take in a local baseball game on a Saturday afternoon there. This is a slice of prairie culture that is full of fun and laughs and colour.

Again, past Carsland, when the road turns north, you get expansive open highway and lovely grainfield vistas. Then you have some choices. The hardy can choose to do the final home stretch on Highway #1. If that is your choice, it has wide a shoulder all the way and you feel perfectly safe even with big trucks going by. But the aesthetics of heavy highway cycling may not appeal to you. The traffic is very much in your face and it is noisy and the road tends to be flat and straight and you have a sense that the view isn't as accessible, maybe because your priority is to hold your own in the traffic. Not recommended unless heavy, fast, super-highway traffic doesn't phase you.

It was a long way in on #1 to the Chestermere Lake turnoff which gives you a quiet alternative to the last leg into town and by then you'll probably be ready for it, (🚻 ♿ ▣ ✂🚗). At Chestermere you can circle under the main highway and take the very pretty and curving Highway #1A into the east end of 17th Avenue SE. And by evening, which it will be if you rode from Vulcan that day, that commercially hectic strip is quiet and an easy route back in.

As an alternative, you can turn left (west) before Highway #1 onto Highway #22/22X and back in on the ever popular 84/88th Street SE entry through Shepard, page 80.

Or you can take Highway #22/22x only as far west as Highway #797, turn right (north) there through Langdon () and north across Highway #1. Highway #797 then becomes #9 and continues north where you can connect with westbound Highway #564 that will bring you into the top of Calgary past Delacour, and the NE Airport Entry, page 77.

Services

Okotoks:

- Shell Snack Shop ()
- Ginger Room, east half a block and south one block from the main stoplight intersection; Sunday Brunch, lunch, dinner and High Tea: ()
- Cappuccino shops along Elizabeth Street ($)
- OK Convenience Store on Southridge ()
- Range of service stations, such as Esso, on Southridge ()
- Range of fast food restaurants like A&W off Southridge ()
- Several grocery stores, such as IGA, on Southridge ()

High River:

- 7/11 with bank machine ($)
- Fas Gas corner of Highway #1A and 3rd Avenue ()
- Convenience store, east on 3rd Avenue ()
- River Roadhouse for dinner– superb prime rib – only served Saturday and Sunday evenings, country dancing in the bar – this is where the ranchers and real working cowboys go ()
- The park in the southwest corner of town ()
- The High River Recreation Centre on 12Avenue SE has benches along the cycle path sidewalk where you can sit and eat your lunch, or snack or warm yourself in the sun ().

Cayley:

- Small, all-purpose grocery store/post office run by a dad and his son, they have regular essentials (🚻 ♿ ☎ 🍎).

Nanton:

- Service station on the hill entering Nanton (🚻 ♿ ☎ 🚗)
- Grocery stores there are closed in the evening
- Aviation Museum (🪑)
- Campground on Highway #533 just as leaving Nanton for Vulcan (⛺)

Vulcan:

- Prairie Past B & B, 485-2998
- PetroCanada in Vulcan where Main Street meets Highway #24 (🚻 ♿ ☎ 🍦 🚗) fresh sandwiches made to order, barbecued chicken, milkshakes, 8 flavours of hard ice cream and lottery tickets - - you're set.
- Trisha's Pantry (🚻 ♿ ☎ ☕ 🍴)

Highway #24 and #542 intersection (🚻 ♿ ☎ 🚗)

Mossleigh:

- One service station/store where you can get a sandwich (🚻 ♿ ☎ 🍎 🚗)

Between Mossleigh and Carsland:

- Wyndham-Carsland Provincial Park campground (🚻 ♿ ☎ 🍦 🍎 🪑 🛏) This park is a beautiful treed contrast to the dry, flat prairie around it. It has a well-maintained campground with a store and ice cream parlour. Their huge deck offers both sun and shade for loafing and eating your ice cream. You also get high standard outdoor bathrooms that are well maintained.

Carsland:

- Large corner/general store, off the highway (🚻 ♿ ☎ 🍦 🍎)

Langdon:

- General Store (☎ 🍎)

Chestermere Lake:

- Porter's Gas and Food Mart, (🚻 ♿ ☎ 🚗) open Monday to Friday 6:30 AM to 9 PM, Saturday 7:30 AM to 9:30 PM and Sunday 8 AM to 8 PM

- Chestermere Landing Restaurant and Lounge: (🚻 ♿ ✕) pizza and steak seven days a week and the dining room, overlooking the lake, is open Thursday to Sunday.

Additional excursions

- Add a night in Nanton: You could spend a night in Nanton instead of, or as well as, in High River.
- A day with the animals: You could stay an extra day at Prairie Past B&B to enjoy the animals, shoot pictures and exchange stories.
- Drumheller: At the end of this ride you could go straight up Highway #9 and start on the Drumheller ride, below.
- Pause in Strathmore: You could shorten the last day a bit by going to Strathmore and spending the night there before heading into Calgary by going straight up (north) Highway #817 and then left (west) on #564. See page 122 for a list of accommodations in Strathmore. For the NE Airport Entry to Calgary, see page 77.

Drumheller

Highlights

A badlands valley that drops below gently rolling, green farmlands and a day to "do" the World Heritage Site, Royal Tyrrell Museum of Palaeontology or explore a vast prehistoric graveyard on Dinosaur Trail.

With the magical attraction children have to dinosaurs, this could be a special ride for children and warrant two days in Drumheller.

Challenges

Main difficulty comes from this involving long days of riding and possibly headwinds. There are hills and gullies, the most demanding being the climb out of Drumheller Valley on the way back.

The shoulder on Highway #9 is rough and eroded. The route is a truck milk run. They travel fast and pass close because they can't give you space if another truck is approaching in the oncoming lane.

You feel in danger of being blown off the road so you have to concentrate on watching the shoulder all the time.

This trip is certainly worth the ride to explore Drumheller and the strange badlands landscape and go to the Tyrrell. But there are more relaxing cycle trips in Southern Alberta.

Total distance: 276 K
Total time: Two long riding days.

Daily breakdown:
Two-day:

Day One: Calgary to Drumheller 136 K

Day two: Drumheller to Calgary 136 K, if you come back the same route you go out the differences in time will depend on wind.

Three-day trip:

Same as the above riding distances but between day one and three insert a day off at the Royal Tyrrell Museum of Palaeontology or riding Dinosaur Trail, a 50 K loop.

Route: Drumheller

Leave early, this is a long trip. Six, if you can, seven at the latest unless you like cycling in the evening.

Take the NE Airport Exit, page 38. That puts you in the country, heading northeast on Highway #564. It passes through two non-towns: Delacour - a community hall, railroad crossing and one house - and Ardenode - an agricultural research station, (🚻 🚰). It would be nice if you could go all the way east on #564, however at this point, a lot of that is gravel so you are best off turning left (north) at Highway #21. It has a wide shoulder, good surface, well-graded hills and nice rolling terrain. Sometimes you'll catch antelope or deer along here. You'll often see ducks, partridges and pheasants.

If it is really hot weather you will have a long stretch here without any convenience stores or service stations so you will have to stop at a farm for water. Be sure to do that. A hot prairie wind can dehydrate you quickly.

Take #21 north all the way to Highway #9, where you turn right (east). It snakes oddly north and sometimes east across the province. Unfortunately it isn't as user-friendly. The shoulder is narrow and chewed up and there are lots of trucks. As a result, you are forced to constantly watch your roadway because a last minute swerve to escape a crack in the pavement could thrust you into the path of a truck from behind you that has not moved over because there is oncoming traffic. This takes the casual, meandering, view-gazing pleasure out of the excursion.

You are now mostly going east over long rolling hills and hoping that there isn't an easterly wind. The only excitement is the

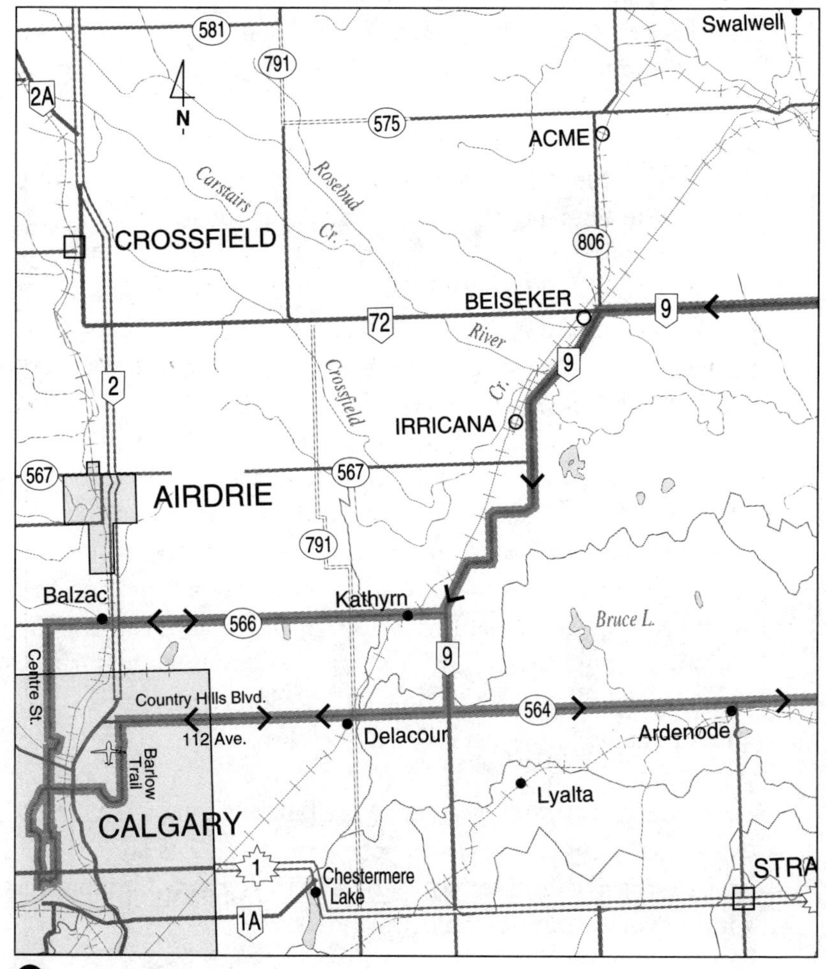

small service station/convenience store at the intersection of Highway #836 and a bit further down the road, That's Crafty, a teahouse in an old dairy barn. Your first sign that you are close to Drumheller is at the crest of a hill when you see the penitentiary complex off to the right. Drumheller is all downhill from there, dropped below the miles of rolling prairies, and looking impossibly different from the surface prairie you have been on.

The winding road down into this deeply carved, pre-historic valley feels like a journey backwards in time. A moonscape and time capsule. The stores, dealerships, fast-food outlets and service stations of a today town seem out of place. So do today's people

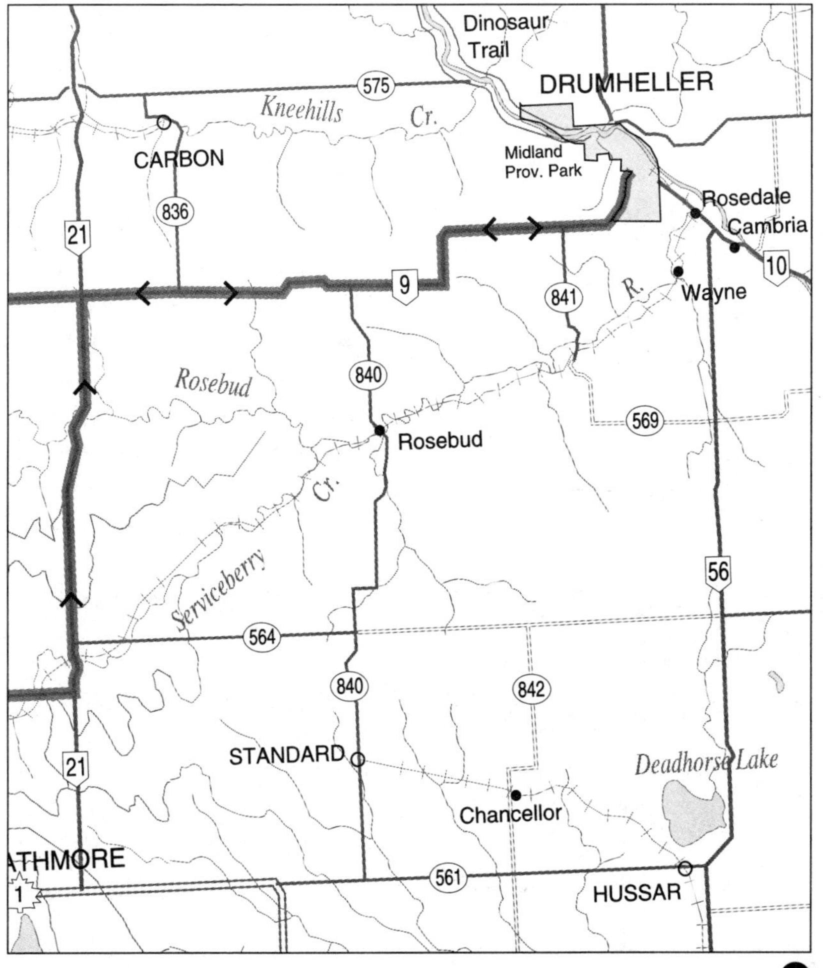

walking around in town looking like hired movie extras. Even during a weekday, Drumheller seems quiet and in the still of a warm summer evening it is positively hushed.

Drumheller is the home of the UN Heritage Site, Royal Tyrrell Museum of Palaeontology. This draws the curious, families and palaeontologists from all over the world so there is plenty of accommodation and plenty of demand.

The town is comfortably laid out and has a population of 6,300. It has all the things you could buy in most cities on a comfortable scale. There are B & Bs that make the perfect destination when you come out of a hot, windy, bleached-out prairie day to the oasis of peaceful riverfront residence. Huge, dark green lawns and big trees. Dinosaur Valley Bed & Breakfast was a well-kept 1950's built house, the kind of house that has built-in storage for everything. The retired farm couple who own it are reserved and pleasant. Wall to wall carpet. Squeaky-clean, tidy, comfortable. A quiet period piece. My room was on the main floor. It would have once been a child's room. Small. Twin beds, dresser, closet.

Eventually, when you leave Drumheller, your first order of the day is getting up THE hill. Whether you are heading back to Calgary or going further north to Stettler, you face a significant climb out of this valley. The earlier you leave the better. If it is still cool, that helps with the climb, which will warm you up.

> ***Cool it with the early rising demands***
>
> *If you pride yourself in being a morning person, don't make a big fanfare to your B & B host about how you want to be on your way by 7 AM or anything dumb like that because when your first eye opens at 8:15 you'll feel ridiculous. Even morning people get knocked out by a day of cycling. When you climb into bed you'll drop like a rock and sleep without rolling over.*

You can come all the way back to Calgary on Highway #9 as it snakes around west and south. This is still pay-attention cycling. At Beiseker, Highway #9 turns southwest then south then west, then south as it seems to jog around farms that didn't sell right-of-way. So whatever the direction of the wind, it will sometimes be sideways, sometimes front or back.

Snake around on Highway #9 and then turn right (west) at Highway #564, the way you left, or for a change, #566. In the latter case go west to Highway #782/Centre Street and use the N Centre Street Entry, page 76. If you take #564, enter Calgary on a similar route that you left with some changes to adjust for the late day traffic patterns, page 75.

Services

Ardenode experimental station, ( ) The people working there say that the water has an awful taste but is safe to drink. I didn't find the taste that bad, but I would of if I hadn't been warned.

Farm houses ( )

Highway #9/836 Junction

- Small, independent convenience store/service station where you can get water and sandwiches and get into the shade, ( ).

Drumheller

- Everything plus places to stay, ($)
- Dinosaur Valley B&B, 823-9250

Beiseker

- Gas station/shop on the Highway, ( )
- Grocery store in town, ( )

Additional excursions

- Dinosaur Trail: You can explore the banks of the prehistoric Drumheller Valley northwest of Drumheller by following the Dinosaur Trail. The moon-like landscape reveals more than 70 million years of geological history cut out of the prairie by ancient rivers and ice. The 55 K loop Trail includes several stops of interest and you see eroded hoodoos, weathered bluffs, steep-sided gullies, cacti and columns of clay shaped like mushrooms. Whole dinosaur skeletons have been found in here. Half way up the trail you cross the river on one of the last cable car ferries in Alberta.

- Royal Tyrrell Museum of Palaeontology: 6 K from downtown Drumheller at the start of the Dinosaur Trail. You can "do" the Tyrrell Museum in one day but the consensus is that it is worth more. Displays are described as some of the most stunning reconstructions of dinosaurs anywhere in the world. A prehistoric garden shows the original dinosaur habitat. You can join in a dinosaur dig or watch experts release skeletons from their tombs of stone. Interactive exhibits and computer simulations ensure that everyone in the group will find something of interest.

- Drumheller Farmer's Market: Saturday 9 AM to noon from May 4th to October 31st, Memorial Arena: 823-8478

- Extend the trip to shorten the days: You could stay overnight in Acme, Big Valley, Airdrie, any number of towns dotted around this part of Alberta and travel some of the other paved highways.

From the 'Hat

The ride from Drumheller to Medicine Hat on the southeast of the province is even better. Highway #1 to Bassano and Highway #56 north to Rosedale and there's a short trot into Drumheller, add up to a nice day's ride.

All the pleasures of Drumheller, without Highway #9

Triumph of the will

I hit gravel construction and lost time. And almost fell. It was 27 degrees. A hot, long ride. The headwinds were the last straw. The wind was steady and strong and got more so as the afternoon wore on. The ride became a struggle. Bum sore, neck and shoulders sore. Tired and dispirited, I would have accepted a lift from the Hell's Angels.

It is evening as I pull into Calgary. The skies had darkened, the wind whipped in all directions. I was tired but I knew I would make it. The lightening over Nose Hill felt like a triumphal fanfare celebrating my victorious return. I pedaled slowly. The universe reaching down to administer a blessing – soft rain. I felt charmed, and AN ATHLETE. I made it. I cycled to Drumheller and back.

High River and Millarville

Highlights

A short first day, beautiful foothills, a B& B that defies description, a quiet, deserted alpine road, long stretches of traffic-free cycling and the thrill of being away on a bike for several days.

Challenges

The hectic traffic on your S Midnapore exit, an unreliable shoulder on a short stretch of #22 where traffic can be annoying and you have some challenging hills.

Total distance: 226 K
Total Time: Three days – comfortably.

Daily breakdown

Three day trip:

Day one: Calgary to High River, 60 K - which means that you can even leave it for an evening ride if you want to get away at the end of a work day, but you will face heavier traffic getting out of the city.
Day Two: High River to Millarville 72 K
Day Three: Millarville to Calgary 94 K

Travelers' Respite - a Magic Kingdom

On the phone the owner of Travelers' Respite says, "an old Victorian House", but at first glance you know this is more than a nice old house. You are approaching an experience.

You enter an exploding garden when you step through the wooden arbour with a little shake roof. In early summer it is a mass of daisies and poppies growing in random mounds banked with river stones, pathways between. Chaos, profusion, the fantasy of how a garden could be. Have we found the Secret Garden? The fence sheltering the back yard has carvings hanging on it. The house is a dignified wood frame with elegant porches and arches and begs to be explored.

You feel like a child entering a magic kingdom. My knock wasn't answered so I sat in the sunny yard eating my picnic lunch.

I wrote in my journal – "I've landed in paradise." Then, out of the front door steps Debra, a wild child beauty mellowed by years of struggle, raising children, creating special worlds like this one. She is burnished to bronze, hair a disorganized halo, faded summer dress a billowing sail around her softened frame – the magician.

She takes you inside to a world that even having seen the yard, transcends what you expect. This is not restored as in the-White-House-was-restored-by-Jacqueline Bouvier/Kennedy. Debra has taken a beautiful old house and, inspired by that, created delightful corners, visual adventures, found objects to be found, lush fabrics in unlikely places, out of time, out of location, it is like nowhere else. To be inside Travelers' Respite is to waver between keeping your bearings and surrendering to a shifted reality.

If you are travelling singly you'll probably be put in a little jewel-box room, with an antique bed tucked under the front eave. A big bowl of perfect fresh summer fruit awaits you when you return from an afternoon strolling in town. For breakfast Debra bakes fresh croissants and offers yogurt, fresh fruit, granola, and whatever else you ask for. Friends I sent there a month later said that they had a three-course breakfast brought to their room, wave after wave, and then went back to bed.

Having said that, I need to add that I have not done this place justice. I haven't talked about the grand piano, the bathtub, the secluded back yard, the conversation - - it is a place to escape from Calgary; by whatever conveyance you have, and refresh your soul. Phone ahead. Debra only accepts guests who appreciate magic.

Route: High River & Millarville

Take S Midnapore exit, page 47. You can leave any time of the day but before 7 AM means that you avoid city traffic as you leave. If that's not an issue, this first day is a short ride and you will easily do it in 5 hours. So you don't need the full day. Follow the exit direction to the junction of Highway #2 and Highway #2A that goes southwest into Okotoks. Follow #2A into Okotoks.

If you are going right through Okotoks, (versus stopping for a picnic, a coffee, a cup of tea - $) you go down the hill to Elizabeth Street, the big main intersection in town. Now continue south on what was Highway #2A coming into town, is Northridge in town, and once you cross the bridge and are climbing up the south side of the river valley becomes Southridge – kind of delightful logic.

Apart from the scramble of traffic at the bridge, this is all pretty easy cycling and as soon as you are up the hill, a manageable hill, you are virtually out of town. Southridge curves around a bit as it leaves Okotoks and then heads straight south to a four way stop:

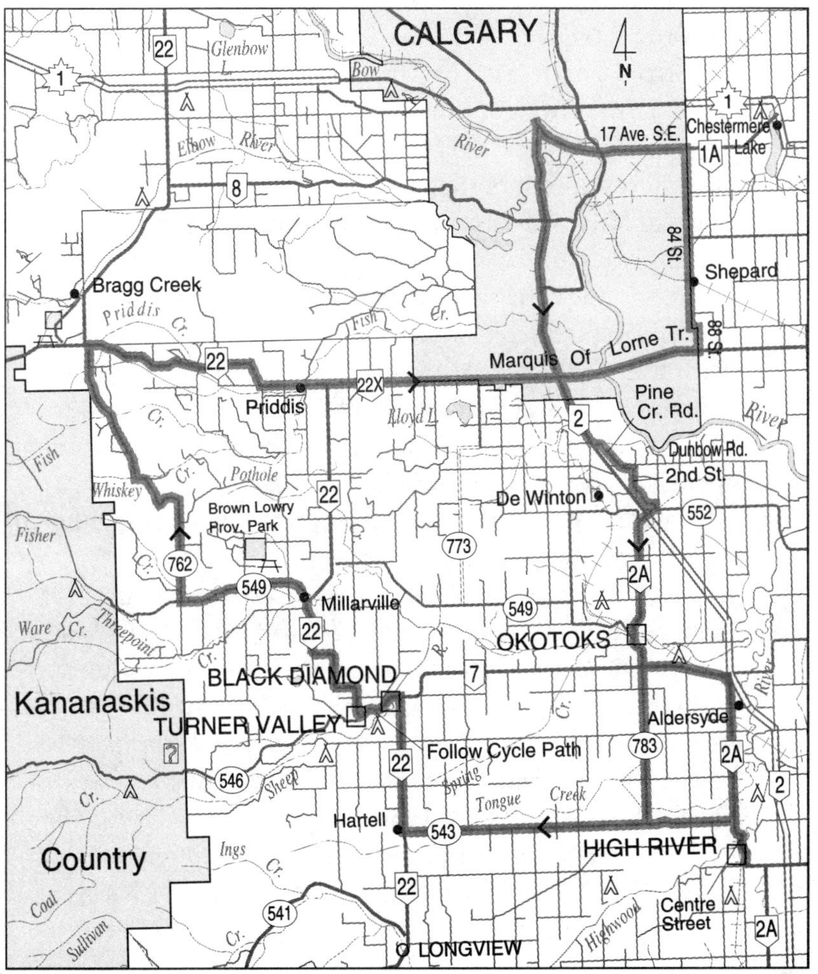

Highway #783 south and Highway #7 east/west. Go east (left) onto #7, which becomes Highway #2A and eventually curves south, paralleling the major #2 highway on the east side of it.

You could go straight south on Highway #783 which, with #543 east, will take you to High River as well. But the next day you would be retracing some of your route.

Highway #2A goes straight to High River. Mostly downhill, rolling, beautiful, wide shoulder, not much traffic. Apart from the smell at the Cargill meat packing plant (which isn't that bad) a thoroughly delightful ride. This, again, is one of those roads that makes you appreciate biking in the area.

Highway #2A then takes you right into downtown High River, ($) and the main east-west street, 3rd Street. Go left (east) on Third Street to 3rd Avenue to find the B& B. Then turn right (south) onto 3rd Avenue.

Whether you stay over or head on, High River traffic is not an issue. If you are out of High River by 9 AM you have plenty of time to get to Millarville before dinner. If you are happy biking in the evening, you can leave even later.

You leave High River the same way you came into town, going north on Centre Street - which immediately becomes Highway #2A. Turn west at the rodeo grounds, onto Highway #543. This is a peaceful stretch of road with rolling hills and a coulee to dip down at Tongue Creek. Heading west there is a slight climbing trend and possibly a headwind.

In 22 K you reach Highway #22 where you turn right (north). At the corner where the two highways meet, there is a dot on the map: Hartell. All that remains of Hartell are seven houses scattered along the road and a tiny general store with a bit of stock, ( ) still run by the original proprietress. She and her husband started it in the early 1900's when, she proudly boasts, Hartell had 23 houses and a hotel and was thriving. She has old

Golden moments

I ditched my loaded panniers and cycled off from my B&B to get dinner. Riding with two fully loaded panniers is a little like waddling around pregnant – you get used to it but it always feels ungainly.

photos of herself and her husband in front of their well-stocked shelves. She is wearing a depression-era bib apron with frill around the edges. The photos could be out of an old school textbook with the caption, "The General Store in a small prairie town."

Your introduction to Highway #22 is a long hill. And after that another, even longer one, not terribly steep just really long and if you are feeling weary they are not a cheery sight. But, the good news is that as soon as you get to the top of the second hill you see a long wide plain stretching away below you and in the distance you can actually see Black Diamond – and it's all wonderful downhill to get there. And green. And picturesque. It feels as if you are looking at a view from an airplane. So it suddenly wasn't that far and you are half way to your destination for the day. Reason for a complete change of attitude.

Both Highways, #542 and #22, are good roads with adequate shoulders although there's much more traffic on #22 than #542. But the road is straight and you feel safe.

Highway #22 takes a right angle turn at the main intersection inside Black Diamond. At that point Highway #7, which you crossed south of Okotoks, enters from the east. You turn left (west) on #22 to continue on to Turner Valley, the site of Alberta's first major oil strike. The ride from Black Diamond,() to Turner Valley, () can be done on a cycle path that parallels the highway and is in excellent condition. This gives a nice break from traffic and an altogether different scale from road travel.

You could B&B in either Black Diamond or Turner Valley to break up the day and build in time for town exploring.

From Turner Valley to Millarville, Highway #22 gets busy. The local people sneer that it is the most dangerous highway in the province with the highest fatality level. It sounds a bit like a public posture to support a plea for improvement but it is worth treating this stretch with respect.

The highway winds around and changes direction. The shoulder here isn't wide and in places it has been eroded away so you are cycling on the edge of the traffic lane and there is too much traffic on this one for that to feel great. However, surroundings are beautiful, scenery is fabulous: little valleys, clusters of trees, smaller fields. It has a European feeling after the great open prairie.

Just before you cross a bridge immediately south of Millarville, following the B & B owner's instructions, you turn left (west) onto a gravel road that takes you up a hill to the B & B. The gravel has been swept out of the main car tracks and the hard dirt underneath is smoother than pavement.

Three Point Creek B & B is 1 K along the gravel road. This is one of these farm/ranches where they now raise cattle but have done other farming over the years. A solid 1970's house nicely sited on a knoll with a huge deck facing south, overlooking lovely, rolling, green lawn. The guest bedrooms are in the basement but the basement isn't deep so the windows are big. They are decorated in comfortable ruffles and are a restful dusty blue. Deep wall-to-wall carpet. Clean. Peaceful and inviting. You can join your host and hostess upstairs to look out their big windows or sit on the deck.

When I was there, a couple who "run" cattle on this land dropped in. Everyone sat around the table talking agriculture-talk in that tip-the-chair-back style that belies the financial pressures of farming. The story is told of an old farmer who had owned land adjacent to Calgary. "He still had a privy!" Everyone laughed. When the developers offered him $14 million for the land he said, "I don't know what I would do with $14 million". So he turned them down. "I guess his kids got it".

The next morning the table will be spread with homemade jams and jellies. You can get pancakes and a mountain of delicious bacon, syrup and great conversation. Cycling alone, you look forward to these chats.

The fabric of life: family history on the farm; years of living with in-laws; eventually building their own house; raising boys and meeting their girlfriends; then marriages and things that work out and things that don't. You get a window into the world of a farm wife.

Millarville,(), is nothing but a store and some new, country houses on large lots. Affluent city people who like a country escape build most of them. The horsy crowd. About 3 K further north along Highway #22 from the store, and still calling itself Millarville, although there is no Millarville in between, is the High Country Cafe. Two more kilometers east of that on Highway #549, and still calling itself Millarville, without any Millarville in evidence between, is the Millarville fairgrounds and racetrack, site of the Farmers' Market.

The B & B owners told me that Highway #22 was always busy but at 5 PM that particular day 75,000 people from the annual Millarville Horse Race would be hitting the highway. You want to watch for that - June 30th and July 1st. Call the Racetrack to check: 931-3411. Also the Saturday morning Millarville Farmers' Market draws huge Calgary crowds from mid June to September 20th.

There isn't really a getting-out-of-Millarville issue. You cycle away from the B & B, down the hill, turn left (north) onto Highway #22. You could cut this day short and go straight back to Calgary, north on Highway #22, past the High Country Cafe and right (east) on #22X. But you would miss a wonderful morning of cycling in the hills. To enjoy that, turn left again (west) as if you are going to the Millarville store. But you don't take the service road, again off to your right, into Millarville. You just keep going and are already on Highway #549.

Highway #549 west is beautiful. Well paved, good shoulder almost no traffic. This feels like your reward for getting out this far. Although the road winds around you are heading in the general direction of Bragg Creek.

The surroundings are increasingly breathtaking and alpine. It is quiet. The hills are bigger and when you reach the junction of Highway #762 turning north you are looking up at the biggest mothering double hill you can ever remember seeing in your life. This is a long climb but you can do it without standing up on your pedals if you pace yourself. After that, rolling hills, winding curves up the sides of small mountains. The climbs continue to be a bit challenging but thoroughly rewarding.

Suddenly you are upon Highway #22, just south of Bragg Creek. Now you need to make a decision. Are you going to go further west and into Bragg Creek, get hot chocolate and a sandwich, coffee, cappuccino, ice cream, cookies – any of those essentials? (🚻 ♿ ⛽ 🍦 ☕ ✕ 🍎 ⛱ 🚗 🛏 ⛺ 👪 📞) In that case, by all means go into Bragg Creek, left onto Highway #22 and then immediately right where Highway #22 turns north to Bragg Creek. If you do that you'll probably return to Calgary via Highways #22 north of Bragg Creek and W Highway #8 Entry, page 89.

If you don't need snacks, you can take Highway #22 that goes in the opposite direction, east/west along the south boundary of Calgary. This route takes you east to Calgary where you enter the city from the south. This stretch of Highway #22/22x offers divine riding to just east of Priddis. Wide shoulder, perfect pavement, lovely views, beautiful countryside. But soon after Priddis the shoulder disappears and, although you still have four-lane, divided highway, the cars don't always give you much room. So there you have it. After that point it seems like a long haul, up hill, down hill, grind. In spite of that, when you get to SW 37th Street Entry, page 87, the only southwest entrance into the city, you may decide to bike further east on #22x to the southeast corner of the city. Then you can come in the East Entry, page 80, an excellent road - better surface and WAY less traffic than 37th Street SW.

Services

Okotoks

- Shell Service Station corner of Northridge and Elizabeth Street (🚻 ♿ ⛽ 🍎 🚗)
- Cappuccino spots (🚻 ♿ ⛽ ☕)
- Shopping centres lining Southridge with fast food outlets like A&W (🚻 ♿ ⛽ ✕ 🍎 🚗)
- Restaurants (🚻 ♿ ✕)
- Ginger Room, a giant old house remodeled for classic tea: sandwiches, scones, Devonshire cream; plus, Sunday Brunch, lunch and dinner, (🚻 ♿ ⛽ ✕) one block east and one block south of the stoplight.
- Okotoks Lions Sheep River Park, a huge park south of the river with giant trees. It feels like a forest in the middle of a town. The Park has 60 campsites and a picnic area and is lovely for a walk in trees, particularly in the fall, (🚻 ♿ ⛱ ⛺). Phone 938-4282 for reservations.

- B & Bs: book ahead (🛏)
- A wonderful little park, east and one block north of the Northridge/Elizabeth Street intersection. This used to have a war memorial and wonderful low benches for picnicking. At the time I was last there the benches were gone. The grass was gone. The cenotaph was gone. The wall of evergreens around the edge was cut down. The whole park had been taken apart. We need to see what they will come up with new. (π)

High River

- Town Office, 652-2110
- 7/11 convenience store has a bank machine, (🚻 ♿ ☎ $)
- Gooseberries' Tea Room, on MacLeod Trail, right at the first intersection in town, specializing in home-made pies, (🚻 ♿ ☎ 🍴)
- Travelers' Respite is an amazing B&B on a peaceful residential street of lovely older homes speaking of a once extremely prosperous town. Phone ahead, Travelers' Respite is not always available: 652-3797
- Second hand stores, clothing stores, art stores, not a ton of great stuff but a nice scale for strolling, (🍸 👫).
- Fruitstand beside the railway tracks during the summer, you can buy wonderful black cherries and apricots and other fruit in season to be well provisioned for the next day of biking.
- Unfortunately, the town bakery specializes in very white bread, mass produced kinds of white buns, so that is a bit disappointing.
- "Roadhouse Tavern", remembering that High River is down there in cattle country, you can find excellent beef . The prime rib, served only Saturday and Sunday, is the best you'll get anywhere. You passed it on Highway #2A just north of town, (🍴). Country dancing in The Roadhouse bar is always fun with real working cowboys and ranchers.

Hartell @ Highway #543 & 232

- Hartell General Store – limited stock, if the store is still there, but well worth the stop, not only to support this little business, but to take a journey back in time,(🚻 ♿ 🍎)

Black Diamond

- Black Diamond has figured out that travelers are bored and have money to spend so they have encouraged delightful craft shops, cappuccino shops, a fun odd store, ( ).
- Old-fashioned hamburger stand ( ) with ice cream, hotdogs, hamburgers and generally great snacks and lots of green grass, brightly painted picnic tables, a raised patio and a feeling of outdoor play.

Turner Valley

- Town Office, 933-4944
- Tea house ( )
- Tourist information hut, the latter with beautiful rolling lawn where you can park yourself to rest, picnic, look at maps or do nothing for a while. Unfortunately, it does not have a washroom. You need to go to a service station for that, ( ).

Millarville

- Three Point Creek Ranch B&B, 931-3217
- The High Country Café at the intersection of Highway #22 and #547 has outside picnic tables and umbrellas, salad, wonderful homemade soup, pie and ice cream. This is a widely known and popular spot,( ).
- The all-purpose Millarville store is excellent. You can get plenty of provisions for riding the next day and magazines for your evening, ( ).

Additional excursions

- Okotoks antiques: There are real antique stores as well as craft stores you can visit on an afternoon of browsing.

- Ginger Room: You won't have trouble finding the Ginger Room. It is in a huge, redone house by the railroad tracks and everyone in Okotoks knows about it. A bit Disney-esque but very pleasant and great food. You can plan your ride around going there for Sunday Brunch. They also have lunch, dinner and High Tea.

- Big Rock: You can cruise south and then 10 K west of Okotoks on Highway #7 to see one of the largest erratics in the world. It looks bizarre sitting there in the middle of a flat field.

- Okotoks Lions Park: If you only make one stop in Okotoks consider this being it. This park is virtually on the edge of downtown and undoubtedly is a great place for local teens to go drinking and partying. It has lovely trails among huge trees. It is hard to believe it is so close to civilization. Particularly beautiful for walking in the fall leaves.

- Houses in old Okotoks: Whether you slowly cruise them on your bike or lockup and walk them, the old residences of Okotoks are worth a look. They offer lovely gardens and a fine example of prairie architecture of several decades ago. Walk along Elma Street, parallel to the main drag, Elizabeth.

- Coffee houses: Like many other small towns, Okotoks has heard that tourists need regular infusions of cappuccino, cookies, nanaimo bars and carrot cake. So you'll find them here.

- Big Valley Country Jamboree: This is an annual Woodstock-gone-country event that brings big country entertainment names and big crowds to a temporary city in a field outside High River (). Find out when it is being held this year. Even if you don't want to attend, it is worth the trip out to the highway to gawk at an instant city of campers, motorhomes, cars and PEOPLE with a stage at the epicenter lit up and blasting music into the country night. As if that isn't enough, there are also carnival rides, covered with lights, whirling beside the stage. A sensory explosion. Best viewed at night.

Golden moments

The sun had been shining and hot but as I walked back to Travelers' Respite, big clouds rolled in and the time seemed right for the luxury of an afternoon sleep. So snuggled into my big, old bed tucked under the eaves, I slept through the summer afternoon storm.

- Museum of the Highwood in High River: portrays rural pioneer life including several train cars dating from 1945 to 1960.

- High River walking tour: there are 18 historical murals painted on buildings in High River that are described in the guide available at the town office, 652-2110.

- Add-a-night: You could add an optional fourth day by staying a night in Black Diamond or Turner Valley, only 4 K apart. Or you could stay a second night in your Millarville B&B and dedicate a day to exploring Highway #549 and, if it is Saturday morning, taking in the popular Millarville Farmers' Market. Or by going into Bragg Creek, page 142, and spending a night there before heading into Calgary on #8 or #22/22X and through Shepard.

- Black Diamond poking around: There is a tiny strip of odd shops that are fun tourist traps in Black Diamond. You can pick up small, bike-packable gifts and tokens.
- Head south: You could go south at Hartell and take Highway #22 to the far southwest corner of the province through Longview and carry on the Grand Tour, starting on page 193.

Acme and Carstairs

Highlights

Open prairie and beautiful rolling foothills, some quite level terrain far away from traffic; tiny scale towns to explore. This is one of the best cycling treks in Southern Alberta. Treat yourself to trying this one. The stretch from Madden to Calgary can be integrated into a day trip. Go and have a look. The landscape is breathtaking, rolling hills of deep green. No traffic and great, curving, rolling highway. Highway #772 has dramatic rock outcroppings along the sides of the valley, looks a bit like a movie set.

Golden moments

Confronted with the huge pair of hills I reminded myself that biking is the perfect icon for life: you just keep pedaling and you get there. It worked on the Connor Pass in Ireland. It can work here. I can always get off and walk my bike for a while. I can stop and rest. I remember that my body seems to adjust to a long hill and my mind does too: back off push, just keep pedaling, breathe deeply, exhale all of it and remember the last big hill I successfully climbed.

Armed with that and a fresh drink of juice and a couple of plums, I tackled two giant hills. And of course I made it and of course I felt like a hero and of course I celebrated at the top with another snack.

Challenges

Day one of this ride is a long ride but the terrain is comfortable. There is one wide valley to climb out of but it is not steeply graded. You can split the ride up by staying overnight in Airdrie. Drawing close to Carstairs from Acme there are a few major coulees to cross. All of them are graded to be manageable. The most ambitious climb is a short one out of Madden. Wind can be a factor at any point on this ride but if it is hot it is a blessing.

Total distance: 251 K
Total time: Three days

Daily breakdown:

Three day trip

Day One: Calgary to Acme: 107 K
Day Two: Acme to Carstairs: 49 K - an easy half-day ride.
Day Three: Carstairs to Calgary: 95 K

Route: Acme & Carstairs

The first day is a long ride so I suggest being away by 7 AM at the latest unless you like evening riding. Take the ever-popular NNW Simons Valley Exit, page 63. One morning I was sharing this road with an unending fleet of dump trucks that came pounding up behind me, but this is unusual. Every other time I used it this was a reliably peaceful exit.

Go north on Simons Valley Road, which becomes Highway #772, until you hit Highway #567 east at the north end of Airdrie. It is easy to mistakenly turn too early at the intersection marked "567 west" that points left. Looking at that, many sane adults would surmise that if #567 west is left, then 567 east is right. Wrong. But not to worry because if you fall for this you will still get to Airdrie but at the south end of town. Which is fine. All these are nice roads, with lots of downward rolling hills, virtually no traffic. "No traffic" is one car every fifteen minutes.

If you end up taking the southern road, when you reach the south end of Airdrie you can take Main Street, the first street into Airdrie, to get back on track. It will carry you through town to the north end of Airdrie, meandering prettily through the southern suburbs, and eventually become very main-street-ish with stores and banks and parked cars and pedestrians and all, ($).

Airdrie is a nice little town. Nice feeling. It is clearly a bedroom community but there is a self-pleased sense of being there by choice so that children will be safe and roads will be quiet and the community will support family-focused values. You'll see signs for a community bus that will pick up on call. You'll see hand made signs for a town hall meeting. It all feels small town John Updike-ish. You can stop in town for a snack, a coffee, a cold drink, a rest and then you are ready to head east.

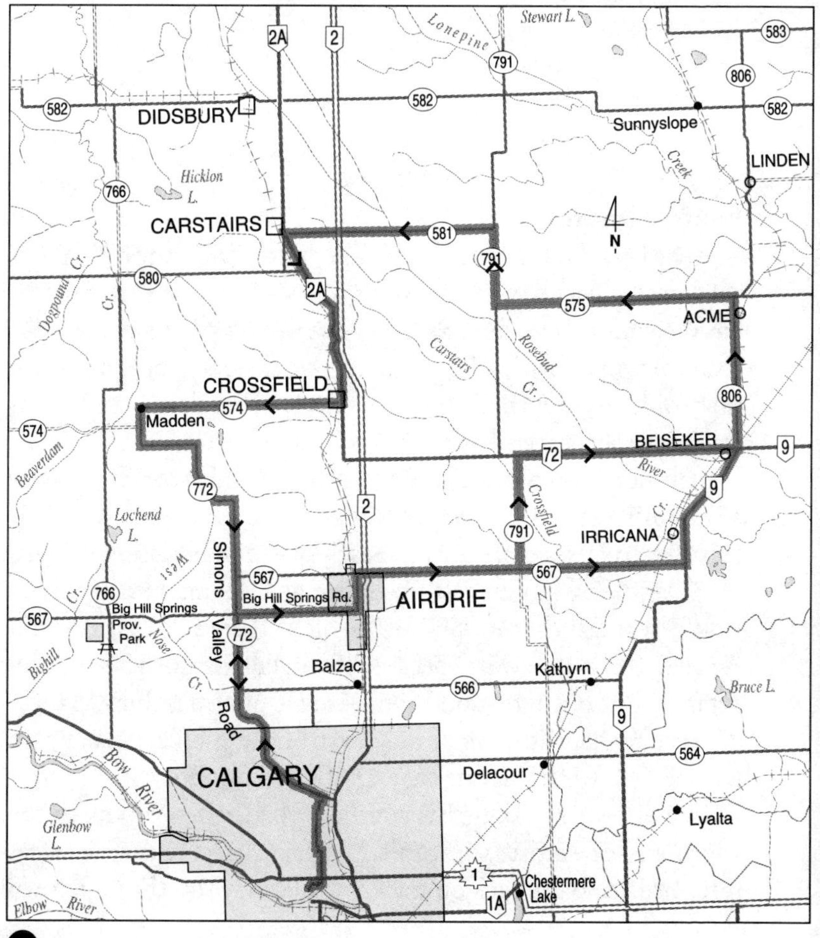

North through town and - bingo - there is #567. Either way, it is about 11 K from the place you turned off Highway #772 to Airdrie. Leaving Airdrie on Highway #567 again, you pass a noteworthy building, the Nova Gas Transmission Office. It combines brick, metal and some unknown bright yellow material into an interesting statement about industry in the prairie landscape. Looks good.

You can go all the way east on #567 to Highway #9 – about 29 K. Then you would turn north to Beiseker where you continue north on Highway #806 to Acme and your B & B. Or, you can take advantage of a newly upgraded road that the map still claims to be gravel. This beautiful, new highway, #791, runs north from #567 and connects with #72, which will take you east to the north end of Beiseker. It is paved.

When I got there it was brand new, black as night, no lines on it yet, no dust, rolling out in front of me. You always wonder at this point – is it paved all the way? Will I run into the paving crew over the hill? Does it turn to gravel and leave me struggling to get to #72? So you have the choice and take on the adventure of finding out. For me the reward was that the road rolled out wonderfully, peacefully, traffic-less to #72. It had a wide shoulder, and flawless, smooth surface - - probably because I was the only person in Alberta who knew that it was paved having shown up as the paving crew packed up and went home.

It is one of those discoveries that make you feel smart and capable. What it doesn't show on the map is that just before this road connects with #72, running east-west, it turns sharply and dips down into a coulee where the intersection is marked with oversized stop signs. It feels like the bottom of the world.

After turning right (east) onto #72 you have about 20 K left to Beiseker, which you can first identify by its grain elevator standing above the tell-tale cluster of trees in the middle of prairie, ( ).

Beiseker store is a good place for jujubes and humbugs and, essentials. The wide "main drag", as we used to call them, sits empty in the shimmering prairie heat. Memories of childhood summers and the freedom to wander around without supervision, even when small. The smell of hot asphalt.

At the other end of the two-block-long main street, with more space than buildings, there is a small store that is worth exploring: Olive's Place. It has everything. Just inside the door is a rack full of homemade B & B brochures. Most of them in the neighbourhood and many that are not listed in the Travel Alberta Accommodation Guide. By the time you get into the neighbourhood you probably already have your accommodation but they will be helpful for next time.

Still in Olive's you come to a second hand bookrack with 60's and 70's Readers' Digest condensed novels plus a few contemporary bodice busters and some horror. This is bible belt reading? Further into the store you find beautiful hand-made wooden toys, strange things made out of Popsicle sticks and crocheted whatnots.

The other side of the store is a tearoom with several kitchen chairs and tables and a silex of hot coffee and two plates of squares and donuts. The local women breeze in and out, at home. All know each other. It's the women's small town coffee shop. The place to share and support. The back of the store is the bus depot.

Whether or not you pedal into Beiseker, which is easily accessible, you will turn north onto Highway #806 as soon as you leave Beiseker, at the northeast corner of town. This is a beautiful road, going straight north, 12 K, to Acme.

Now it is probably late afternoon. A superb stretch of flawless highway that lets you cycle your heart out, feel relaxed, get in tune with the waving crops on either side of you.

Acme is off to the side of the highway. Its water tower stands above the cluster of trees that mark the town, (🚻 ♿ ⛽ 🍴 🍎 🚗 🚲). You enter Acme on Nolan Street, the only street that links it to the highway, so you leave the same way. The departure time out of Acme is flexible if you have three or four days for this trip because you do not face a long day's ride to Carstairs. So choose whether you like riding morning, afternoon or evening and do so.

Acme is fun to explore. This is a town where the town fathers ran out of money between the sidewalk contractor and the paving contractor. Excellent curbs. Solid poured concrete sidewalks, churned up, gravel streets.

Every era and style of house imaginable, none of this suburban developer control here. Some loved gardens, some junkheeps. Here, the main drag is a block long and even though it is already 8 PM – on the Friday of a long weekend – there are still guys working in the offices of the Pig Improvement Project. You may have passed vehicles with the P.I.P. logo in Beiseker or on the highway. They are everywhere. Clearly improving pigs is critical work.

You have two restaurant choices: Chinese/Western (How well are Chinese people received in small town Alberta?) and a homemade country style kitchen restaurant – with a real salad bar, just like downtown.

The B & B owner strongly recommends the homemade restaurant and it is certainly popular with the locals. There are steadily three other tables active. Again, lots of people know lots of other people, single working guys and families with young children.

Their Special is a half-fried chicken with mashed potatoes and gravy. The helpings are huge and this comes with salad bar. And dessert comes too. Vegetables aren't their strong point, the mashed potatoes and gravy are as mashed potatoes and gravy should be and the chicken is wickedly wonderful.

The Country Village B & B in Acme wasn't officially open when I stayed there. I only found out about it from a B & B in Beiseker, which was full due to a reunion but knew of this one opening in Acme. And fortunately had the phone number because they weren't listed anywhere. It was my last chance to find a place to stay in that area. If they couldn't take me I would have had to find another ride because I wouldn't be able to bike far enough in daylight to get to another place to stay.

Golden moments

My first Southern Alberta multi-day ride – three days. I sing to my walkman tunes. I see the world through the curious eyes of a traveler. I relished the freedom. I wasn't on a bike RIDE. I was on a bike TRIP.

It is not much outside, an average house. But inside, a cool, serene, flawlessly clean pastel world. The main floor has a dusty blue rug and pale aquamarine furniture. It feels like stepping into an aquarium. My bedroom was peach with a pale, lush, peach rug and mountains of cotton eyelet pillows on the white bedspread.

After a day of cycling, you can feel nothing short of filthy. Pigpen. You may be covered with alternate layers of sunscreen and sandblasted prairie dust. But that's what makes the bath so delicious. And that's why some of us don't camp. The lovely, gentle lady who owns the B & B is instantly comforting and makes me feel like an athlete because she can't believe I cycled from Calgary. After dinner she offers herbal tea.

If you have trouble sleeping, just ride a bike for 12 hours in the hot sun, then have a bath and eat a big, fried chicken dinner. You won't even roll over in the night.

Then there is the breakfast. The hostess serves breakfast on crystal and china. A glass of fresh berries, homemade muffins and homemade blackberry jam. She has heated the jam in the microwave. Unbelievable french toast made with homemade bread. Thick back bacon. Coffee or in my case, hot water is served in a lovely, delicate china cup.

She may even press extra muffins on you as you leave and these can prove to be useful later because there are zero stores between Acme and Carstairs. Reminder: consider asking BB hosts to pack a lunch or just sandwiches for you when you'll be on an unserviced stretch.

As many B & B owners do over breakfast, she chats about her life: about her teaching, her husband's work as an electrician in Calgary, their decision to renovate and open a B & B. You get a glimpse into the ways small towns are different and the ways they are the same. And as always, it is hard to leave. But you will. The road calls.

Back onto Highway #806, which brought you from Beiseker, you are continuing north to Highway #575 running east and west. You get there in the equivalent of two city blocks. Turn left (west) onto #575.

There is very little traffic on this highway, another one of those prairie gems. Mostly level, straight west, farms on either side, an uneventful strip. Just peaceful pedaling. Eventually you come to an intersection and stop sign. Highway #575 continues west but is gravel from there on. You turn right (north) onto #791, which is rougher pavement, oil and aggregate. But the car tires have created tracks of hardened oil that is smooth as glass in places.

Highway #791 takes you north to Highway #581 going west straight into Carstairs, 18 K. Go left (west) onto #581. There are several dips and one serious coulee on this stretch. The highway blithely shoots straight down one side and straight up the other. You will do okay with them because they are well graded and not all that steep. It is nice to see the rivers in the bottom, the cattle grazing in pastoral kinds of situations. All seems as it should be.

The overpass across the big #2 Highway that joins Calgary and Edmonton, comes as a startling return to civilization. Once you have crossed that it feels as if you are on the west side of the province. It is then mostly downhill into Carstairs. You pass a B & B on your left, a huge old house with a big yard. I have no first hand knowledge of it. It was booked, as was most of the rest of Carstairs, ($).

You sail into Carstairs on one of the three main streets that dominate the layout of the town. Carstairs is at the intersection of Highway #581, that you are already on, and Highway #2A that parallels the big, north-south traffic super-slab you just passed on the overpass. The first street you hit in Carstairs is the #2A road. If you continued straight ahead you would cross the railroad tracks and then you would cross the main street. Carstairs lies along these three north-south lines: #2A, the railway and Main Street.

But you aren't going straight ahead if you are staying at The Golden West Motor Inn. You are turning right (north) up #2A for one block. The motel is easy to find and a wonderful 1970's classic: varnished knotty pine paneling, wrought iron second story balcony all around, coke machine outside the office and a lovely garden. On the way there, you may notice a stunning garden in the block before the motel. It is worth going back for a second look later.

Alert: the day I checked in, the owner told me that there were no other rooms between there and Banff, 219 K away. Calgary was full, people were calling trying to find a place to sleep that night. So book ahead. When you are travelling by bike you can't just zip on another 100 K in the evening when there is no room at the inn.

Carstairs is bigger than Acme. Some lovely old houses, magnificently loved gardens and an ice cream store. Interestingly enough the paving crew still hasn't shown up in Carstairs either.

The motel is on Highway #2A as it passes through town and leaving town to return to Calgary you want to stay on that road to avoid the heavy, high-speed traffic on Highway #2. So head south right out of the motel parking lot on #2A which takes you south to Crossfield. There is little shoulder when you start out here, and then it widens and gets smooth and comfortable. It also has little traffic at 6:20 AM. It is 15 K from Carstairs to Crossfield, (🚻 ♲ ▣ ✂ ☼ 🚗 🛏 ✆).

Highway #2A combines with the big #2 a bit south of Crossfield and would leave you sharing a superhighway with traffic going 130 K. Some call it superslab. You go west instead. By going west at Crossfield, you get into some very pretty country and will eventually re-enter Calgary via the popular NNW Simons Valley Entry. All away from traffic.

So go west out of Crossfield, for Madden, 18 K away. This is another superb cycling road. Little traffic, big rolling hills, rich farmland, you feel truly lucky to be on it. Like almost all of the land in Alberta, your surroundings are under intense agriculture. It is raked, plumped, fluffed, carved, clipped, sprayed and harvested with more attention than a golf course. This is noticeable out here because when it is raining, which it happened to be when I did the trip, it is odd to see such evidence of intense human activity and still be in silent, windswept solitude.

If it is overcast, or raining, the views from Crossfield to Madden are second to none. The landscape takes on the rich deep colours that we notice in colour photos shot on heavily overcast days but rarely notice in reality. The grain beside the road glistens with drops of hanging rain jewels. The yellow mustard is almost too beautiful to look at. Dark greens have become black. When I did it, I realized that I have always liked walking in the rain and have always avoided biking in the rain. Yet there I was, alone in a water world that I will never be able to do justice to.

And when you pull into Madden you realize how important it was to have bought snacks when stores were open in Carstairs – especially if Crossfield will still be closed up when you go through. Madden doesn't even have a service station. It does have Dodd's General Store but their hours are brief, ( ).

You climb up a hill out of Madden on Highway #574, a bit rough for a short stretch but very soon excellent highway. This road takes several right angle turns and becomes #772 then becomes Simons Valley Road at the city limits.

You can come in the NNW Simons Valley Entry page 93. The beauty of this route is that even when it is "busy", it isn't busy.

Services

Symons Valley Ranch ( )

Airdrie

- Seventh Day Adventists Church on Main Street, which overlooks a lovely lagoon, ( )
- Gas stations, 7/11's, grocery stores, full restaurants, Macdonald's and every other fast food. All you could need, ($)

Beiseker

- The general store in Beiseker is cool and dark after the prairie glare so you can take your time in there, stroll all the aisles, cool off. You can refill with some bottled, cooled water they sell ( ).
- Service Station/store on Highway #9 ( )

Golden moments

I felt privileged to be on the isolated alpine hills. No traffic. Not a car. Silence, but for the murmur of the rain and the bike tires on wet road.

Acme

- Town Office, 546-3783
- Country Village B&B, 546-4478
- The only corner-store-video-store-service-station-bus-depot in Acme, Gas Plus, is on the next corner west from the B & B, ( ).
- Cal's Cycle is north of Acme: 546-4007 ()

Carstairs

- Golden West Motor Inn, 337-3333
- Temarest B&B, 337-3069
- Ice cream parlour, you'll find it off the main street ()
- A tiny, beautifully clean, empty Chinese restaurant in an A-frame. If you are alone, you can get variety with one of those combination plates. Delicious. ( )
- Early Sunday morning nothing is open in Carstairs. The motel owner says places will be open for breakfast – but she probably wasn't thinking 6 AM. Be careful because none of these towns have any eating places open early on Sunday morning. If you aren't in a B & B, and therefore being fed, you can get stranded without food. Plan for that the night before.

Crossfield

- It has a hotel and service stations, corner stores, but none operating early Sunday, ( ).

Additional excursions

- Browsing in Airdrie: This new town has a pleasant scale and comfortable atmosphere. You feel like people like being there. It is nice just to walk around in for a while.

- Nose Creek Valley Museum in Airdrie includes Southern Alberta Native artifacts

- Start the ride with a night in Airdrie: You could split up the long first day of riding by only going as far as Airdrie. You could get there comfortably in a summer evening. Then leave Airdrie the next morning with 91 K ahead of you. Or get to Airdrie and your B&B there early enough to enjoy the human scale "downtown" and the long winding park on either side of Nose Creek through the southern suburbs.

- Hanging out in Beiseker: Beiseker has so little happening it is like "The Last Picture Show". And that brings back a pensive nostalgia that is quite pleasant.

- Beiseker Station Museum is in a former CPR rail station under the same roof as the town office and library. It has homestead artifacts, a furnished bedroom and kitchen and old-time music items, 947-3744.

- Explore north and east of Acme: You could take Highway #575 east from Acme or #806 north and add additional days of cycling in this pretty country with trees and rolling hills.

- Take time to look at the Carstairs garden: You can stroll to the magnificent garden that you saw on your way into Carstairs, one block south of the Golden West Motel. And like all gardeners, she may invite you into her world and tell you how her garden gave her comfort and courage over the many years that her husband was ill. She also might tell you all the secrets of setting up a bed to grow outstanding lilies. Her pink, orange, yellow, white, and peach lilies are tall and healthy and full. The day I stopped by she was putting together bouquets for a family wedding. She handed me what looked like a flawless bloom that she had rejected so I took it back to my room and put it in a water glass beside my bed.

The Carstairs Paper says

Carstairs has a new doctor moving into town who is thrilled to be getting his family to a small community. Carstairs also has a serious problem with teenaged vandals and some of the citizens think a curfew would be a good idea. Carstairs is staging a major fair in a couple of weeks that will include a parade, displays of crafts, sale of homemade goods, merchant support, a square dance, pony rides, children's games, a wonderful day thanks to the teamwork of the tireless committee. Now that would be a fun weekend to turn up in Carstairs. Read the paper. It's all there.

Golden moments

Just ahead of the 75,000 horseracing fans about to spill onto the Highway from the Annual Millarville Horse Race, I decided discretion was the better part of valor. I turned back to the B&B as the afternoon storm clouds were massing and lightening flashed over the adjacent hillside. The first few big, cold drops thudding down just as I pulled up to the door. Then the sky opened and it poured. Pelting rain. Sheets of it. Huge, heavy drops pounding into the ground. I stood at the panorama livingroom windows with my B & B hosts and watched pounding rain and howling wind whip through the dark green grass on their rolling lawn. I made it.

The Grand Tour of Southern Alberta

Highlights

The world famous badlands with their remarkable cache of dinosaur remains, an up close view of the Rockies as you cycle along the rolling foothills, flat ranchland and endless fields under cultivation. The birds, the trees, wildlife caught unaware, the people and the delightful B&Bs will entertain and teach you.

Challenges

Road surface conditions and hill grading will be more varied than on the shorter rides but it is all manageable. You have to deal with a city when you go through Medicine Hat. There are two long stretches without accommodation and one with limited water and few humans. You may have wind problems but the ride is routed going east in the stretch of most relentless west winds.

Total distance: approximation - 1,200 K
Total time: Two to three weeks

Daily breakdown

Rather than restrict you to specific lengths of cycling each day and specific places to stay the guide describes the route and places to stay and you can choose where and when you want to stop. If there is a long stretch between places to stay the guide will alert you. You choose where you want to stay an extra day or the different excursions you want to add. Below we give you a route. Do with it what you would like.

Route

Take the S Midnapore, page 47, or the East Shepard Exit out of Calgary, page 43. If you take the latter, go west on Marquis of Lorne Way/Highway 22/22X to MacLeod Trail. At the intersection of MacLeod Trail/Highway #2 south and Marquis of Lorne you want to get heading west on Marquis of Lorne which becomes Highway #22/22X west.

Highway 22/22x is a source of confusion because it winds around, changes direction, even goes in three directions from one intersection. And that's just what it does at 208th Street SW. You are on Highway 22/22x going west. And there, off to your left, going south, is also Highway 22/22x, which is sometimes called 208th Street. Don't ask. Just turn left (south) onto 208th Street/Highway 22/22x. You are going to wind around on Highway #22 almost all the way to the southwest corner of the province.

Into the Foothills

This is a pleasant road with lovely views of the foothills. You will be constantly riding up and down rolling hills that are well graded. Traffic can be busy on the weekends and you'll hit spots with limited shoulder and some of it chewed up.

Highway 22/22x takes you right to Millarville, 20 K from the edge of Calgary, (🚻 🚲 ☎ 🍴 🍎 🚗 🛏). Millarville scatters along the highway with big gaps between. At the intersection with Highway #549 one of the most popular parts of Millarville, The High Country Café, perches on a rise to your right. It just sits by itself beside the road. If you cycled east, down #549 a bit, another piece of Millarville, the site of the Millarville Farmers' Market and Millarville Annual Horse Race also stands in isolation. Continuing 2 K further south along #22, with no town in evidence in between, you come to "downtown" Millarville with an excellent general store and some country houses on large lots. This is a popular spot with the horse-y crowd. This is around the corner on the continuation of Highway #549, right (west) of #22. Highway #549 continues west and a service road that, once again, goes right off the road, takes you into the store and the most concentrated cluster of houses in Millarville.

Back on #22, southbound, Three Point Creek B&B is down the next right (west) turn after Highway #549. You travel about 2 K along gravel that in fact is smooth dirt to this comfortable home with the big open sun deck.

Continuing south past Millarville you are surrounded by terrain and vegetation reminiscent of Switzerland. Vegetation is deep green. There are smaller fields than usual in Alberta, pretty

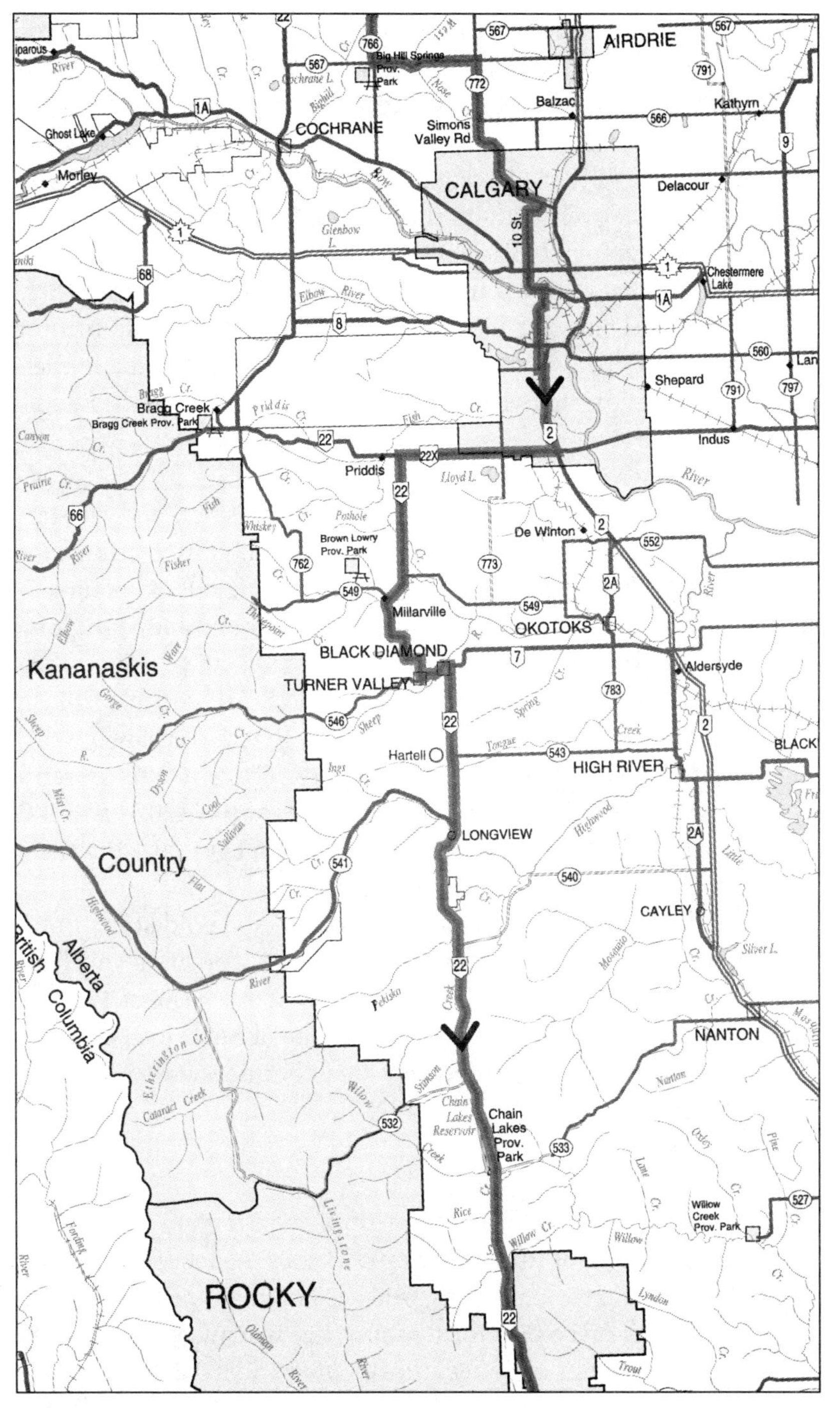
AIRDRIE
COCHRANE
CALGARY
Balzac
Kathyrn
Delacour
Chestermere Lake
Shepard
Indus
Big Hill Springs Prov. Park
Simons Valley Rd.
Ghost Lake
Morley
Bragg Creek
Bragg Creek Prov. Park
Priddis
Brown Lowry Prov. Park
Millarville
De Winton
OKOTOKS
BLACK DIAMOND
TURNER VALLEY
Aldersyde
Hartell
HIGH RIVER
LONGVIEW
CAYLEY
NANTON
Chain Lakes Prov. Park
Willow Creek Prov. Park
Kananaskis
Country
ROCKY
British Columbia
Alberta
10 St.

little old barns and everything on a hillside. There is a petting zoo along this stretch. Traffic can be heavy here and the shoulder is challenging in places until you get to Turner Valley, ( ), 18 K form Millarville. It is small and pretty and pleasant to be in. For a change of pace from highway cycling you can take the cycle path on the north side of the highway for the short 4 K stretch to Black Diamond. These two towns are so close together that they each seem as if they are a suburb of the other.

Black Diamond has gone to an effort to provide fun for tourists ( ) so poke around in their strange little shops where the highway turns south in the middle of town.

Going south out of Black Diamond you face an increasingly significant climb for about 10 K before the hill crests and you start down the other side toward Hartell and the intersection with Highway #543. At the crest of that hill stop and look around. A wonderful vantage point back to Black Diamond and to the long ride ahead.

Accommodation alert: There is a B&B 6 K south of Black Diamond and less that 1 K west off the highway. You have traveled about 76 K from downtown Calgary. There is one more in Longview. From Longview until the next town is 120 K, and 140 K to the next bed. It will be a long ride. Don't get stuck out there at nightfall if you don't have camping gear.

Through Hartell, (with a depression style old store and 5 houses - worth stopping into the store), continue south to Longview, ( ). Longview is quiet, isolated and an increasingly popular spot with people who like to "head out to the back country". Longview is very small but does have a tourism information centre.

Rugged country

From Longview you continue south down Highway #22 for 111 K before you come to any services: no B & Bs, no food, nothing but Chain Lakes Provincial Park, which is popular for fishing. ( ) Embark prepared. Quiet, rolling, trees for miles. This is some of the most stunningly beautiful country you'll see on this ride.

Finally you reach Highway #3 that, to the west, leads through Crowsnest Pass. If you tried to cycle west into BC on this road you would usually face monumental headwinds up to reach 160 K. But one thing makes it worth taking that on: the Frank Slide. At 4:10 AM, April 29th 1903 the side of Turtle Mountain broke away. In 100 seconds 82 million tons of rock plunged to the valley below. It buried forever half of the town of Frank and 70 of its citizens. Now the highway goes right over top this gigantic rock pile and the scar on the side of the mountain still shows. If you want to take on the wind, pedal 20 K west on Highway #3 to Frank and up the hill to the excellent Interpretive Centre. You have to see it to believe it.

If not, go for the tailwind and turn left (east) on Highway #3. Lundbreck Falls, ( ) is a tiny bit east of where Highway #22 meets #3. You'll probably have to go the additional 24 K to Pincher Creek:, which is 3 K south of #3 on Highway #6, in order to get a place to stay. Stay on #3 until you get to the turnoff to Highway #6 and Pincher Creek (different than Pincher). Turn right (south) onto that. So it has been a long ride, 137 K from Longview.

Pincher Creek is small but you get motels as well as B&Bs, ($). Pincher Creek may have more B&Bs per capita than any town in Alberta: 13 B&Bs and a population of 3,660. After your long ride yesterday, you may want to take your time before leaving Pincher Creek, even spend the day there. But when you do leave, you continue south on #6 for about 60 K to Waterton Park. After 40 of those, you turn left (west) off Highway #6 onto #5 to get to Waterton. Chances are you will fight a strong headwind all the way south on Highway #6.

Into the mountains

Waterton is worth seeing but involves some serious uphill as well as headwinds that are hard to believe. The town of Waterton is in Waterton National Park, which is the Canadian part of border-straddling Glacier National Park. Suddenly you have gone from foothills into mountain peaks. Many say that this park seriously rivals Banff.

The Park is noted for interesting geological formations and wilderness hiking. Boats ferry hikers across to the more isolated spots around the lake for day hikes. The town of Waterton is built for play. There is a campground right inside the town, ( ). You can rent delightful side-by-side double bikes with a little surrey roof so you could probably get bike repairs done there in an emergency. This also happens to be prolific Saskatoon berry territory. In late summer, watching for

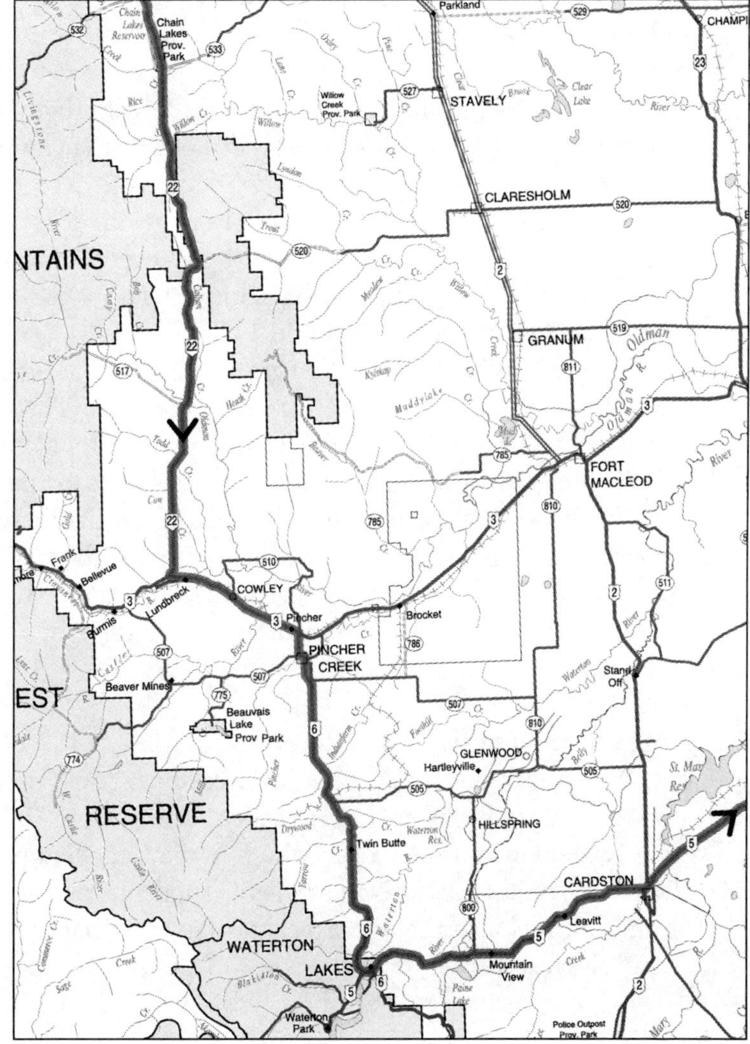

bears with the same idea of course, you can quickly gather a large pail, popular locally for pies.

Rather than staying inside the town, which is fun and active, you can stay at the spectacular, 'wedding cake' Prince of Wales Hotel sited on the hill overlooking the lake. This corner of rugged Southern Alberta was popular with the Prince of Wales who subsequently married Mrs. Wallace Simpson. He spent considerable time hunting and fishing from private lodges in this area.

Out onto prairie

Or you can forget about Waterton all together and turn left (east) as soon as you reach Highway #5 and continue on 45 K to Cardston, (🚻 ♿ ⛽ ✕ 🚗 🛏). If you had gone into Waterton it would be 54 K from there to Cardston.

For accommodation, in Cardston you have the Historic Granite Inn B&B made of the same stone as the Mormon Temple. On the way, 20 K east of Waterton Park, you passed Mountain View B&B as an alternative, (🛏). There is also a motel and a couple of ranches in the area.

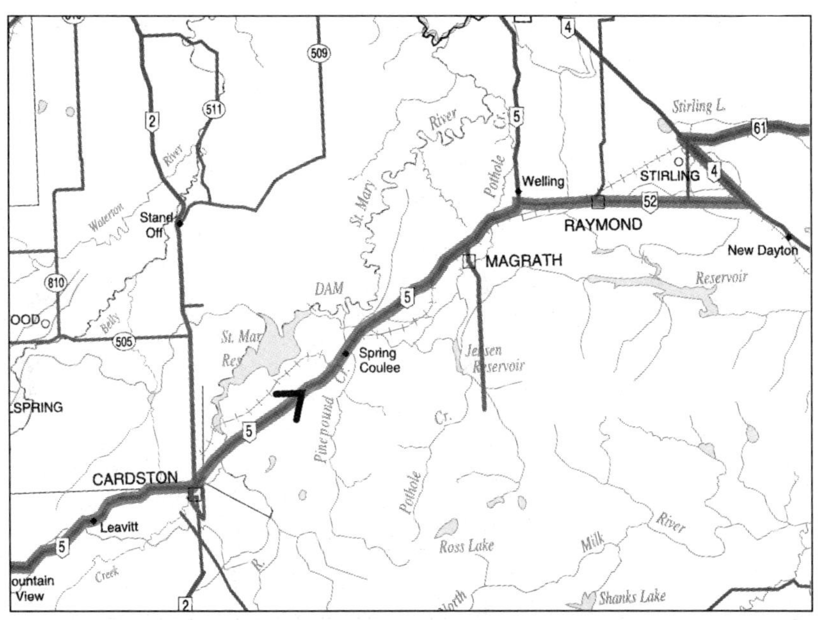

Eleven Mormon families traveled north from Utah in one of the last great covered wagon migrations to found Cardston. Regardless of your religious views, the Cardston Mormon Temple is an architecturally stunning example of heroic early 20th Century design. The grounds are beautifully landscaped and the building sits solid as a rock. Have a look.

Cardston is small and quiet. You have come about 100 K from Pincher Creek, depending on whether or not you went into Waterton. This is a good place to stay over night unless you have some other priority.

Leaving Cardston you continue traveling northeast, gradually getting further away from the American border, the mountains and eventually away from green and into brown prairie. In 50 K you get to Welling. From here #5 goes north to Lethbridge and much busier highways. You will encounter less traffic by continuing east on Highway #52, which, in just 7 K more, gets to Raymond and a B&B.

Tiny towns and arid prairie

If you do not stay overnight in Raymond, consider going on to Taber, your next chance for accommodation, another 65 K.

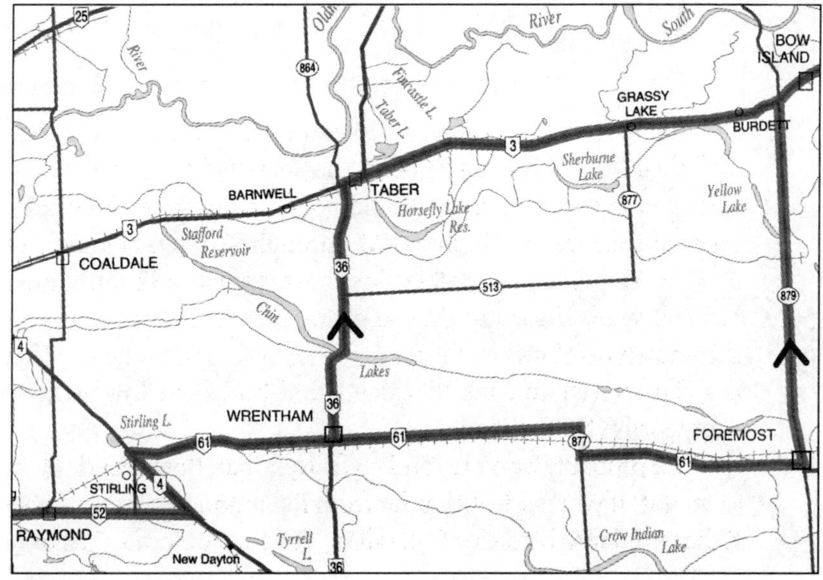

You get there going east out of Raymond on Highway #52 and then turning north to Sterling on a secondary highway. At Sterling, where there isn't much, you get on Highway #61 to Wrentham where you turn north on #36 to Taber. Taber doesn't have a B&B but it does have three motels, (). It is then 43 K east on Highway #3 to Bow Island, where there are also motels and a full range of services ($), and then 59 K on to Medicine Hat.

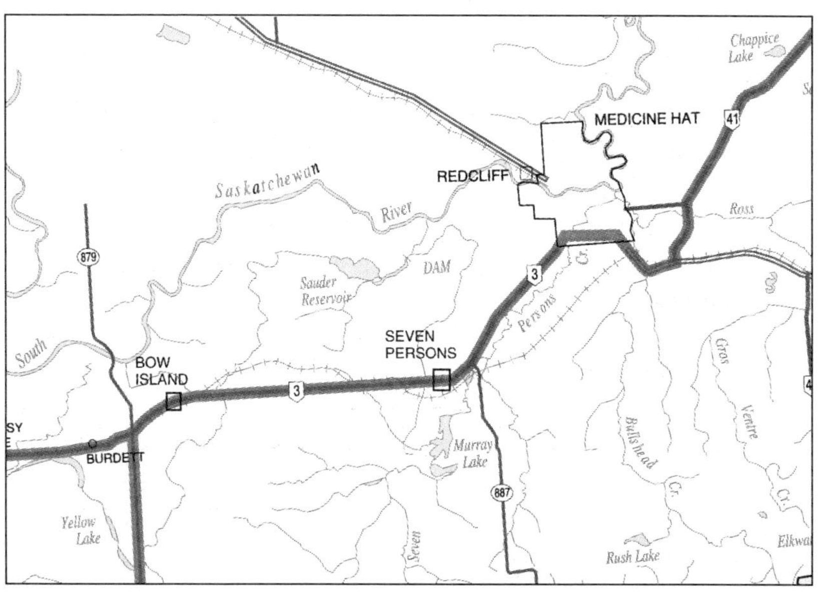

If you stayed overnight in Raymond you may want to try making it the 150 K from Raymond to Bow Island in one day. You start out on the same route but do not turn north at Wrentham. You continue east on Highway #61, through Skiff to Foremost, ($). Foremost is small, 582 souls, but has full services for travelers and one motel. At Foremost you turn north on Highway #879 up to the busier Highway #3. This is a flat stretch and the highway is old but there will be little competition for the road.

You probably won't try and go further than Bow Island () if you made it that far from Raymond so that leaves 43 K the next day to Medicine Hat, called "The Hat" by locals. The only services on the way are at Seven Persons (🚻 ♿ ▣), about 39 K from Bow Island, where the store has an outside table, nicely sited under a tree.

In, out & through Medicine Hat (🚻 ♿ ▣ 🍦 ☕ ✕ 🍎 🍸 ⛩ 🚗 🛏 🚲 $ ✚ ☎)

Medicine Hat is one of Canada's sunniest cities: 1,440 hours of bright sunshine each year. This is the largest city on the Grand Tour once you are out of Calgary so special instructions on getting in and out are included here to minimize traffic problems.

Heading east on Highway #3 from Seven Persons, you can get off the highway into Medicine Hat at the city limits near the airport. Go right onto 30th Street. Go to the end of 30th and turn left onto 10th Avenue SW, through a light industrial area. Turn right onto 16th Street SW and following it to the end into downtown. This route positions you to get accommodation and then to connect with Highway #41 out of the city.

The Visitors' Centre there, (527-6422) is open Monday to Saturday, 9 AM to 5 PM, "...and a little longer in the summer." They can give you a city map. There are plenty of places to stay and services available in Medicine Hat - a real city -and for accommodation you can choose a hotel, motel or B&B, but no camping. Whatever your choice, you will have to stay in Medicine Hat because once you head out on Highway #41 there isn't anywhere to stay for 95 K. You will be on isolated road with few services for two days.

Wherever you stayed, you want to leave town by getting onto 16th Street SW, through downtown to the end of 16th. It ends at a little road, Bullivant Crescent, which goes north. Take Bullivant all the way to 5th Street SW where you go right. After about three blocks you go left onto Division Avenue and down quite a steep hill. This gives you access to some of the particularly pretty part of Medicine Hat.

At the end of Division go right at 1st Street SE. You go under a train overpass and immediately turn right without proceeding to the traffic lights that you can see ahead. This has you on North Railway Street. Stick with it. It becomes Highway #41A and

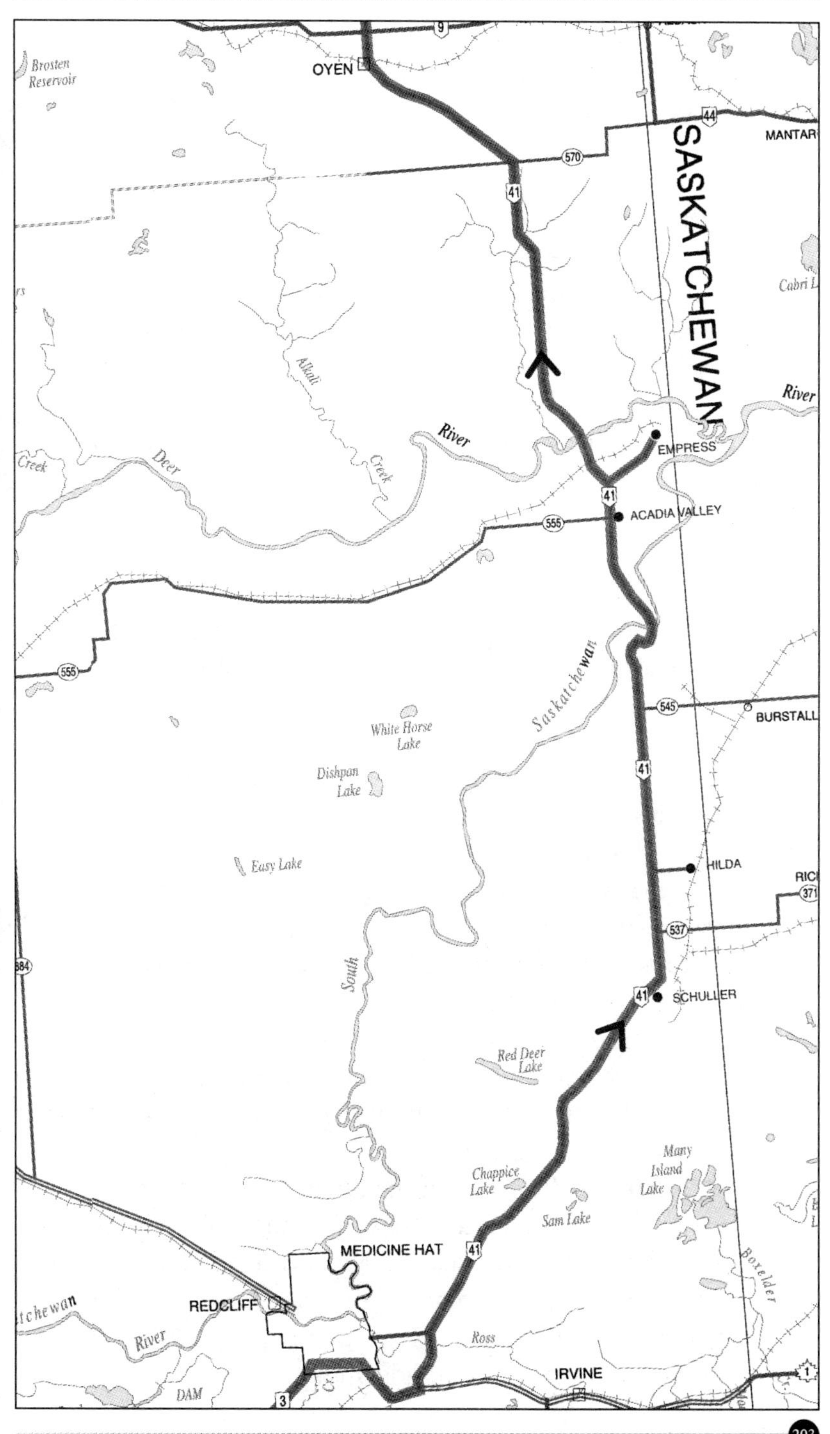

OYEN
Brosten Reservoir
SASKATCHEWAN
MANTAR
Cabri L
River
Alkali
River
Creek
Deer
Creek
EMPRESS
ACADIA VALLEY
BURSTALL
Saskatchewan
White Horse Lake
Dishpan Lake
Easy Lake
HILDA
South
SCHULLER
Red Deer Lake
Many Island Lake
Chappice Lake
Sam Lake
MEDICINE HAT
Boxelder
REDCLIFF
River
Ross
IRVINE
DAM

that carries you painlessly to Highway #41 and on your way out of Medicine Hat and onto the next leg of your adventure.

You have an alternative to all of this. Heading east from Seven Persons toward Medicine hat you can turn off onto Township Road #120, and then skirt around the edge of the city to get out to Revival Ranche. Township Road #120 is only marked with a small, blue city street sign. Go right (east) and travel about 5 K along Township Road #120. Before the railroad tracks you see another street sign. Range Road #61A. Go right (south) to Revival Ranche at the end of the road, 1 K.

Once you are at the Ranch, you can get bottled water at a nearby convenience store and the owner will pack food for your next day. To get from there onto Highway 41A and then 41, you can skirt the east edge of the city. Beth will draw you a map to #41A.

Hot, dry isolation

The next couple of days will be on quieter highway that takes you close to the Saskatchewan border, through hot, dry country that the locals consider boring. This sandhills area is bare. If you hit a warm spell, be careful about water, sun protection, shade and overheating. You are looking at up to 30 K between ranches out here. This is where the depression turned the soil and everyone's dreams into a dustbowl and broke the farmers financially. Plan places to stay carefully. Book ahead. You may have to go off the highway up to 15 K to find a place to sleep. And you will probably have to ask a restaurant to pack a picnic for you to carry for the next day.

You will have steep climbs when you cross two big river valleys, the Saskatchewan and Red Deer Rivers. Between them the road is fairly flat. It is single lane highway that usually has good shoulder. Some stretches are excellent.

Empress is the centre of the dry belt here. The first to turn brown, the last to turn green. The wind is predominantly northwest. It is stronger in early May than later on. You may hit thunderstorms in July but there is not going to be a great deal of precipitation at any time. You will see antelope, deer, coyote maybe a fox and possibly rattlesnakes as you ride this stretch.

Alert on rattlesnakes: Worst case scenario: you get bitten. You stay calm. This seems the critical piece. Keep the heartrate down. Sit down. Keep the bitten area below your heart. You can tie a scarf above the bite but just snuggly, not tight.Flag down a car to take you into Medicine Hat for an anti-venom shot. If they happen to have ice, put ice on the bite. You will at least get a terrible headache for three to four days. You may wish it would kill you but it won't. The people in danger are those with serious allergies. They know who they are and should have a kit from their own doctor to protect them from anaphylactic shock.

The fact is that rattlesnakes hate you even more than you hate them. They would prefer to have nothing to do with you. They stay off the road during the hot part of the day. When they hear you coming they are out of there. You won't get bitten on the road but when you go off it to go to the bathroom or look at something, your possibilities increase. They are most aggressive during shedding season at the end of May or beginning of June. Best protection is heavy leg coverings.

Look at it this way – you are getting a chance to see wildlife in its natural setting. This is the world that early settlers came to and contemporary ranchers get rich on. Watch, listen and appreciate what you get to see and hear.

Water Planning

Between Medicine Hat and Empress there are few houses so you should leave Medicine Hat stocked with all the water you would need on a long, hot, dry full day of riding. From Medicine Hat it is 43 K to Schuller(), 61 K to Hilda() and 105 to Empress, the first place you will find to stay. The road is good to here having been re-surfaced last year.

If you are camping, or having emergency camping essentials with you, you can consider a campground, before Empress, where the highway crosses the Saskatchewan River ( ). Empress is small – 189 people, but there are services, ($). North of Empress there is 10 K of rough road with many bumps. This is barren, quiet country that goes forever.

If the weather isn't too hot and you are feeling like this is the day you are going to find out how far you can go, it is 174 K from Medicine Hat to Oyen, your next accommodation opportunity on the stretch from Medicine Hat. It is 40 K from Empress to Acadian Valley, which is at the intersection of secondary Highway #565 (). This is the first town since Empress. 28 K north of there, Oyen is even bigger: 1,106 humans, an inn and a tea room, (). If you stayed in Empress, it is 49 K from there to Oyen.

Please don't try and do this stretch in one day if it is hot and windy.

You may want to spend a day in Oyen imagining what it would be like to live in a tiny prairie town and resting from your long, hot haul. After your Oyen sojourn, however long it lasts, you eventually will head north again. This time straight north to Highway #12, 68 K. Few inhabitants, good highway. It is a total of 85 K from Oyen to Consort, your next accommodation but there is sometimes camping at Sedalia along the way, 40 K north of Oyen and 5 K left (west).

New Brigden, just past that turnoff is a town with people in it but it doesn't have any services so you will have to go to someone's house for water, (). It is 68 K from Oyen north to Highway #12.

Back to civilization and westward bound

Highway 12 goes all the way west to the Rockies. It has an excellent shoulder and smooth surface. Traffic will increase as you go west but there will be plenty of room for you all. You will not encounter hills until further west. Once you turn onto #12 it is an additional 17 K west to Consort. An 85 K ride from Oyen may feel like a breeze after the long ride prior to that.

In Consort you are at the northeast corner of your Grand Tour. It is still dry in this area but you are out of the isolation of Highway #41 and there will be towns and services every 30 K or so. You will have choices of where to spend the night instead of needing to make it to the next bed.

Consort is the original home of singer/songwriter k.d. lang. Her anti-beef television commercials years ago have left ranchers, and by association the whole population there, peevish about this amazing Canadian star. They forget that the courage with which they pride themselves has made k.d. a hero to people who believe in the power of the human spirit. Tread lightly on the k.d. issue in rural B&Bs up this way.

Consort is a small town but has all the basics: ($). No B&B but there is one motel, so call ahead. Refreshed by a night in a motel and back in populated terrain you are ready to move into the second half of your grand tour, heading toward the Rockies in the west.

You leave Consort heading northwest through Veteran and Throne to Coronation. It is 46 K through undulating countryside to Coronation, ($) from

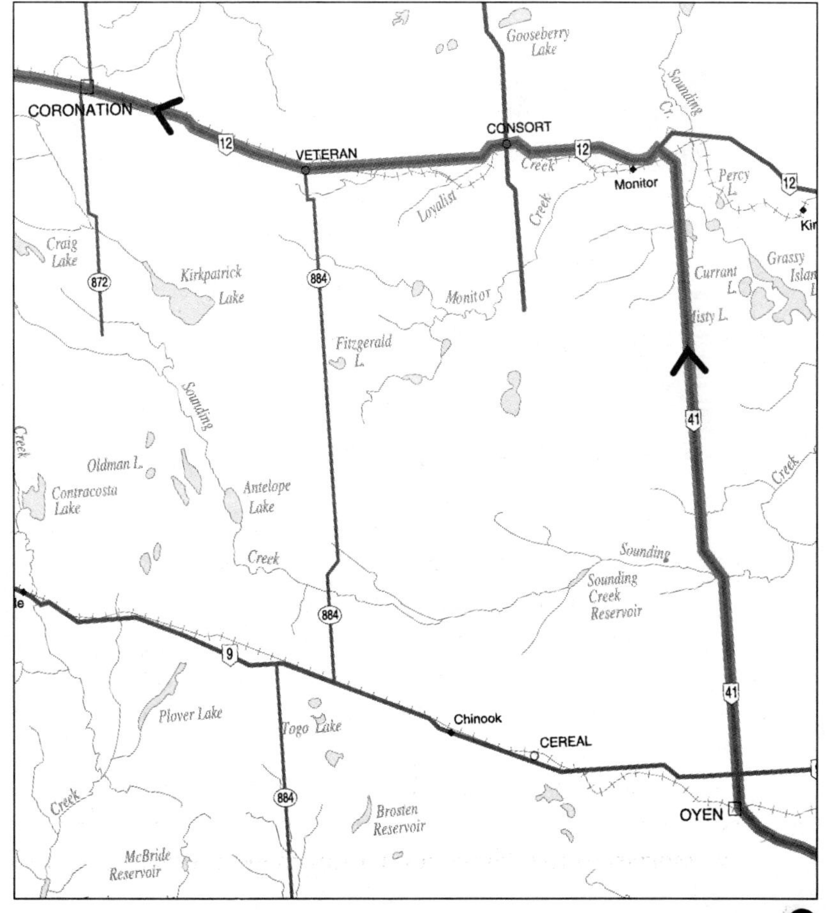

Consort. There are 1,184 people and one motel in Coronation. Don't be caught with no-where to stay due to a reunion. Call ahead.

Accommodation galore and water sports

If you can make it all the way to Castor, (boating, swimming, free camping on Castor Creek) from Consort - 81 K - you have a B&B and motel, (). Now you are starting to get back into some green and some trees. It feels less parched-prairie-badlands and more Canadian northland.

It is then 64 K to Stettler, the biggest centre you've hit since Medicine Hat- 5000 citizens. There are two B&Bs and five motels. The Grandview Motel is an excellent, award winning vintage 1950s motel and it has kitchenettes in some rooms if you want to do some cooking.

Thirty-nine K west of Stettler, your next accommodation is in Alix – a B&B and a motel. If you didn't stay in Stettler you would have ridden 1i6 K from Castor to get to a bed in Alix. Another substantial ride. There is a B&B and a motel in Alix, (

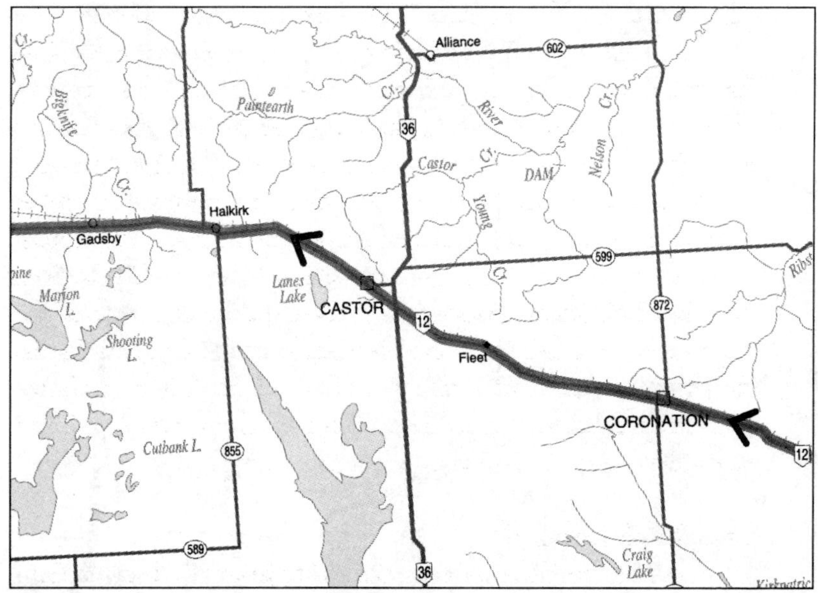

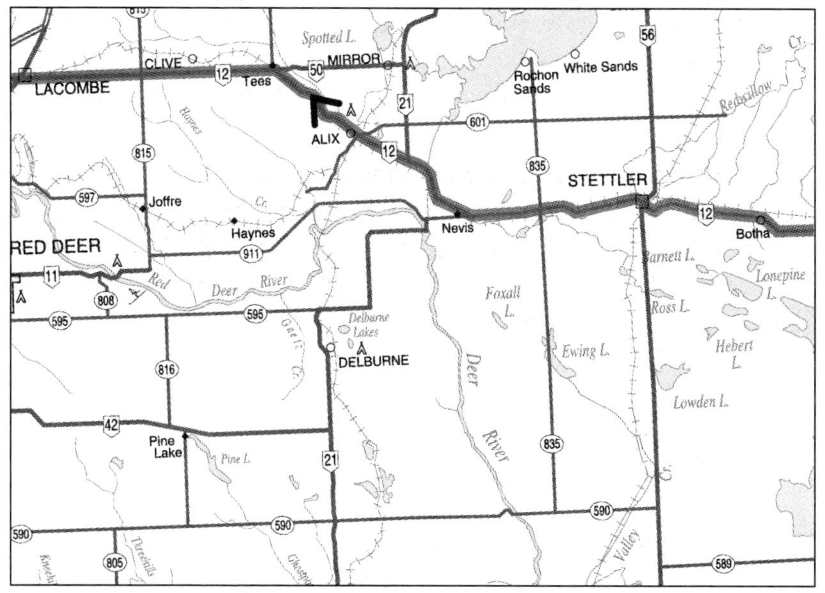

) and swimming - which is quite a bit for a little town of 782 people. Just be sure you have space reserved there before you breeze in on your bike. Continuing west you hit some substantial hills for the last 27 K before you get to Lacombe.

From Alix it is 45 K to Lacombe. From Stettler it is 82 K to Lacombe. So you have some accommodation options that give you flexibility on length of riding day. Lacombe, is the next centre big enough to insure accommodation and give you a range of services ( ). There is one B&B right in Lacombe, and one 12 K east, before reaching Lacombe. There are four motels.

Leaving Lacombe, still going west on Highway #12 you cross the big #2 Highway. As soon as you are on the west side of the highway it seems like the Rocky Mountains are not far away. In this northwest corner of your ride you will wind around to maximize your sampling of Southern Alberta, stay away from Highway #2 and enjoy the mountains on your way back to Calgary.

Into the playground

It is 21 K from the spot your cross Highway #2, through Gull Lake ( ) to the little town of Bentley ( ) where you turn south on Highway #20 to go to Sylvan Lake. It is a 50 K ride from Lacombe. Sylvan Lake ( )is a jumping little resort with water slide, speed boats, camping, teenagers sunning and drinking beer, the great Alberta playground. There are three B&Bs and 5 motels but book ahead. People come back here year after year during July and August. It is booked solid.

If you choose to get back to your solitude as quickly as you can, pedal on. Head south on Highway #781 to Highway #54. That is 22K. Turn right (west) onto #54. It is 15 K to Spruce View ( ), another accommodation opportunity and 25 K further to Caroline with two motels. It is 50 K Lacombe to Sylvan Lake, 87 Lacombe to Spruce View and 117 K Lacombe to Caroline. You choose how far you want to go.

If you choose to stay out of this altogether, continue west to Rocky Mountain House from Bentley: #12 west, #761 south and #598 west again. You would have traveled close to 100 K from Lacombe, so you may overnight in what locals call Rocky ( ) before going 46 K south to Caroline.

Trees, foothills and rolling terrain

Caroline is the northwesterly corner of your Grand Tour of Southern Alberta and you are now going south and back toward Calgary. This is foothills country again, with the mountains towering in the west and rolling hills. Caroline ( ) is a few extra K west of Highway 22 on Highway #54. If you go into Caroline you retrace those few K to get going south on Highway #22 to Sundre ( ), about 34 K. There are five sources of accommodation in Sundre and it is 25 K to continue on from there to Cremona.

From Sundre you pedal east again on Highway #27 before hitting the continuation of Highway #22 where you go south to Cremona. Cremona has a B&B and basic services, ( ).

After Cremona you leave Highway #22 and head east along Highway #580 to get to Highway #580 south toward Madden, in about 20 K. The maps are a bit hazy about Madden. You may have to come at it from the side and you may face a short stretch of

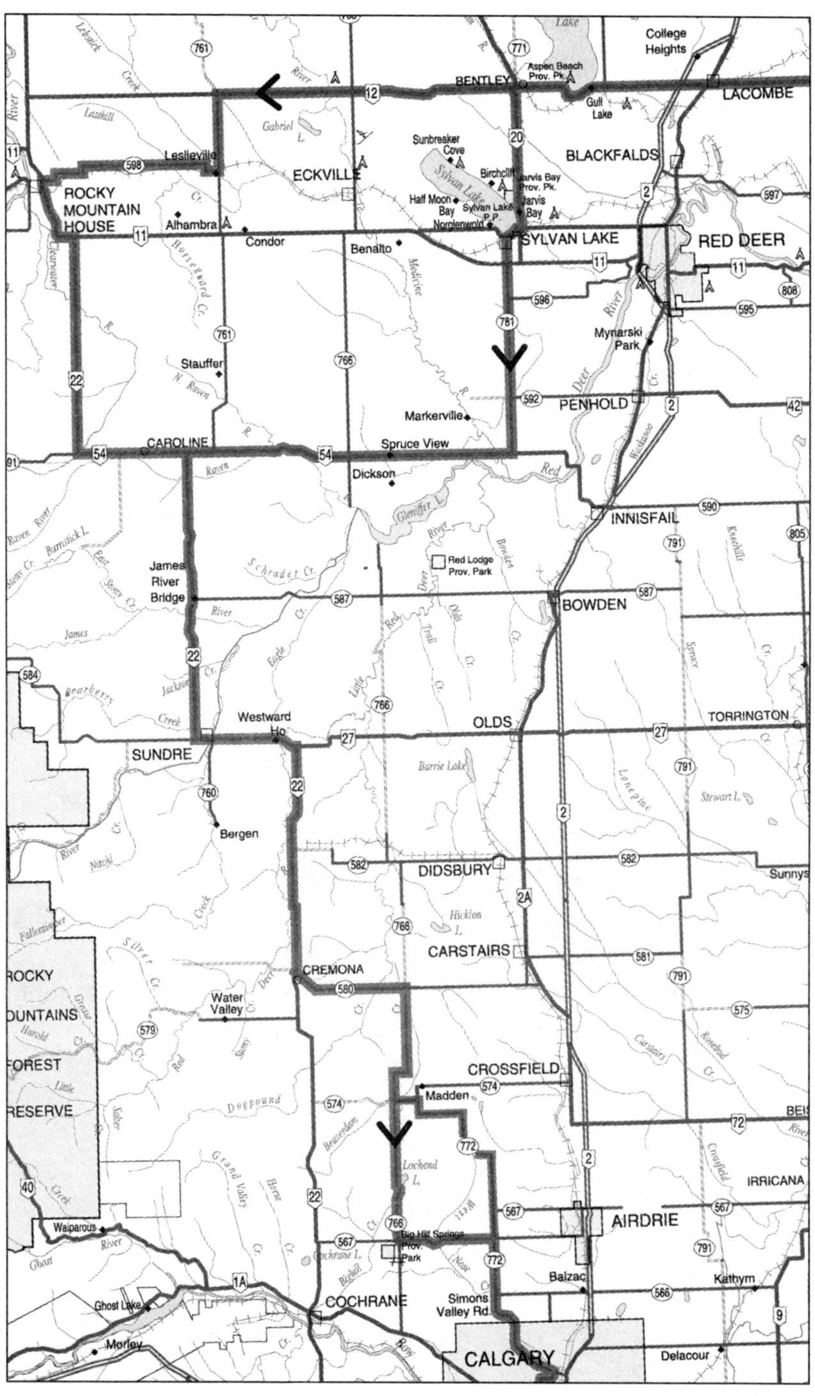

College Heights
LACOMBE
BENTLEY
Aspen Beach Prov. Pk.
Gull Lake
BLACKFALDS
Sunbreaker Cove
Leslieville
ECKVILLE
Birchcliff
Jarvis Bay Prov. Pk.
Sylvan Lake
Half Moon Bay
Jarvis Bay
Norglenwold
ROCKY MOUNTAIN HOUSE
Alhambra
Condor
SYLVAN LAKE
RED DEER
Benalto
Mynarski Park
Stauffer
PENHOLD
Markerville
CAROLINE
Spruce View
Dickson
INNISFAIL
Red Lodge Prov. Park
James River Bridge
BOWDEN
Westward Ho
OLDS
TORRINGTON
SUNDRE
Barrie Lake
Bergen
DIDSBURY
Sunnys
CARSTAIRS
CREMONA
Water Valley
ROCKY MOUNTAINS FOREST RESERVE
CROSSFIELD
Madden
Lochend L.
IRRICANA
AIRDRIE
Waiparous
Big Hill Springs Prov. Park
Balzac
Kathyrn
Ghost Lake
COCHRANE
Simons Valley Rd.
Morley
CALGARY
Delacour

gravel, but last I was on it, it was quite ride-able gravel. Madden doesn't really have services. It has Dodd's Store with limited wares and limited hours: take your chances. But by then you are close to Calgary and will probably just come back into the city.

Immediately south of Madden you get onto #772 which becomes Simons Valley Road which brings you into Calgary on the best entry route in the whole city at any time of the day, any day of the week, page 93.

Congratulations

Welcome back to Calgary. You have just completed a major ride. You've been on the road for days and you have explored new territory with little protection from what the riding day brings your way. I sincerely hope that this little guide has been helpful and easy-to-use.

Services

Millarville

- The High Country Cafe at the intersection of Highway #22 and #547 has outside picnic tables and umbrellas, salad, wonderful homemade soup, pie and ice cream. This is a widely known and popular spot,( ).
- The all-purpose Millarville store is excellent. You can get plenty of provisions for riding the next day and magazines for your evening, ( ).
- Farmers' Market with produce, crafts, you name it – Saturday 8:30 AM to noon, June 15th to October 5th, 931-3411
- Three Point Creek B&B, 1 K south and 2 K west of Millarville, 931-3217

Turner Valley

- Town Office, 933-4944
- Tea house (🚻 ♿ ▣ ☕)
- Tourist information hut, the latter with beautiful rolling lawn where you can park yourself to rest, picnic, look at maps or do nothing for a while. Unfortunately, the tourist info hut does not have a washroom. You need to go to a service station for that,(⛱).
- Bathrooms in service station (🚻)
- Restaurant in Quonset hut, to the right of the highway T-intersection in the middle of town, this Korean run restaurant has delicious food and is popular with the locals.
- Variety store, the old fashioned kind with items you haven't seen since you were a kid. I can't remember where it is and don't know if it is still there, just poke around until you find it.
- Grocery/convenience store, just south of the Highway turn in town, wide selection for a convenience store.
- One motel, a hotel, two B&Bs and a B&B Association phone: 933-4174 (🛏)

Oh... and By the Way

Medicine Hat Day Trip

You can get a good workout and a fun ride east out of Medicine Hat. Head east on Highway #1 for 17 K. Turn Left (north) onto Highway #41 which shortly takes you to #41A back to town. Go left (west) onto #41A back.

A Pleasant 38 K Loop!

Black Diamond

- Triple A Motel, 933-4915
- Black Diamond has figured out that travelers are bored and have money to spend so they have encouraged delightful craft shops, cappuccino shops, a fun odd store ($)
- Old-fashioned hamburger stand ( ) with ice cream, hotdogs, hamburgers and generally great snacks and plenty of green grass, brightly painted picnic tables, a raised patio and a feeling of outdoor play.

South of Black Diamond

- Welcome Acres B&B, 6.4 K south and .8 K west of Black Diamond, 933-7529

Hartell @ Highway #543 & 232

- Hartell General Store – limited stock, if the store is still there, but well worth the stop, not only to support this little business, but to take a journey back in time, ( )

Longview

- Highwood River Inn B&B, 558-2456
- Blue Sky Motel, 558-3655
- Grocery store, convenience store, ( )

South of Longview

- Bar U Ranch is 13 K south of Longview and less than 1 K west of the highway on a good quality, oiled road. It is an historical site and there is no accommodation but there are services, ( )

Chain Lakes

- Chain Lakes Provincial Park (– outdoor-) camping, boating, water play, about 55 K south of Longview

84 K from Longview

- Maycroft Camping, open May 1 to Thanksgiving, ( ) outdoor toilet

Lundbreck

- Campsite and scenic waterfall with fishing ( )

Pincher Creek

- Town Office, 627-3156
- Farmer's Market, Friday 3 to 5 PM in the MCC Arena on Main Street from mid-July to mid-September: 627-4589

- B&Bs, 13 () plus six motels, due to the ski hill: Allandale Lodge & Retreat, 627-5598; Evergreen B&B, 898-5111; Prairie Schooner B&B, 627-3800 – accepts Visa and M/C
- Plenty of ()

Waterton

- Town Office, 859-2224 ()
- Pat's Gas rents bikes, pedal carriages and scooters, they may repair a bike: 859-2266 ()
- Three B&Bs and 13 motels/inns ()
- Prince of Wales Hotel, 859-2231

East of Waterton

- Mountain View B&B, 653-1882

Cardston

- Town office, 653-3366; tourist hut, 653-3787
- Husky Service Station () open Sundays, as well as during the week
- Cobblestone Manor Dining Room () designated an Alberta Historical Site, outstanding interior, thousands of inlaid woods and antique furniture from Europe; open seven days a week – 4:30 to 10 PM; 653-1519
- Mormon Temple, dedicated in 1923, 9 AM to 9 PM; May 1st to September 30th the Information Centre and grounds are open to the public: 653-3552
- Historic Granite Inn, 653-3157

Wellington, ()

Raymond

- Crystal Butterfly B&B, 752-3100 ()

Stirling and Wrentham, ()

Foremost, ()

- Cedar Villa Motel, 867-3611

Taber

- Taber Motel, 223-2223
- Taber Provincial Park for picnics and camping, 5 K from town, 223-7929
- Farmer's Market, Thursday 7 to 9 PM at the Agriplex July to September, 223-4915

Bow Island

- Town Office, 867-3804
- Farmer's Market, Friday 2 to 5 PM at the Golden Age Centre from July to September, 545-6936
- Golden Bell Motel, 545-6060

Seven Persons

- Convenience store on the highway ( )

Medicine Hat

- Tourist Information centre, corner of the TransCanada Highway and Southridge Dr., 527-6422
- Cyclepath Bicycle Club, Mike McAllister, 528-4818
- Cyclepath, a bike shop in a mall, 526-2274 ( )
- Farmers' Market, Monday, Wednesday and Friday from 9 AM to noon, mid-July to October 1, across from City Hall, 527-6128
- 19 hotel/motels and two B&Bs: Country Breeze, 527-9987 ( )
- Revival Ranch, 528-3918 is outside the city and you can get to it from Seven Persons without going all the way into Medicine Hat. Turn right (east) onto Township Road #120. After about 5 K, you get to Range Road #61A. Go right (south). The Ranche is the only building along the road.

Schuller and Hilda - ( )

Empress (Sask.) - ( )

- Town Office, 565-3938
- Empress Motor Inn 565-3952

Acadia Valley - ( )

Oyen - ( )

- Town Office, 664-3511
- Antelope Inn on 1st Avenue ( ), 664-3886
- Alberta Hotel with rooms above the bar and rooms in behind ( )
- Convenience store ( )
- Oyen Golf Course, in case you get the urge - 4 K north of Oyen at Highways #41 and #9 intersection
- 24 hour convenience store and gas station, restaurant, open 6 to 11( )

New Brigden -(Ⓢ)
Consort -(Ⓢ ⛽ 🍴 ⛩)
- Day's Motel, 577-3847

Veteran, Chinook and Throne -(Ⓢ)
Coronation - (🚻 Ⓢ ⛽ 🍴 ⛩)
- Town Office, 578-3679
- Court West Motel, 578-3534

Fleet - (Ⓢ)
Castor
- Town Office, 882-3215
- Robin's Nest B&B, 882-2701
- Grey Goose Motel, 882-3444
- (🚻 Ⓢ ⛽ 🍴 ⛩ ⛺) and swimming and boating, camping right in town

Halkirk, Gadsby and Botha (Ⓢ) tiny towns
Stettler
- Eilleen's B&B, 742-3827
- Garden of Eden, 742-0986
- Five motels, including award winning Grandview, 742-3391
- (🚻 Ⓢ ⛽ 🍴 🍎 ⛩ 🚗 🛏 $ 📞) and ⛺ at several sites outside town

Alix
- Connie's Country Cocoon, 747-2217, with environmental priorities and reflexology – try it.
- Alix Motel, 747-2761
- (🚻 Ⓢ ⛽ 🛏 ⛺) and water sports

Lacombe
- Sunset Country B&B, 885-4691
- Four hotels/motels
- (🚻 Ⓢ ⛽ 🍦 🍴 🍎 ⛩ 🛏)

Bentley and Gull Lake (🚻 Ⓢ ⛽ 🍎 🍸 ⛩ 🚗 ⛺ 📞)
Sylvan Lake
- Town Office, 333-4477
- Three B&Bs: Kozy Korner, 887-4070; Sheila Turner's Office & Guest House, 887-5422 and Sylvan Lake B&B, 887-3546
- Jarvis Bay Provincial Park camping and picnic area, 887-5575
- (🚻 Ⓢ ⛽ 🍦 🍴 🍎 ⛩ 🚗 🛏 ⛺ $ 📞) plus water sports

Spruce View

- Spruce View Motel (🚻 🚲 ⛽ 🍎 🚗 🛏)

Rocky Mountain House

- Country Cabin B&B, 845-4834 and Riverside B&B, 845-5901 (🚻 🚲 ⛽ 🍦 🍴 🍎 🍸 ⛩ 🚗 🛏 ⛺ $ 📞)

  Caroline

- Tourist Information, 722-3781
- Caroline Gateway Motel, 722-3322
- Caroline Motel, 722-3000
- (🚻 🚲 ⛽ 🍴 🍎 ⛩ 🚗 🛏 ⛺ 📞)

Sundre

- Town Office, 638-3551
- Farmer's Market, Friday 5:30 to 8:30 PM, at the Curling Rink May 3rd to October 11, 403 638-2201
- Five motels, several with kitchenettes: Chinook Country Inn, 638-3300; Parkwood Motor Inn, 638-4424 etc.
- (🚲 ⛽ 🍴 ⛩ 🛏)

Cremona

- Spruce Hollow B&B, 637-2277
- Sunset Guiding & Outfitting to add some western outdoor experience to your cycling tour: 637-2361 to phone or fax
- (🚻 🚲 ⛽ 🍴 🍎 🚗 🛏 ⛺)

Additional Excursions

- Calgary: Contact the Convention & Visitors Bureau, there are an enormous number of possibilities in the city. 1-800-661-1678

- Millarville Farmers' Market: If the timing works and you want to sample local produce and crafts, stop at the market on Saturday morning.

- Turner Valley Tea Room: Any town is improved by the addition of a tea room. Try this one.

- Black Diamond weird shops: Black Diamond's answer to tourist traps is a delightfully cobbled together strip of shops that are truly odd. And fun. A good spot to pick up little gifts and bike-packable souvenirs. (🚻)

- Bar U Ranch Historical Site: 13 K south of Longview, this ranch portrays the history of ranching in Canada with old buildings, equipment, corrals and vignettes acted out by staff.

- Frank Slide Interpretive Centre on Highway #3, 20 K west of Highway #22.

- Lundbreck Falls: The Falls are a bit off the highway but a nice picnic spot and any falls is a pretty thing to see.

- Pincher Creek Museum sounds extensive and interesting.

- Head-Smashed-in Buffalo Jump, a UNESCO World Heritage site, documents the buffalo hunting culture of the Plains Indians. To get to it, rather than going south on Highway #6 to Pincher Creek, turn north onto Highway #510 then #785. They take you right there. That will leave you 16 K west of Fort MacLeod and off the track of the Grand Tour. To get back on track, go into Fort MacLeod and connect with Highway #3 at the south end of town. This will take you east, through Coaldale to Taber where you can pick up the tour on page 200.

- Waterton Park and Town: We all know the reasons not to bother going west 9 K to get to Waterton National Park and the Town of Waterton and the Prince of Wales Hotel. The reasons to bother are that this may be one of the most spectacular town sites in the world and is a truly untouched natural area. The town is fun with many treats, an in-town campground and waterside diversions; hiking, fishing horseback riding, golf and boat excursions. The Prince of Wales Hotel has to be seen to be believed. A drink on their outside patio overlooking the lake takes you back to the turn of the century posters promoting the Great Canadian Rockies.

- Cardston: It is worth taking time to cruise the exterior of the Cardston Mormon Temple. This building and its grounds are a stunning example of heroic, 1920s architecture.

- Taber: This town supplies all of Alberta with corn and hosts the Taber Rodeo.

- Bow Island: You'll go through the Island in the middle of the prairies – and it really does have an island. Take pictures.

- Medicine Hat: Many options: the historic Medalta Potteries Plant, art gallery, Police Point Park – a 400-acre natural reserve of wildlife and wildflowers and the greenhouses in Redcliff, 10 K northwest of Medicine Hat. Contact the local tourism office, 527-6422, for information. There is a lot to do there.

- Historical Walking Tour of Medicine Hat: Medicine Hat has some of the nicest old prairie architecture in Alberta and the self-guided walking tour helps you find it, from the Tourist Centre, corner of the TransCanada Highway and Southridge Dr., 527-6422.
- Stettler steam train excursion: This little railroad does circuits, 4 to 8 hours, of small towns in Central Alberta stopping for shopping, picnics, sightseeing and historical spots of interest. Vintage cars include a 1919 passenger car, a 1921 deluxe sleeper converted to a lounge and two Pullman day coaches: 742-2811
- Sylvan Lake water play: Sylvan Lake is the place that Albertans go to swim, sail, motorboat, water ski, jet-ski, lie on the beach, suntan and go camping with their friends before their parents would think of letting them go traveling any other way. Lots of beer gets drunk, music gets played, backs get sunburned and slurpies get sloshed. It is fun and jivie and Coney Island. There is a huge water slide for the kids. Settle in for a day or so and watch young Alberta at summer play.
- Sylvan Lake Wild Rapids Water Slide Park for really hot weather and big crowds, 887-3636
- Caroline Rodeo, mid May
- Sundre Pioneer Village Museum: depicts turn of the century rural life, school, log cabin, blacksmith's shop, free.
- Sundre Rodeo, just past mid June

***Note:** There are parts of this ride that I am only doing while this guide is being printed. If you want more detail or questions answered, call, fax or email and I'll share all the information I have. And if you have additions or suggestions for changes to make, likewise, let me know.*

Oh... and By the Way

Into the Wild Blue Yonder on the David Thompson Highway

From Rocky Mountain House at the northwest corner of the Grand Tour, you could head north and then west on the David Thompson Highway. Everyone loves this road, but it does require camping gear. It eventually carries you west to the Jasper/Banff Parkway _ which is an ambitious cycle itself. This is a long demanding wilderness ride on an excellent highway. Go prepared to fend for yourself.

- Day One: 80 K to the Hanlech Campground (🚻 ♿ ⛺) - which isn't listed in the Alberta Camping Guide but is there.
- Day Two: 15 K gets you to breakfast in Nordegg, where the coffee shop waitresses are reputed to be particularly friendly. After a total of 100 K you get to Thompson Creek Campground.
- Day Three: 92 K to the enormous Lake Louise Campground - including a demanding 37 K climb to Bow Summit.
- Day Four: Lake Louise to Banff on Highway #1A - 60 K

Things to take: less being more

You are always packing to minimize what you are carrying and still have all your essentials. That is obvious but hard to do. It is not just a matter of disciplined paring down. It is first a matter of some cagey predictions of all you may face in weather, health, alternate activities, social events, and even emotional needs.

Any items that will serve multi-purposes are helpful. Swiss army knife items, so to speak:

- ❑ Shampoo for hair and for hand laundry,
- ❑ Bathing suit for swimming/ sunning and for women, as an aprés cycle top, even under a skirt
- ❑ Long, soft socks for socks and a neck warmer
- ❑ Towel for lying on, drying yourself, using as a pillow and as a picnic table cloth.

If you are on the road for an extended time you will keep discarding as you acquire. You will trade and give away books, T-shirts, food. It is a marvelous exercise in simplifying life, which is easier on a bike than at home.

Handlebar bag:

- ❑ Pens, journal and little list pads
- ❑ Sunglasses
- ❑ Sunscreen – see note page 228
- ❑ Nail file/nail clippers
- ❑ Orange sticks or something else to get road dirt out of fingernails
- ❑ Knife, preferable a multipurpose Swiss Army Knife
- ❑ Knife/ fork/spoon set to expand your eating options - - yogurt, chunks of cheese
- ❑ Camera and one roll of extra film. A camera that comes with a remote is fun for taking pictures of yourself if you are traveling alone.
- ❑ Maps, guidebook, accommodation details

- ❑ Handi wipes, Kleenex or a cotton handkerchief
- ❑ Food for that day

Optional:

- ❑ Small pair of binoculars for bird watching
- ❑ Current reading material
- ❑ Business cards so you can easily leave a trail with people you want to

Other:

- ❑ ____
- ❑ ____
- ❑ ____
- ❑ ____
- ❑ ____
- ❑ ____
- ❑ ____

Handlebar bag side pockets:

- ❑ A couple of bungee cords to strap on extra items or a pair of wet runners
- ❑ Plastic bags for garbage and food
- ❑ Cable lock for your bike

If you make a habit of putting your lock away locked, you have to produce a key before you can lock your bike so the chance of being stuck with a bike you cannot unlock are reduced. You can then attach a spare key, using a loop of string, to a ring sewn inside the pocket of your riding pants.

Other:

- ❑ ____
- ❑ ____
- ❑ ____
- ❑ ____
- ❑ ____
- ❑ ____
- ❑ ____

Fanny pack:

This goes everywhere you go - restaurants and bathrooms - because these are the things you are guarding carefully or accessing often.

- ❑ Walkman and extra batteries
- ❑ Cash
- ❑ Credit cards
- ❑ Identification
- ❑ Health insurance documentation
- ❑ Medical alert notices
- ❑ House/hotel key
- ❑ Telephone card and payphone coins
- ❑ In the Alberta telephone system, it costs $.25 to activate a payphone before you can tell them your phone credit card number.
- ❑ Lipgloss of some kind, ideally with sunblock, which you'll use over and over
- ❑ Current, in use, handkerchief

Other:

- ❑ ____________________
- ❑ ____________________
- ❑ ____________________
- ❑ ____________________
- ❑ ____________________
- ❑ ____________________
- ❑ ____________________

Around your neck

- ❑ Bicycle key
- ❑ Compass

In your panniers

Tools

- ❑ Easy to use hand pump - mounted on your bike, not inside your panniers - Zefal is a commonly available and reliable pump.
- ❑ Kit for changing tires

This should include several of the tools below plus a set of prying tools specifically designed for prying the tire off the rim. One brand is called "pry babies"

- ❑ Tube patching kit
- ❑ Spare tube, the right size for your tire - so you can do your patching later
- ❑ 3-in-one oil or WD-40 with tiny, plastic tube held on it with elastic, so you can reach difficult places
- ❑ Your chain needs oiling every few weeks. It means you will constantly be getting oil on your leg – but your chain will be happy. This is another reason to buy your cycling pants secondhand.
- ❑ 8, 9, 10 and 15 mm crescent wrenches
- ❑ Tire gauge
- ❑ Needle nose pliers
- ❑ Small Phillips screw driver for adjusting the gear derailleur
- ❑ Full set of metric Allen key wrenches and extras of the most crucial ones
- ❑ Multi purpose glue
- ❑ Liquid hand cleaner and small wipe-up rag
  All packed inside a zip-lock plastic baggie

Optional:

- ❑ Chain repair kit
  This seems like a luxury but a damaged chain is one of the few problems that render you immobile. This tiny mechanism gives you peace of mind if you are going to be isolated. It removes damaged links out of your chain and puts the chain back together shortened.
- ❑ Spoke tightener

Other

- ❑ ______________________________
- ❑ ______________________________
- ❑ ______________________________
- ❑ ______________________________
- ❑ ______________________________

Toiletries

- ❑ Towel
- ❑ Toothbrush and toothpaste, dental floss
- ❑ Comb
- ❑ Q-tips
- ❑ Handsoap and carrying baggie
- ❑ Shampoo
- ❑ Insect repellent
- ❑ Range of sunscreens and moisturizer combinations - see note below

Optional:

- ❑ Condoms
- ❑ Deodorant

Other:

- ❑ ____________________
- ❑ ____________________
- ❑ ____________________
- ❑ ____________________
- ❑ ____________________
- ❑ ____________________
- ❑ ____________________

❑ Sunscreen

This information is for both males and females. The effect of sun on skin is not gender specific. You have heard the news. Dermatologists are describing tanned skin as skin in crisis. Southern Alberta, with its high altitude, has the second highest rate of skin cancer in the world. Being exposed to sun all day long on a bike is quite different from three or four hours lying beside the swimming pool. And once you are out there, a burn developing at 3 PM is going to be a problem by 5 PM and a bigger problem the next day when you are back in the sun again.

In spite of all this, we still love the look of bronzed skin so we need to learn some balancing around looking healthy, outdoorsy this summer and doing ourselves harm. If you are unwilling to live a zero-tolerance policy, at least learn to monitor your skin closely and take preventative action when conditions call for it. Think in terms of accessing your sunscreen many times a day. Carry a range of strengths and apply different ones to different parts of your body. Pick the right range of sunscreens to suit your colouring. Use clothes that cover up skin as one of your sun management options. A judicious cover-up at just the right time in the early afternoon can head off a burn when the highest sunscreen in the world just won't protect you any more.

Be obsessively careful about your face. This is the last place you want to have chunks cut out of your skin ten years from now. This is where the investment in a high-end moisturizer/sunscreen combo is worthwhile because wind will be a factor as well. Moisturizer with SPF of 25 to 30 applied to your face every morning, whether you ride or not, is a good habit to get into. All year round. There is an expensive brand called Clarins that combines excellent moisturizer with SPF 25 and comes in a little canister a bit bigger than a lipstick and squirts out tidily. It is too expensive for anywhere but your face but I wouldn't ride without it. Lasts a long time

In Canada you can get a brand of sunscreen called Ombrelle. Their Extreme Lotion 30 contains the titanium dioxide that skiers put on their noses only this doesn't stay white on your skin. It gives amazing protection. However sometimes you just have to get fabric between skin and sun.

For most body skin (versus face skin), a daily layer of SPF 15 is minimal. Early in the season the minimum is higher, particularly for areas that get pounding sun exposure such as top of shoulders (a common skin cancer location in men) and top of the thighs (a common spot for women). When you start the season, going out there in your cheesy whiteness, slap on a good layer of maximum coverage on these spots. Do likewise for any spot that gets that suspiciously warm feeling, which can happen as quickly as half an hour. Consider these sunscreens part of your first aid kit that is kept immediately at hand all day. Don't run out. Keep slathering. As the sun builds during the day, match the sunscreen to the need.

First aid kit

- ❑ Matches for on-the-road sterilizing
- ❑ Tweezers
- ❑ Nail scissors that will be your all-purpose scissors
- ❑ Hand mirror, for getting something out of your eye or examining a face wound
- ❑ Tiny bottle of alcohol
- ❑ Cotton swabs
- ❑ Range of band-aids in a plastic bag, including butterfly band-aids to hold a wound closed
- ❑ Moleskin for blisters
- ❑ Gauze
- ❑ Antibiotic cream
- ❑ Fungicide ointment
- ❑ Polysporen
- ❑ Antihistamines

  Even if you don't consider yourself allergic, you'd be amazed how easy it is to come upon something your body doesn't like.
- ❑ Allergic eyedrops – Vasacon A, because eyes are often the first thing to react and eyedrops go into effect quickly.
- ❑ Aspirin or equivalent
- ❑ Tums or Pepto Bismal tabs
- ❑ Post insect bite cream (Dermocaine)
- ❑ Rescue Remedy

  This is one of the Bach flower remedies, an all-purpose naturopathic remedy. It is popular with the 20-year-old trekking-on-a-budget crowd for warding off illness, managing injuries and handling stress.
- ❑ Cough drops

Optional:

- ❑ Anti-inflammatory prescription
- ❑ Prescription for pain
- ❑ Imodium for diarrhea
- ❑ Something for constipation

Other:

❑ ______________________________

❑ ______________________________

❑ ______________________________

❑ ______________________________

❑ ______________________________

❑ ______________________________

❑ Weather gear

Keep your raingear on top inside your pannier, on the side that is easiest for you to reach around to. Weather can change so fast in Alberta that if it isn't handy you can be tempted to ride it out and then regret it.

A multi-purpose rain/all weather, hooded jacket, with plenty of zippered pockets, Velcro wristbands and maybe zippered underarms is central to your comfort. If it is bright yellow, it helps with visibility. Some people like a rain cape and even put elastic around the bottom so it can hook over the handlebars and the back of the seat, making a little rain tent with air circulation below. It would be a problem in high wind but worth trying. Some people use a shower cap under their helmet to keep the rain off if they don't have a hood or find that a hood restricts vision.

Wind pants will help you stay warm even though they aren't waterproof, rainpants can be too warm. Spandex pants without rainpants keep your legs warm in light rain when it isn't too cold and they dry quickly.

Take gloves and a warm headband and neck warmer because sooner or later you will be caught out in sudden cold. They are versatile and you can experiment until you find exactly what works for you.

You can get nylon or Gore-Tex rain booties to go over or under your shoes but bread bags work almost as well. You can also just let your runners get wet.

❑ Clothes

You already know about layers of clothes and about fast drying fleece for warmth, even when wet. Put layers on and off every few minutes if conditions call for it. Be ready to deal with a change when clothes get wet. Think of your body as the motor driving this machine and keep it in conditions it likes.

- ❑ Change of underwear and socks, not cotton that stays wet, but synthetic or a blend
- ❑ Two tank tops or minimalist T-shirts, which are a warm weather staple
- ❑ Light turtleneck t-shirt, ideally with a zipper front
- ❑ One warm sweater, or fleece liner, turtleneck if that is your preference
- ❑ Long-sleeved, Gore-Tex, undershirt to wick away the sweat or rain, and doubles as your multi-purpose warm top
- ❑ Cycling gloves and warm gloves
- ❑ Multi-purpose jogging shoes or cycling shoes that you can walk in
- ❑ One pair of lycra or spandex biking pants and one pair of similar shorts

A note about lycra and spandex. This figure clinging stuff is very comfortable and keeps you warm even if wet. It is revealing. If you are not used to wearing spandex or feel like your body isn't out of a magazine you may decide the self-consciousness effect of this outweighs the advantages. Many mature cyclists avoiding spandex as long as they can. The fact is that spandex works extremely well for comfort, drying and versatility. But brand new, spandex pants are frightfully expensive. Buy a pair at a second hand store (like Value Village) for $3 to $5 to try them out. Don't look in the mirror. Get on the bike and ride. Now what do you think?

Options:

- ❑ Sandals
- ❑ Change of running shoes
- ❑ Bathing suit
- ❑ Additional warm sweater

Other:

- ❑ ____________________
- ❑ ____________________
- ❑ ____________________
- ❑ ____________________

Miscellaneous:

- ❑ Watch
- ❑ Day pack
- ❑ Business card sized calculator
- ❑ Envelope for receipts
- ❑ Extra plastic bags and Baggies in various sizes
- ❑ Extra film & camera batteries
- ❑ Day-Glo ankle straps
- ❑ Cover up you can throw on quickly for bathroom trips at night
- ❑ Music tapes
- ❑ Tiny, high intensity flashlight
- ❑ Sewing kit
- ❑ Packing tape, which you move to your handlebar bag when you are putting your bike on a plane
- ❑ Mosquito coil
- ❑ Envelopes, stamps, writing pad
- ❑ Toilet paper - easily accessible

Other:

- ❑ ____________________
- ❑ ____________________
- ❑ ____________________
- ❑ ____________________
- ❑ ____________________
- ❑ ____________________

Women:

- ❑ Sanitary supplies

It is smart to take at least minimal sanitary supplies (one tampax, one maxi-pad, and two pantiliners) to get you to the next shop. A change in exercise, particularly if you have traveled here from elsewhere, can result in surprise periods or part periods.

Your potential for vaginal infection can also change when traveling, changing your diet and sitting on a bicycle seat for long periods. Cutting out sugar for a couple of days can help. The rule of cotton underpants for women is best ignored on a bike. Cotton stays damp - - either from rain or sweat and holds that dampness against you all day. Any synthetic or no underwear at all, just spandex shorts, gets dry fast.

❑ Tiny samples of perfume

These are so packable and can give you a lift any time, anywhere. They remind you, with a simple daub daub, that you are a woman as well as an adventurer and having something nice to smell for a few moments and then again when you put the same clothes on. It is a little gift.

❑ Makeup

You'll find that traveling on a bicycle gently loosens the hold of makeup. Rain and wind play havoc with mascara. Bicycle helmets give you helmet-head, however long you blow-dried and chemical-ized your hair. At the same time, the growing pride you feel from meeting the challenges of riding develops awareness of the other things you have going for you, apart from looks. It feels so liberating to get up, get dressed, put on your helmet and go, without that mirror work. And when you clean up at the end of a riding day the pleasure of just being clean sometimes feels like all you need.

Take the makeup you want. Watch what happens. Let things evolve.

❑ Bras

The politics of feminism aside, I happen to hate wearing a bra, damp with sweat, clinging to my rib cage and making me feel chilly. This is a personal thing that I can solve in tomboyish ways because of my build. Jane Russell isn't going to enjoy a day on a bicycle without a bra. I wear either a heavy T-shirt and no bra or a cotton sports bra, which looks more like a swimsuit top. Sometimes I just wear a halter top, by itself or as a bra underneath a T-shirt. I envy guys on this issue. I'm working with a designer to develop a female version of the fast drying, synthetic cycling top that men wear yet can be worn bra-less without nipple flaunting. Good luck solving this one for yourself, in the meantime.

❑ Dress-ups

You may want some dress-up, aprés cycling clothes. A sarong skirts packs easily and gives you enormous off-bike versatility. For exploring a town after an end-of-day bath you may want a comfortable sun dress or walking shorts and sandals. For some reason I really love that switch when I am roaming in a town. I take the toiletries I need to feel clean, pampered and pretty at the end of the biking day: moisturizer, orange sticks, perfume.

Safety

Always wear a helmet. There isn't a whole lot more to say about it. The head hits the pavement first. People fear they will be hot and uncomfortable. Personally I haven't seen much difference. It is the wet-chin-strap-under-the-neck that drives me crazy. And I still wear one.

With children along

Sharing bicycle travel adventures with your children can become a special bond between you. But if they don't yet drive a car, their sense of what traffic does on the highway will be limited. Get a copy of *From A to Z by Bike* by Barbara Lepsoe.

An orange whipper flag is seen from far away, by you and by vehicles. Helpful in both cases. You can get a little orange flag that sticks out the side of the bike to encourage vehicles to give them plenty of room.

The sound of a standard bicycle bell carries quite far and you can establish signals among you for emergency communication.

Energy levels in children need to be monitored more carefully than in adults. Make sure that they get plenty of food and keep getting enough liquid. Their breaks and stretches are also important to keep them alert, flexible and strong and therefore able to ride steadily and keep on enjoying themselves.

It takes anyone, including children, a bit of conditioning to get used to seeing a passing car come barreling toward them on a two-lane highway. Even though you understand that cars and trucks are passing you from behind at the same speed, and probably just as close to you, it can get you wobbling to have them in your face. Your first reaction may be to bail out in the ditch. You can help a child prepare for this. In spite of your urge to gape in horror at the source of your impending demise, you have to apply the same principles that stop you from staring into headlights when you first learned to drive a car.

There are two steps. First of all, fix your gaze on the shoulder ahead of you and keep it there. Watch exactly where you are going. Second: say over and over to yourself, out loud or silently, "steady, steady, steady, steady..." I still use this and it seems to prevent that wavering that could be so deadly at a time like that. Coach your kids on this and get them to practice.

Keeping warm

Hypothermia quickly moves from uncomfortable to dangerous. The key is to keep your extremities warm. When they are cold, the body reduces circulation to the extremities to protect the central system. This reduces your strength and co-ordination. When the body can no longer sustain the central body temperature, you have a serious problem. Even if you don't die, it leaves your body so drained you will be short of energy for days, vulnerable to getting sick and feeling emotionally down.

Get used to your body's tolerances and act quickly. Keeping your body temperature up is worth your constant attention on a bike. My performance drops quickly when I feel chilly.

Manage heat loss in your extremities and anywhere else that matters to you - - in my case, my neck. Have dry clothing handy. That means they are individually wrapped in plastic bags inside your panniers, which are lined with plastic bags. This double layer is necessary because however careful you are, some of your bags will leak.

Experiment with the best routine to adopt because you are managing moisture both from outside and inside. For example I only put my rain jacket hood up under my cycle helmet when it is raining hard or cold. Otherwise I get wet from my own perspiration generated by climbing hills, even though my extremities are cold. I adjust my neck zipper up and down constantly and have started opening it from the bottom to manage perspiration. Next time I'll get a jacket with underarm zippers as well.

It's personal and subjective. If I have a wet helmet chin strap against my neck I am cold and miserable. So I go to great lengths to keep something dry - - even a dry sock – between that and me. You may need leg warmers or rainpants. Rainpants may be too hot; wind pants may keep you warm enough.

I dry out my clothes at a short stop if I can but without finding a clothes dryer that's a bit of a lost cause. I switch to dry clothes if possible making sure that I'll still have dry clothes to put on when I get to a place that I can stop for the day.

Although I normally don't drink caffeine, I've learned to quickly get three cups of sweet, milky tea or coffee if I have to continue riding in the cold and wet. For my constitution, three cups of caffeine keep me warm, give me energy and make me cheerful. Find what works for you.

Think prevention, always. Ask others what equipment and habits they use. Keep trying out items that might work for you. A fast drying, fleece neckwarmer has been key for me. It has a drawstring at the top to manage airflow.

Likewise a pair of puffy, full finger gloves with leather palms, padded spandex on top and velcro wrist straps keeps me warmer than other gloves – even when wet.

An emergency pair of fleecy socks can reduce heat loss from your feet. Rainbooties are good if you can find them to fit over your footwear. Bread bags remain the old standby of most cyclists.

Some people find a cape is hard to control yet one ingenious rider has elasticized the bottom and loops it over his handle bars and the back of his seat making a little tent that gives free circulation and keeps him dry. He admits that in strong winds it becomes a problem or asset.

Think of synthetics to wick moisture away from your body. A cross-country sky instructor said, "cotton kills". Invest in your comfort and safety. There is a relationship between the two.

Surviving and thriving in the rain

Dozing off in the evening I overheard one of those vivid conversations that drift in your motel window: "It's a cold night", "Yes and supposed to get colder", "I hear it's going to rain tomorrow." That's all. That's enough. As it floats in and out of my mind during the night I reassure myself that I can cope with whatever it does

Woke early. It is Sunday. It is pouring. It is windy. It is still dark, even after I pack. I stall. I meditate. I put on rainpants. I put on my great jacket. I'm ready for this.

It is finally as light as it is going to get on a seriously overcast morning and I'm keen to try this out. I put plastic bags over my feet inside my running shoes. I'm not particularly hungry and am sure this town is not open yet so I might as well be on my way. And if the wind is still from the north I'll have a — yippee — tailwind. So I'm off.

I notice that I am riding braced against the elements and have to make a conscious effort to relax. Relax my arms, shoulders, back. Everything is fine. The rain isn't blowing into my face. Inside my cocoon I am warm and dry. In fact, inside wetness may become the problem. This is going to work just fine.

Then, within five minutes I feel rivulets of water on my skin, running down from my knees, down my shins. The rainpants are leaking along the top of the thigh. A moment of panic. Then I realize that I am warm enough and now I know about the rainpants so that's that. I am able to enjoy the pattering sound of the rain around me.

By the time I get to Crossfield I am wet several places and know a service station cup of coffee would be smart. I remember the borderline hypothermia when caught cycling in a spring snowstorm and realize that I need to take my condition seriously. Unfortunately the most likely service station to be open, the one by the highway — isn't.

No coffee shop is open in the hotel. This town is dead as a doornail. I cruise some of the residential streets and fall in love with some creatively modified houses. No restaurants, no other service stations, nothing open.

A teenager creeps down the street in his Dad's pickup while his little sister delivers newspapers from it. He thinks the service station at the far side of town will be open and it has free coffee. But he is too new to driving. He really doesn't have a clue. No such luck. So there is nothing to do but head west.

I remember that the next town, Madden, was just a little enclave of houses at the bottom of a hill. I can't remember any commercial activity but surely it has a service station? How can any town survive without a service station? And it is going to take me a while to get there so by then it will be open. Even on a Sunday, the service station will be open by then.

So west it is. A pickup truck passes me just after I leave Crossfield. I guess I am looking a sorry sight by then. He rolls down his window and says kindly, "Can I give you a ride somewhere?" I tell him that, in spite of what I look like, I'm comfortable inside and I think I can get coffee in Madden. He doubts it. I say I'll try anyway. I thank him for stopping. I'm left feeling as if there is a network of caring people who will be there when I need them.

Now there is rain running down my face. And I can't believe it but it feels wonderful. I'm wet inside and out. My plastic bags over my feet are torn and flapping. My wool gloves are heavy with rain. And I'm happy. I can't believe it. The vivid, rich colours of the landscape in the rain have created a surreal world. Raindrops decorate every stalk and blade. I see beauty all around me.

But I am getting cold and I am going as slowly downhill as I can to prevent the velocity from cooling me more. And it seems to be all downhill. I am thrilled when I see a hill that needs climbing – I can get warmed up. I know I have to get food and coffee in Madden. I will have the hypothermia problem again if I don't. This is for safety. This is no longer an option.

Madden is looking pretty quiet. Pretty people-less. Ah, there's a guy stopping at the mailboxes in his Bronco or Roughrider or Cherokee or whatever guys in the city drive in their Marlborough Man fantasies. I stop and ask him if there is any place in Madden where I can get coffee.

He says no. That's it. No. I pause long enough for him to realize how slow he is being. Now it is time for him to rescue me. This guy is really slow. I'm still standing there and he ain't peeping. He rolls up his window.

To hell with him. Goddam jerk. Uptight city jerk playing country squire and doesn't know that in the country you don't leave people to die by the side of the road. Well there's a house on my right. It looks as good as any.

Let's just hope that it is late enough on Sunday for people to be up. I've really no idea what time it is. I squish up to the door and a big granny in a giant flannelette nightie opens it.

"I'm sorry to bother you. I'm trying to cycle back to Calgary and I haven't been able to find any place open to get a coffee. Could I buy a cup of coffee from you?"

"You certainly could not. But you can have one. Come on in"

I refuse and gesture at my dripping self and she has none of it. I say I will take off my shoes. She waves that suggestion away and takes me into her kitchen and feeds me three, milky sweet cups of coffee and three pieces of toast with peanut butter on them.

Never has anything been so good. And there I sit in a soggy lump grinning, slurping, stuffing my face and thrilled to have people to talk to and to be warm.

The odd thing is that I am not particularly bothered to be sitting there soaked to the skin. For someone who hates wet clothes so much that they pull a wet bathing suit off while climbing out the pool, bystanders or no bystanders, I am calmly wet. The thought still makes me shudder now but at the time I was truly happy and comfortable sitting there in my puddle.

She tells me about Madden, about she and her husband opening the only store 40 years before. Her husband is dead now and the store is sold to new owners. We talked about city folks who move out to the country and are shocked when country living doesn't live up to their dream. She told me about their beautiful community hall and the fabulous cooking facilities in it and the number of events that go on there. I would like stay a few days and have her tell me her story. But her kitchen clock says 9:30 and I do my best biking early so I figure I had better get the home stretch covered, particularly if I am going to be cold.

I want to give back to her. I wanted to say "God bless you" as I pulled away but that's never been in my repertoire so I just said "Thank you from the bottom of my heart". She replies "People have done lots bigger things for me when I've been in need. It's a pleasure."

And it is still raining and - - low and behold — the person who never drinks coffee is on a caffeine high. I sing to cows, wave at horses. I feel wonderful. I'm not cold. Not tired. No sore muscles. No discouragement. This is a wonder drug. I feel powerful. And people drink this every day. WOW. How can this be street legal? Love it.

Nearing home I decide that I must have chicken noodle soup so I stop at my corner store and squish my way in and the guy there can't believe that I have just cycled from Carstairs. Makes me feel like an athlete. Proud moments.

In the door at home, I put a sheet on the livingroom floor for my bike to drip on. First off with the wet clothes and into a bath. Then empty all the wet stuff, wash things, drape things around. My biggest loss is that my maps, on which I draw all my routes as I travel them, are wet and the red felt pen has run and bled and faded. But like any veteran, I wear that scar with some pride. I phone the people who will be appropriately impressed with my feat. It is early afternoon and tomorrow is a holiday. I can lie in front of a fire, drink chicken soup and read and gloat. I'm hot. I'm brave. I have stamina. I am wonder woman. Time to go ballroom dancing and show off.

Keeping cool

Pick your cycling locations to match your temperature preferences. Southwestern Alberta is rarely over 30C and the temperature always drops considerably in the evening and stays cool at night. Early morning cycling starts are cool. Even during a brief hot spell it will be dry and chances are it will be windy which will help cool you. Then your main issue is keeping enough water with you.

Farther away from the Rockies, particularly in the southeast corner from Drumheller south and east, you can get long dry, hot, spells. So your main task is still sun and water management.

It takes extreme heat and exertion to put your body into crisis if you are keeping your water levels up. When you have any hint of feeling weak, dizzy, nauseous or light-headed you are not going to cycle through it. If that happens: STOP!

Wave down a motorist or go to the closest farmhouse. Get out of the sun and rest. It may help to eat something. Negotiate a ride to the next place you'll spend the night.

Learn your body's preferences and protect it ahead of time. Your cycling trip will suffer if you damage your body with overheating. The next day you'll have less energy and less enthusiasm and be even more prone to heat sensitivity.

Build in shady drink and snack stops. Drink water constantly and start looking for a place to replenish when half your water is gone. Along with your two water bottles, add a large or two medium bottles to the outside pocket of your pannier if it is really hot and windy. Treat yourself to some juice as well, for variety.

Stop for a swim or a wade in a pool, river or creek. Change your plan and don't go as far. If you don't like hot weather, take a day off and explore a town, go to their museum, do a photo journal of a day in the life of a town. Get your hair cut, get a pedicure, have a massage, buy gifts to send home, read your journal and write reflections on your trip, write all the postcards you've avoided - - lie low and have fun and wait for cooler weather.

Sun

We are all well educated now on skin damage from sun. Be warned: the high altitude of Alberta creates one of the highest skin cancer rates in the world. Err in the direction of overkill. You may want to go home with a tan and looking healthy and sporty but trust me – being outside will do that even with high SFP sunscreen.

Travel with a range of sunscreens so you can thoroughly protect high vulnerability areas - - back of neck, back of shoulders, nose, ears and, in women, top of thighs. Have cool clothing that covers shoulders, back, anywhere you are getting too much sun.

Consider investing in high quality, face moisturizer/sunscreen combo, particularly if your skin is sensitive. (See page 228 on specific sunscreen brands.) Windburn is often as much or more a factor than sun. If you like to stop for lunch, stop in the shade during that sun-intense time.

Be kind to your skin and you can still go home looking healthy and outdoorsy - - and smart.

Dogs

This is a big fear for some riders. And in fact dogs can be a nuisance but I personally have never been in danger, been bitten or been seriously attacked by a dog while riding a bicycle. There are two separate issues here: when you are truly in danger and secondly when dogs are just being annoying.

Be careful about reading more danger into a situation than is appropriate. If you are nervous about dogs in general or have had a bad experience - - on or off a bike - - this can happen. On the other hand, if you feel a dog's teeth, you are in danger. You can try to cycle through it. If you are a steady, one-handed cyclists and you see it coming, you can have your bicycle pump in your hand and try to land one good, strong blow while you keep riding. Even water squirted or dumped on some dogs will make them back off long enough for you to get out of range.

Resist the temptation to kick at them. Even if a dog isn't vicious, some owners roughhouse with pets by encouraging them to grab a sleeve or pant-leg and hold on and tussle. They may react to a kick by grabbing on.

In an extreme case, a veterinarian suggests getting your bike between you and the dog. Then keep walking. Any dog loses interest when you leave their territory. Flag down the first passing vehicle. Together you can discourage even the most stubborn dog.

The small-time criminals who have vicious dogs tend to be in cities. Those dogs are usually tied up. They are big and dangerous. Stay out of their leash length, out of their yard and away from them. Stay away from their owners. Country dogs on the loose in Alberta do not fall into that category.

As I say, I've cycled many places and seen many dogs and been chased by many and never has a dog come close to biting me.

In most dog situations you are not dealing with danger, you are dealing with annoyance. Just keep riding. Ride steadily and ride out of their territory. It doesn't take long. Try talking to the dog as you keep riding. It doesn't discourage the dog but it makes you feel better.

And watch for situations in which the dog has come rushing out to make friends and get a pat and a chat. These can be very rewarding visits. If you suspect a dog is actually friendly (tail wagging, maybe whole back-half wagging, a playful, bouncing gait) you can confirm this by talking "nice doggie" talk to them. When this makes them just wag more, lower their head, even roll over, you know your biggest problem is how long to stand and pet them.

If you have a phobia about dogs, cycling gives you an opportunity to work it through. If you don't have dog fears, just be ready to act decisively if the bizarre happens and you need protection.

Fatigue

The pleasant fatigue of a long day riding is one of the great rewards and pleasure of traveling by bicycle. If that shifts from fatigue to exhaustion when you are on a bike, you need to stop immediately. Wave down a car or go to the closest house. A rest, drink and food can be rejuvenating, even in weather extremes but if a rest doesn't rejuvenate you, it's time to stop cycling for the day.

The issue here is to be flexible about goals. When it isn't fun any more, stop doing it. You're on holiday. Who cares if you got a lift or stopped early? In response to my own time-to-quit instincts I was once registering in a hotel at 9 AM when everyone else was checking out. I had been struggling on the bike since 6 AM and I felt weak as a baby. I climbed into bed and slept until 11:30 AM - - and woke proud of my willingness to be flexible.

Cyclists get stubborn and goal driven. "Rode the whole way," "Did 150K every day", "Never cycled less than 10 hours." These are cycling boasts. How about "We never cycled longer than it was fun," or "We were slow that day and got wonderful pictures." This is holiday cycling, not racing cycling.

Problem people:

This is more of an issue for women (which we will deal with separately) but anyone can feel nervous about a car full of young yahoos who have been drinking and travelers everywhere wonder if they are being ripped off by the locals.

Alberta is as safe as anywhere on the planet. There is no politically dissident group with angry young followers, there is little serious poverty in the countryside, the seriously poor are in cities and tend to be women, and there is no history of resentment of strangers. Canadian natives, who have reason to be angry, direct it at themselves and their families with appalling rates of suicide and family abuse.

Rural Albertans are cautious and responsive. They know they are vulnerable to strangers coming onto their property but warm immediately when they find out you need directions, water, coffee, shade etc. They do not hassle cyclists and they try to help. They are by inclination, fair and it is unlikely anyone will try and charge you unduly.

You can ride safely in Southern Alberta.

For women

In general, Alberta males are impressed by women riding on their own and show respect and even a bit of envy. However women have enough first and second hand experience with problems created by men that women traveling solo will not be lulled into taking safety for granted. In Alberta, as everywhere in the world, your best protection is to be clear about your own boundaries. And cycling alone is a great way to cultivate this.

The air of a no-nonsense, sportswoman who is friendly and capable is respected. You can be friendly and open but be careful with whom you choose to flirt. They may become a pest and require harsh discouragement. If you are interested in sexual activity on your holiday be clear with yourself about this and be conscious of whether you are sending a generalized message of availability to all people. And take condoms.

If you have trouble saying "no"; establishing boundaries and keeping people the distance you want, make it a goal to experiment with this while you travel on your bike.

Southern Alberta is a safe place for women traveling alone. Be as alert as you would be at home. Stay away from situations that worry you in the least. Err in the direction of caution. And gain confidence in your ability to look after yourself.

Flat tires

First of all - - go for prevention. Get your bike fitted with tires that are durable and can stand up to some rough road. You don't need to go all the way to mountain bike tires but they should be a bit knobby and wider than a racing bike's tires.

If you continually have flats, make sure your tires are inflated enough. If so, go to a bike shop you trust and ask them to help you change to a different tire, or even wheel to reduce this aggravation.

Then you want to arm yourself with the tools that make it as easy as possible to change a flat when it does occur. (See the tool kit list on page 225.) Wrenches to loosen the bolts and get the wheel off and any small tool, like the blade of a Swiss Army knife, to depress the valve pin and release the extra air when you are packing up the old tube. You need three specialized prying tools that come in a set from a cycle shop, for prying back the rim of the tire to get the tube out. If you carry extra tubes, the right size, you don't need to patch the tire right there beside the road. Once the new tube is in, you need a bike pump to pump it back up.

You want a patch kit so that when you inflate the damaged tube you can find the hole and patch it later. This is all simpler than it sounds.

It is impossible to tell you how to repair a bicycle tire in writing without it sounding much harder than it is. The following is a crude attempt to walk you through it. Get someone to help you change tires and to coach you doing it. Ask a child.

When it happens to you

Monitor the on-going health of your tires. Be ready to change one as soon as you see that more air pumped in isn't holding. Look for a level spot where you can get far enough off the road to feel comfortable with cars passing.

Take off your panniers and turn the bike upside down. If it isn't a quick release wheel, get a wrench on each of the visibly obvious nuts on either side of the wheel. One bolt goes on way, one the other. Turn them both, at once, one against the other. You'll figure out which goes which way.

If it is the back wheel, you'll have to get it disentangled from the chain. That's easy when you increase the slack by pushing forward on the derailleur. Even if you don't know what a derailleur is you'll figure it out just looking at it, touching things, moving things. Don't worry about upsetting things. If you can move it with your hands, you can move it back.

Wheel off. Next get the tire off the rim - - a messy process requiring some brute strength but entirely within the capabilities of women and children. (So teach your children now, if they aren't the ones teaching you.) You pry one edge of the tire out from inside the wheel rim by pushing three prying tools under the edge and flipping it out. (Have someone demonstrate.) You work only on one side of the tire. You space out the three prying tools until you have one whole side of the tire out of the rim. You see the tube inside. Push the valve stem through the hole in the rim (easy and obvious with a tire in front of you) and lift out the tube.

Your choice now is to find the leak, repair it and put it back OR, put in a new one. The catch is that if you don't find what caused the leak to start with you could immediately puncture the new tube. So regardless of your choice you need to do some investigation.

Help and the psycho killers

While I worried about my ever-flattening tire I also worried about psycho-killers. In the aftermath of full saturation media coverage about an appalling couple who had tortured and murdered two young girls, I was convinced that just such a couple lurked in one of these farms. Waiting, right now, for a new victim. Locals described them as quiet and keeping to themselves. It's hard to get that kind of idea out of your head when it once gets into it.

I stalled. I scanned the horizon for a farmhouse with a sign that said "Psycho killers don't live here". But flat is flat and eventually you just have to stop and change it, regardless of psycho killer dangers.

I got the wheel off the bike but I couldn't get the tire off the wheel. And along came an elderly Englishman farmer in his unrestored vintage pickup. He changed it. We chatted. I hung around and chatted some more, trying to make up for the thoughts I had had.

Eventually I waved my way off, awash with platitudes: people are there when you need them; country people will never see you stranded; you can't beat the English; no one ignores a broken-down cyclist; if you reach out to people they will always be there for you and so on.

Pump up the inner tube and look for the leak. Put it to our ear and listen. With really fine ones you may have to submerge it or soap it which you probably can't do beside the road.

Either way, feel and look along the inside of the rim and the inside of the tire. If you have found the hole in the tube, figure out where that sat inside the tire and look there first. (To help with this task, you can mark with a yellow highlighter the side of the tube and the side of the tire and rim adjacent to the valve stem before removing the tube. Them you know which way the tube lay inside and when you find the hole in the tube you can check that spot on the tire.)

You may find glass, a nail, or a rough spot on the rim. Whatever you find, get your coach to show you ways of dealing with it before putting the tube back. You may find nothing. Fair enough.

Place the new or patched tube inside the tire around the edge of the rim. Don't be surprised if there seems to be a whole lot too much tube for the tire. Then pump it up a bit. Look all around inside the tire to make sure that the tube is lying flat and even all around, that it isn't doubled over. Then push the edge of the tire back into the rim (amazingly easy considering what was involved to get it out) and pump it up further.

Put it back on the bike, fitting the chain around the gear rings - - this is when you are really glad the bike is upside down. Tighten the nuts on each side equally and be sure the chain is sitting right. Top-up the air if need be and pack up your tools.

A small jar of the cream hand cleaner used by mechanics with a small rag to wipe off the grease will be a much-appreciated part of your tool kit at this point. Pack up and you are away.

A tire change is easy when shown and well worth the time for a lesson. Otherwise a flat tire has you dependent on others.

For out-of-towners

Arriving with your bicycle in a new city or a new country necessitates dealing immediately with practical issues. And if you have had little sleep the night before, while traveling, you are best off to cope with the minimum necessary, get somewhere you can settle for two or three days and let yourself adjust.

At the time of writing, the below list is accurate. It will change. The more you travel with your bike the more you will be used to sniffing out these services wherever you go.

Currency

Most bank machines in Calgary and rural Alberta are connected to Cirrus and Interac. This means they probably accept your card, wherever it is from. This is the easiest way to stay solvent. You find bank machines in most banks and in some convenience stores. The guide includes any rural ones that I know about. If you find others, please let me know.

There is a foreign exchange booth at the airport just outside the International arrival area. Most hotels and merchants accept American Express or Thomas Cook travelers' cheques until you get into really small towns. B&Bs probably won't. Most banks will give you cash advances on VISA or MasterCard depending on their affiliation.

There are two American Express offices in Calgary, one downtown and one at the south end of the city. Call them, 1-800-668-2639 for information on getting money on your American Express card. You can get up to $1000 of what they call emergency cash every 30 days by writing a personal cheque drawn on your own account of your financial institution at home and presenting it with your American Express card and your passport.

There is a sophisticated Money Exchange office in downtown Calgary where you can buy or exchange almost any kind of currency from around the world.

There is no provincial sales tax in Alberta but the Canada-wide Goods & Services Taxes applies.

Metric System

Alberta, with all of Canada, uses the metric system so distances in this guide are in kilometers (K) and meters. All the highway and street signage is in kilometers. One kilometer equals 5/8 mile. Fifty K speed limit equals 30 mph and 100 K equals 60 mph. The exception to this is when the source, such as a topographic map, was in feet or miles. Although Canada switched to metric several years ago people in rural areas still tend to talk in terms of miles.

Phones & electricity

The Alberta area code is 403. To dial overseas dial 011 + country code + area code + local number. By dialing 0 you can get the country code and area code for other places. To dial within Canada dial 1 + area code + local number. To dial within Alberta dial 1 + 403 + local number.

All the phone numbers in the guide are in the 403 area code so assume that is required if you dial from elsewhere.

Plugs and voltage are the same in Alberta as in the United States. If you bring small appliances from areas using other systems, consult the local electrical authorities before using them.

Maps

Before you can even find a place to stay it is helpful to have a map. The ones in this guide should cover the most common cycling out of Calgary. There are specific cycle route descriptions here for people arriving at the airport (page 65), bus depot (page 67) or train station (page 70). If you have read these and feel you have your bearings, you are fine. Otherwise, you can pick up a Calgary Pathway and Bikeway Map in a bicycle shop or any of the other sponsors. If you are in the downtown core, Map Town, at 640 6th Avenue SW is your best source.

The Calgary Tourism & Convention Bureau has a booth at the airport and another in the base of the Calgary Tower, which is upstairs from the train station. Both places give away Calgary maps.

Accommodation

If you have traveled more than four hours to get to Calgary, we recommend one night in the city to rest before heading out.

The Calgary Airport Hotel is virtually part of the airport complex. Or a brief daylight cycle to Airdrie – straight north 16 K, will get you out of the city without an ambitious ride. See NE Airport Exit,, page 38 and Airdrie under "Additional Excursions", page 109. From there you can plan rides to anywhere in Southern Alberta.

Otherwise consult the accommodation resources listed on page 11 or the directory of accommodation in the bus depot or airport. You can also call Travel Alberta from anywhere to get help with accommodation: 1-800 661-8888. For the Calgary Convention & Visitors Bureau the toll free number from anywhere in Canada or the US is 1-800 661-1678.

For an Internet browse see: http://www.visitor.calgary.ab.ca or e-mail: destination@visitor.calgary.ab.ca.

If you already know where you want to cycle, pick Calgary accommodation convenient to your exit route. There are B&Bs within Calgary that offer excellent value.

Holidays & Events

The Calgary Convention and Visitors Bureau and Travel Alberta, phone numbers above, can help you pin down the exact dates of annual events. Some worth watching for are:

- Caribbean Festival, early June in Calgary
- Jazz Festival, late June in Calgary
- Canada Day, July 1
- Stampede, early July in Calgary
- Folk Festival, late July in Calgary
- Heritage day, early August
- Mozart on the Mountain, late August in Kananaskis
- Spruce Meadows Equestrian Events, late May and early June, late June/early July and early September

Each town has their local summer fair and rodeo that you find out about as you travel through. When you phone to reserve accommodation you can ask about what is going on locally. Throughout Alberta, holidays to watch for during the cycling season are: Victoria Day in late May, Canada Day July 1st, Heritage Day early August, Labour Day in early September and Thanksgiving in mid-October.

The Bow and Elbow Rivers

To avoid confusion it is worth being aware that the Bow River flows from the west, originating at Bow Glacier in the Rockies, and bisects Calgary as it flows east. At the east edge of the city it turns and flows south, bordering the east edge of the city before heading southeast across the province and joining the South Saskatchewan River just east of the Alberta-Saskatchewan border.

The Elbow River, which originates in the foothills southwest of Bragg Creek, is dammed in the Glenmore Reservoir in the southwest corner of the city. It then flows northeast and joins the Bow inside the city at Fort Calgary. Several city cycle paths run along these rivers so getting them straight in your mind will help prevent future confusion. The Elbow is smaller than the Bow.

Navigating in Calgary

Calgary streets (north/south) and avenues (east/west) are arranged in a logical, right angle grid. Centre Street and Memorial Drive (which follows the Bow River except in the east part of the city after the Bow turns south) are the main axis. Where they cross is the hub. From that point the street and avenue numbers rise as you move out.

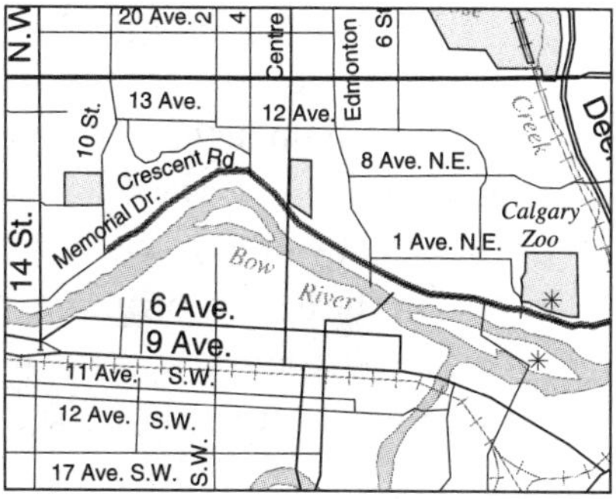

In the suburbs this disintegrates into popular, curved configurations of lanes, gates, closes and whatnots. You will probably only deal with them if you cycle to friends there.

Calgary has some in-city throughways that are direct and convenient for cars but some are unpleasant, unsafe and even illegal for bicycles. If it is called "Something" Trail, be careful. This guide will only put you on trails for brief, safe stretches. We do this cautiously.

Like many cities, Calgary has dealt with downtown congestion by instituting a series of one-way streets. As a result, instructions for exit and entry routes from the train station and bus depot are more convoluted than seems necessary.

But the compass grid of the city makes it easy to figure out where places are. You will quickly be comfortable getting around the city.

On the right

In Canada, traffic travels on the right hand side of the road and you should ride over on the right shoulder. It takes a bit of getting used to if that's not how it is done at home so keep out of tight spots or riding when tired until you are acculturated. Both are situations when you can revert to old habits.

It is smart to get into a habit of not hugging the right curb. That may leave you no-where to go in an emergency. It also tempts cars to share the lane with you. Give yourself some safe space and judge each situation on its own.

Traffic

Depending on what you are used to, the traffic in Calgary is either worse or better. It moves quickly and drivers are impatient during Chinooks and Friday afternoons – particularly before a long weekend.

A few things to be cautious about:

- In the early morning, driving east, a driver may be blinded by the low sun and simply not see you. Assume as much when you are leaving the city early.
- Drivers everywhere have a bad habit of parking and opening their door to get out without looking back. Assume a row of parked cars that you are cycling past has just such a genius in it, waiting to swing their door open the second you are along side.
- Another common problem happens at corners when cars stop beside you or slow down beside you and then turn immediately in front of you. Your only hope is to hit the brakes fast. If you are aware of this, you can almost be ready. This is a worldwide phenomenon.
- Dealing with turning lanes is also an issue everywhere. When you want to go straight through and one or two lanes are

mandatory turning lanes, you have to get across them intact. The law states that you are to stay against the curb until the last minute when you then cross the exit lane and start riding against the curb in the lane that continues on. In other words you are not to swing out a lane and cycle between two lanes for a distance ahead of the turnoff. Be forewarned.

A word about the annual Calgary Stampede. This is held for ten days starting in the second week of July. There is more traffic not only from visitors in town but also because many Calgary employees are driving from party to party - - even during the day. Some downtown streets will be closed at unexpected times not only for the grand opening parade but also for street dancing, pancake breakfasts, mini-parades and events that go on throughout the Stampede. Take in some of the free pancake breakfasts. They are easy to find. Enjoy some of the street events and even jump into the epicenter at the Stampede grounds. (But don't take your bike there. Park it somewhere and catch the C-train, 262-1000, which takes you right to the grounds.) Just don't be surprised by changes in expected traffic flow.

In city bike transportation

During non-rush hour in July and August you can take your bike on the local light rail transit system, called the C-Train. That opens another option for getting to the edge of town. However most of the station platforms are eight steps above street level so you'll be dragging your fully loaded bike up the stairs. Calgary Transit information is 262-1000. More information on riding the C-Train in and out of town is listed at the beginning of the section on Routes out, page33 and again in Routes in, page 75.

You can order a station wagon taxi. It costs more but it fits your bike. Tell them when you order the taxi.

Your bike on trains, planes and buses

Each airline and bus company requests different things of you when you are sending your bike as baggage. One wants air out of tires and handlebars turned and pedals off. Another wants the chain wrapped in paper but doesn't care about the air. Another wants the whole thing in a box.

The key is to have tons of your own packing tape and be ready to buy newspaper. Have Allen key wrenches handy to loosen and turn the handlebars. Have a wrench to take off the pedals. Most ticket agents who insist that you box or bag it have the materials to do it. You have to pay for them, usually around $20 and they say you have to do it yourself but you get used to that quickly, and they usually help if asked.

If they want you to box it and demand that you have a box with you, even the most rule-bound official backs down when you quietly point out the impossibility of you cycling to there with a box big enough for your bike - on your head?

If you can't get the pedals off, I never can, just hand them the wrench and say pleasantly that you'll need some help with that. Never once have I seen them try. They discard that rule immediately.

You can always buy newspaper at an airport/station to wrap your chain and tape it. Then just cut it off when you arrive. This rule makes sense because you already know from riding how much grease your chain gets on you. It also gives a bit of protection to a vulnerable part of the bike. The most common problem you will experience when you get your bike back is the chain jammed into the gears.

If you take the air out of the tires, leave a bit in because chances are someone will wheel it and you don't want it on the rim. Have them plaster Fragile stickers all over it. Might as well try.

In a big bus they may have a compartment at the back where they hang your bike. Otherwise they can stand it up underneath if the compartment is tall enough. Either way, this is a good time to have bungee cords.

It isn't advisable to check your helmet even though it can feel like a nuisance to carry it around. If it is roughly handled and gets a hairline crack, you may not be able to see that damage with the naked eye but its effectiveness would be sharply reduced.

Bike repairs

Apart from changing a tire, page 244 you'll have little things that required adjusting from time to time. Your handle bars tip up or down too far (a common one because other people often pick up the front of your bike using the handle bars and it is really hard to tighten them enough that this doesn't move them) screws come lose, things go out of adjustment.

Given enough time you can fiddle with a bike problem until you eventually solve it. Try one tool and a little adjustment. Ride a bit. Adjust a bit further or turn it the other way. Look at it. Think about what's needed. Improvise. Given time you'll stumble on the solution to most things. And then feel wonderfully competent.

To help you out with major bike problems, or an extensive tune-up, the guide includes any rural bicycle repair options I can find - - which aren't many. And even if there is a repair place listed, don't let that lull you into a false sense of security. These places change their hours, close down and move. A local phone book is your best bet. Within Calgary, the Calgary Pathway and Bikeway Map has cycle shops right on it and there are more in the yellow pages.

Daylight savings

Alberta switches to daylight savings on the first Sunday in April and off it the last Sunday in October. During that period, clocks are moved ahead one hour, which results in long light summer evenings. Southern Alberta is far enough north that there are a couple of weeks at the end of June, beginning of July, when it stays light until 10:30 at night, celebrated as white nights in St. Petersburg, Russia.

Reading and sources of information

Alberta Bed & Breakfast Association 1995 Directory of Member Bed & Breakfasts: available from Travel Alberta: 1-800-661-8888. This has some crude, rather hard to read maps of six sections of the province with B&Bs marked on them and cross-referenced to boxed descriptions of each one, their address, phone and cost. Do not judge the professionalism of the B&Bs by the appearance of this leaflet.

Alberta Bed & Breakfast Guide: by Marg Ruttan, published by Rocky Mountain Books in 1996, comprehensive, useful and user friendly.

Alberta Accommodation & Visitors' Guide: an annual listing of B&Bs, motels and hotels produced by Travel Alberta. Extensive but not exhaustive, particularly for B&Bs. 1-800-661-8888

Alberta Campground Guide: also from Travel Alberta, camping is listed by the name of the closest town. 1-800-661-8888

Alberta Wildlife Viewing Guide: a publication from Alberta Environmental Protection. Phone 422-1053 for details on getting your copy.

Beyond Ararat: A Journey Through Eastern Turkey: by Bettina Selby, a mature cycle adventurer who has written several books. She describes the difficulties of cycling through a Muslim country, and of course all ends well.

A Bike Ride: by Anne Sustoe, Virgin Books. An English headmistress rode around the world on a bicycle after she retired, starting out with no mechanical knowledge of her bike and no training.

Calgary Pathway and Bikeway Map: produced by Calgary Parks and Recreation, available in any bicycle shop from early May until mid summer when they may run out. They cost $1. Phone the City Parks and recreation Department, 268-2300 if you are having trouble finding one.

From A to Z by Bike: by Barbara Lepsoe, published by AMC Media Corporation. This is written for children to read themselves and learn about bicycle safety on the road.

Full Tilt: Ireland to India on a Bicycle: by Dervla Murphy. She has written many others. These are heroic trips by a mature woman who makes any cycle adventure seem possible.

Miles from Nowhere: Around the World Bicycle Adventure: by Barbara Savage, 1983.

Tales of a Traveling Man: by Bernie Halgate. A $70,000-a-year engineer from Toronto spent eight years traveling around the world on a ten-speed bicycle. He did it on $10,000.

Tell me what you find!

As you travel these routes you will notice changes and find new and better options. Where are the new bathrooms? What picnic place has disappeared? Please let me know. It helps me keep this information current. It is a pleasure to add another route and make it your own. If you are willing to share yours, we can pass them on to others.

This is the first of a series on seeing the world from a bicycle. It will be updated. Others will be added. Find out what is coming out to plan your next cycling holiday by checking our homepage: monday@nucleus.com.

The road beckons. Adapt our suggestions to work for you. Enjoy riding Southern Alberta. Happy bike adventures.
And may the wind be always at your back.

TEXT INDEX

Map index

Service symbols:

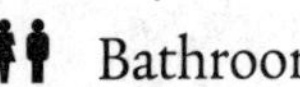

- Bathrooms
- Water
- Snacks
- Ice cream
- Fancy coffee
- Restaurant
- Groceries
- Liquor outlet
- Picnic
- Service station
- Accommodation
- Camping
- Bike repairs
- $ Cirrus/Interac bank machines
- Fun shopping
- Emergency medical services
- Telephones
- Tools

EXCELLENT CYCLING ADVENTURES

EXPERIENCE THE FREEDOM!

Mail to:
The Monday Communications Group Ltd.
212 Hawkwood Drive N.W.
Calgary, Alberta, Canada T3G 3M9

For information on bulk orders,
call: (403) 270-4414,
or fax: (403)283-5983
or E-mail: monday@nucleus.com

Please send the following number of Excellent Cycling Adventure Books to the address on the reverse side of this coupon

Qty.	Title	Each	Total
	Excellent Cycling Adventures in Southern Alberta	$15.95	
Total Qty.	Total Cost of Guidebooks		$
	Canadian Residents add G.S.T. @ 7%		$
	Plus $2.00 Shipping		$
Less $5.00 for every third copy per order			$
Plus International Shipping Expenses (add $4.00 if outside Canada and U.S.A.)			$
Total Amount Enclosed			$

*Special Mail Offer: Order 2 copies by mail at regular prices and Save $5.00 on every third copy per order.
Not valid with any other offer.

Orders Outside Canada - amount enclosed must be paid in U.S. Funds.
Make cheque or money order payable to: The Monday Group
Prices subject to change after December 31, 1997
Sorry, no C.O.D.'s

Give the Freedom of Excellent Cycling Adventures to a Friend

Please send *Marg Archibald's Excellent Cycling Adventures in Southern Alberta*,
listed on the reverse side of this coupon to:

NAME ____

STREET ____

CITY ____

PROVINCE/STATE _____________ POSTAL CODE/ZIP CODE __________

Gift Giving - We Make it Easy!

We will send *Excellent Cycling Adventures* directly to the recipients of your choice - the perfect gift for birthdays, Mother's Day, Father's Day, graduation, retirement, Christmas or any occasion!

Please specify the number of copies on the reverse side of this coupon and provide us with the name and address for each gift order. Enclose a personal note or card and we will include it with your order...

...and don't forget to take advantage of the **$5.00 saving** - buy 2 copies of *Marg Archibald's Excellent Cycling Adventures in Southern Alberta* by mail and **save $5.00** on every third copy per order.

CYCLING ADVENTURES - WE MAKE IT EASY - YOU MAKE IT FUN!